Private Enterprise
and
Public Interest

PRIVATE ENTERPRISE
AND
PUBLIC INTEREST

the development of

American

Capitalism

GORDON C. BJORK
President
Linfield College

PRENTICE-HALL, INC.
Englewood Cliffs, New Jersey

Private Enterprise and Public Interest
The Development of American Capitalism
Gordon C. Bjork

©1969
by Prentice-Hall, Inc.
Englewood Cliffs, New Jersey

Printed in the United States of
    America
Library of Congress Catalog Card
    No.: 69–14531

Current Printing (last digit):
10 9 8 7 6 5 4 3 2 1

Prentice-Hall International, Inc.,
    London
Prentice-Hall of Australia, Pty. Ltd.,
    Sydney
Prentice-Hall of Canada, Ltd.,
    Toronto
Prentice-Hall of India Private Ltd.,
    New Delhi
Prentice-Hall of Japan, Inc.,
    Tokyo

Preface

The title of this book will strike many as being pretentious. I hope those who have this reaction will listen to my explanation of how I came to treat the subject as I have. It was not my original intention to talk about American economic institutions and practices in such sweeping perspective as is attempted in this book. I only wanted to explain why things were organized as they are in order to give a better understanding of the social constraints which structure economic activity in the contemporary United States.

It soon became apparent to me, however, that one could not adequately explain the contemporary forms of American economic organization by merely starting with the classical liberal model of a *laissez-faire* economy—of the sort which exists in economic texts—and then explain the way in which the government had modified it by various types of "controls" and "interferences." It seemed necessary to me to examine the very foundations of a capitalist economy—private property in the means of production and freedom to bargain about its use. This inquiry led me to a consideration of the forms of economic organization which preceded modern capitalism, to an examination of Soviet practices, and to an historical examination of the way in which the rights to the use of property were evolved in the Anglo-American tradition.

It also became evident that it was necessary to understand the political as well as the economic factors which helped to shape the socio-economic framework and the analysis moved away from economics to become a progressively more eclectic treatment

v

of capitalist development. I am fully aware of some of the simplifications
I have made in economic theory and American economic history. I am
not very aware of the extent of the simplifications, omissions, and *gaffés*
committed in other areas and I must simply ask for the indulgence and
sympathy of other specialists for my attempts to bring materials (in
which I have little professional competence) to bear on the argument.

Explaining the evolution of the argument of this book would make the
preface into an intellectual odyssey of greater length and complexity
than the text of the book. And yet, while there is not enough space in
the book to give a full explanation of the evidence and assumptions which
led me to accept one explanation in preference to another, I am acutely
conscious that many a reader will be baffled or disagree with the conclusions and generalizations about the development of economic institutions which come in such a rapid fire progression in the narrative. I
would, therefore, like to make a succinct statement about the important
formative influences on the argument.

The original impetus to write this book grew out of a dissatisfaction
with the classical liberal formulations of political economy. These were
focused for me, as an economist, by the writings and general intellectual
position of Milton Friedman. My objections arose, in large part, to the
way in which the case for capitalism was developed. I thought that
some of the arguments were misleading in their logical development and
overdrawn in their generalizations about how *laissez-faire* would always
lead to the optimum solution to thorny social problems.

As I read economic, political, and legal history to learn how men
actually did change their economic organization, I found it necessary
to deal with the Marxian theory of institutional change. I found the
Marxian critique of capitalist organization and development as misleading as its classical liberal defense. Thus, what is developed in the
succeeding pages is an argument, about the nature of capitalism, which
seeks to avoid the pitfalls of both classical liberalism and the Marxian
formulation of economic determinism. I expect that doctrinaire intellectuals on both left and right will find it unsatisfactory because of my
rejection of their assumptions.

My intellectual debts are legion. This work depends largely on secondary sources for its evidence and I am acutely conscious of the years
of research on primary sources by others on which this volume depends.
I must record a particular debt to John R. Commons. The theory of
capitalist development articulated in this book is closely related to his
attempt to formulate a theory of political economy in terms of a system of
inducements and restraints. I hope my attempt to reformulate some of
his ideas is less obscure. I must also acknowledge the strong influence on
my thinking of R. H. Tawney, Max Weber, Thorstein Veblen, Milton

Friedman, and I. M. D. Little. I hope that other obligations are adequately made in footnotes which I have attempted to minimize.

The Graduate School of Business of Columbia University provided both the intellectual environment and considerable financial support for the writing of this book and I must record my gratitude to the School and particularly to its Dean, Courtney C. Brown, for making this book possible. There has been much "sniping" at business schools from the rest of the academic community on the grounds that they are narrowly vocational with little interest in "true" intellectual endeavor. I can say with some objectivity (since I am no longer a member of the faculty of the School) that I never found this to be so at Columbia. In addition to giving a highly professional training to its students, the School actively promoted scholarly research by its faculty in many areas—some of which were very far removed from the practice of business. Among my colleagues at Columbia, James Kuhn, Ivar Berg, Bruce Bassett, Eli Ginzberg, Paul McNulty, and Giulio Pontecorvo were particularly important over the years in the formulation of my ideas. So were many of my students.

I have benefited from discussions with scholars at several other universities whose interest and help I would like to acknowledge: Roy Church of the University of Birmingham, England; Harvey L. Dyck of Toronto; H. Scott Gordon of Indiana University; John Habakkuk of Oxford; Mancur Olsen of Princeton; Dwight Robinson of the University of Washington; and Dan Usher, now of Queens University in Canada. Finally, I must express gratitude to several former mentors who played an important part in my earlier intellectual development: Basil Mitchell, my philosophy tutor at Oxford; Morris D. Morris and Douglass North who stimulated my interest in economic history at the University of Washington; and Donald F. Gordon who made economic theory exciting and related it to philosophical method and other disciplines.

While my wife claims no responsibility for the ideas expressed in this book, her never-failing common sense and feeling for language have removed some of the jargon and infelicitous style inculcated by the study of economics. Her good humor and devoted care have hastened the completion of the book.

Linfield College
McMinnville, Oregon

Foreword

The world in which the American businessman operates is changing at an accelerating pace. While many of us occasionally express a nostalgic desire to return to the verities of a distant mythical age (about 1925 when the only uncertainties were prices, wages, and sales!) we are learning to live and prosper in a rapidly changing social environment. This book is concerned with the essential relationships among men with each other and with their environment as the groundswells of political and technological changes are imposed on our daily lives. It puts the process of institutional change in perspective and explains its dynamic.

Using some of the tools and techniques of modern economic analysis to explain the social rationale of earlier forms of economic organization and business practices, the author shows why changes came about in the relationships between the organizers of production and the rest of society. Moving quickly from classical antiquity to nineteenth century America, he emphasizes both the compelling economic reasons and the ethical values which came to produce what we call the American "private enterprise" system. He then brings the analysis to the 1970's with a well reasoned critique of individual rights and social interest. The book ends with an impressive marshalling of evidence on the ability of American capitalism to promote greater equality in income distribution as well as expanding abundance, and makes a plea for special treatment for Negro and other minority groups to bring them into the logic of the system.

We are proud of the tradition at the Graduate School of Business of Columbia University from which this volume springs. Before assuming a college presidency, the author taught for four years in a course entitled Conceptual and Historical Foundations of Business which is an integral part of the training of both M. B. A. and Ph. D. candidates at the Columbia Business School. The course, like the book, attempts to place the American business system in perspective to enable the businessman to operate creatively and responsibly within it and recognize the challenges it provides. I believe that Professor Bjork's book makes a significant contribution to our understanding of the logic and development of the American business system. More importantly, he finds embedded in the philosophy of "the commonwealth" which formed the basis for the capitalistic revolution of the seventeenth century in England, a reaffirmation of appropriate guidelines for the conduct of business in the present period of changing purposes and motivations.

Courtney C. Brown
Dean
Graduate School of Business
Columbia University

Table of Contents

This book is dedicated to my *father*:
a fervent believer in private enterprise,
who ran a business to provide
good service at low prices,
employment for those in need,
and profits for the ministries of his church.

1

The Nature
of Capitalism:

mistaken

emphases and

semantic

confusions

Capitalism is a term used to describe a system of economic and political arrangements. It has never enjoyed great currency in the United States. This may be because critics of capitalism have succeeded in investing the term with such negative semantic connotations that even ardent supporters of those arrangements hesitate to use the term. Another explanation is that the term, itself, is an unsatisfactory one because there is no consensus about the distinguishing characteristics of the system which the term *capitalism* purports to describe.

The Nature of Capitalism:

Two Approaches

Economic historians and other scholars of economic institutions have never reached any substantial agreement as to the peculiar features of a capitalist system which serve to distinguish it from other methods of socio-economic organization. Nor has there been agreement as to when particular societies could be termed to have become predominantly capitalist.

Two different approaches to the description of a capitalist system have informed the work of scholars. One approach seeks to distinguish capitalist organization in terms of certain ethical emphasis. This method of approach gained great currency among such scholars of the German historical tradition as Werner Sombart[1] and Max Weber.[2] In England, R. H. Tawney[3] drew attention to the profound changes in man's way of looking at his social responsibilities as the basis of transition from feudalism to capitalism in the sixteenth century. The United

1

States has been short in historians who painted with a broad brush, but such observers as John R. Commons[4] and Thorstein Veblen[5] gave great emphasis to ideology and social values in describing the development of American economic institutions. Americans, themselves, have traditionally emphasized the ideological roots of their institutions.

The other approach to description and explanation of economic institutions finds its classic exponent in Karl Marx who made ideology a function of the mode of economic organization. Marx[6] found the distinguishing characteristic of capitalism in the private ownership of the means of production and the sale of labor as a commodity. This enabled Marx to distinguish capitalism from the feudalism which preceded it and the communism which he predicted would inevitably succeed it.

Marx called attention to some profound changes in economic organization in distinguishing as a characteristic feature of capitalism the sale of labor as a commodity. Yet, insofar as he was calling attention to the shift from the sale of goods to the sale of labor services, he was merely noting the change in the character of technology which occurs in industrialization. For practical purposes, labor is sold to the state industrial enterprise in the Soviet Union in a way which differs from the United States mainly in the prohibition of explicit collective bargaining by the Russian labor unions.

While such economic historians as Sombart, Weber, and Tawney found the advent of capitalism explained by the rationalist spirit of the Renaissance and the individualist emphasis of the Protestant Reformation, Marx found the replacement of the corporate concepts of feudalism by the possessive individualism of capitalism to be the result of changes in agricultural and industrial technology. These changes permitted the ruling classes to alienate part of the increasing surplus of social output over the biological needs of men by the purchase of labor rather than by actual physical coercion.

Generalization in historical studies makes possible the comparison of

---

[1]Werner Sombart, *The Jews and Modern Capitalism* (New York: The Free Press, 1951). See pp. 160ff.

[2]Max Weber, *The Protestant Ethic and the Spirit of Capitalism*, 4th ed. (London: George Allen and Unwin, 1952). *General Economic History* (London: George Allen and Unwin, 1927).

[3]R. H. Tawney, *Religion and the Rise of Capitalism* (New York: The New American Library, 1960).

[4]John R. Commons, *Legal Foundations of Capitalism* (New York: The Macmillan Co., 1924).

[5]Thorstein Veblen, *The Theory of Business Enterprise* (New York: Scribner, 1932).

[6]Karl Marx, *Capital; a critique of political economy* (New York, The Modern Library, 1906).

different cultures and allows perspective on the peculiar and universal features of one's own society. In this respect, the lack of agreement among economic historians over the distinctive features of capitalism is both necessary and desirable. The economic institutions of a capitalist society are structured differently from those of noncapitalist societies by both ethical emphases and the requirements of different technologies. Controversy over whether economic institutions structure values or the opposite is an unresolvable question and most partisans on both sides would concur that they are really arguing about a matter of emphasis— not causation.

A difficulty arises in dealing on a comparative basis with the institutions of societies at different stages of economic development. It is the problem of distinguishing those features which are the result of the organizational problems of a particular technology and those which reflect a difference in values about the proper relationship of man to man in socio-economic organization. Thus, for example, one has difficulty deciding from the historical evidence whether American hostility to corporations and labor unions in the early nineteenth century was the result of the technology of the time which made them unnecessary in most instances or whether it was the result of ideological emphasis on the individual and the impropriety of giving political sanction to the activities of groups which could use that power to coerce individuals for their own benefit. Obviously, technology was very important in determining social practice, but then if one looks at the public stance toward corporations and labor unions during the same period in say, France or Britain, one is struck by the importance of unique historical circumstances and ideological differences.

This book will argue that the logic of the institutional arrangements loosely identified as "capitalist" has been determined both by social priorities and technological demands. Economic factors obviously play an important role in determining both social priorities and the technological structure. Nevertheless, the author wishes to argue that a society has options governed by its values. Economic development need not lead inexorably to Orwell's 1984.

Attempts to Characterize

Capitalism in America

The disagreements of economic historians and scholars of comparative economic institutions about the distinctive features of capitalist economic organization in other societies is matched by the diversity of opinions among observers of every sort about the character of contemporary American capitalism. As noted in the introduction, the term "capitalism" is seldom used. Some speak of America as being a "private enterprise" economy. Others emphasize the characteristic of "free" enterprise. How far these terms are synonymous with "capitalism" in the minds of their users is difficult to determine.[7]

One of the difficulties with Marx's description of capitalism as private ownership of the means of production—a definition which has been followed in the American practice of emphasizing "private enterprise" or "free enterprise"—is that property and freedom are general terms which need further specification. This is not just a matter of linguistic exactness. In legal discourse, *property* is identified as a "bundle of rights" or a "bundle of powers." What is in the "bundle" is decided by society. In a capitalist society, individuals are sanctioned by the state in the exercise of certain rights with respect to assets. But this is also true for practical purposes in such systems of economic organization as feudalism and socialism. Even in a capitalist society, the powers subsumed under the general term *property* vary widely. In contemporary America, the property which an individual has in his own labor, in the land on which he owns a home, or in his shares in an industrial corporation give him very different types of rights or powers.

Contemporary American use of the term *private* in connection with productive assets is likely to be misleading. The modern industrial corporation may be legally owned by individual investors, but the practical rights or powers which they exercise in the control of its policies, like their liabilities, are exceedingly circumscribed.[8] Even the American small farmer, a prototype private enterprise entrepreneur, is both supported and controlled by the state in a variety of ways.

Perhaps no attribute of economic organization is more susceptible to confusion than "freedom." An American has legal freedom to offer employment to another person above a certain age as long as the hours worked do not exceed a legal maximum and the compensation does not fall below a legally established minimum. An American has freedom to offer most goods for sale at any price he wishes but the anti-trust laws deny him the freedom to agree with others as to the price at which the goods will be offered, and fair trade legislation may prevent him from selling goods below "cost" or at a different price than that established by the maker. Much legislation now exists which denies freedom to home-

[7]For an interesting discussion of contemporary American attempts to "explain" the Amercian economic system, see R. Joseph Monsen, Jr., *Modern American Capitalism: Ideologies and Issues* (Boston: Houghton Mifflin Company, 1963).

[8]An already dated account of the changes wrought by the modern corporation on property may be found in A. A. Berle, *Power Without Property* (New York: Harcourt, Brace & World, Inc., 1959).

owners, school boards, employers, or restaurants to practice discrimination on grounds of race, religion, age, or sex.

Conceptual Confusions and
Practical Problems

The difficult problem with respect to the definition of freedom is not its existence or desirability but balancing the freedom of one man to do something with the freedom of another man from having the something done to him. As Justice Oliver Wendell Holmes once sagely observed, "Freedom to swing one's fist is limited by the proximity of another man's jaw."

The lack of agreement about the characteristics of capitalism and the contemporary economic institutions of the United States would be of largely academic interest if different conceptions about the extent to which enterprise in America ought to be "private" or "free" did not constitute the basis of many disagreements about the solution of important problems. The lack of any definition about what capitalism *is* has been accompanied by a failure to develop a consensus about what *ought* to be recognized as the "rights of the individual" and the "public interest."

Let us consider a few contemporary examples. There is a general consensus that economic growth is in the public interest. What *ought* to be the "rights" of individuals displaced by the technological change which makes economic growth possible? What *ought* to be the "rights" of management and of labor unions bargaining over the implementation of technological change and the gains resulting therefrom?

Another general consensus holds that all members of society *ought* to have the right to bargain over the conditions of their employment. What does this entail for compulsory union membership. Does it mean that workers in public services or critical industries *ought* to have the right to withdraw their labor collectively in support of their demands?

The problem of income inequality underlies the problems of urban decay and racial violence. How far is the government justified in dealing with the situation through income redistribution by taxation and subsidies, prevention of discrimination in employment, or even fostering of selective discrimination to aid minorities?

Control of price inflation is generally believed to be in the public interest. Should a democratic government place any restraints on its own actions with respect to the rate of increase of the money supply or price and wage controls? How *ought* the interests of one group of people in stable prices be balanced against the interests of another group in full employment?

Obviously, the problems just mentioned are not going to be solved by a better intellectual understanding of the character and development of American socio-economic institutions. They involve real conflicts of interest between various members of the community. The management of a corporation could increase profits more rapidly and the community at large could benefit from lower prices if management did not have to bargain with the unions over the displacement of labor. In the short run at least, the community as a whole might be better off if civil servants and workers in public service industries were prevented from striking. In practice, a large proportion of the white population would like to have the right to discriminate on the basis of color in order to restrict the opportunities of Negroes in housing and employment. Another such conflict exists between debtors and creditors over the rate of inflation.

While intellectual treatises cannot solve real conflicts of interest, they can make possible more rational compromises to some of the pressing problems which confront our society. We do not have any easy answers to pressing socio-economic problems. Solutions are not going to be found by the reiteration of claims about the "rights of the individual" and the "public interest" when extensive disagreement exists as to what individual rights and the public interest are. Understanding the logic and development of our institutions can only create increased agreement about the nature of the framework in which adjustment to the new problems caused by changing social priorities and technological change must be made.

Much of the debate and controversy over contemporary economic and social problems—economic growth, inflation, racial discrimination, urban decay, labor-management relations, to name just a few—involve one set of people advocating the use of political power to compel other people to do certain things. The "other" people frequently claim that the proposed action by the state would violate the rights of the individual—natural, moral, constitutional, or legal—and would, additionally, be against the long-term public interest.

The intellectual conflict between the two groups stems from a lack of understanding of the logic and development of the rights of freedom and property which structure our economic institutions and political system. One group views the existing distribution of property and effective freedom of action to be a function of political power which can be changed arbitrarily by political power. The other group regards the existing definition of freedom and property as being "natural" or "moral" in its origin rather than negotiated in a continually revised social contract based on bargaining and "consideration" (in the legal sense). There is truth on both sides. People do not often hold views which are completely at odds with reality. It is the extreme forms of both views which merit examination.

Politics and Morals—
Conflict and Confusion

A tradition of criticizing or rationalizing existing distributions of economic power in terms of natural rights, divinely bestowed prerogatives, constitutional provisions, or persuasive appeals to "self-evident" morality has existed in the United States for some time. Instead of inquiring as to the effects of social "interference," the supposedly pragmatic American has often questioned the morality or constitutionality of legislation affecting his interests. Businessmen or their spokesmen have been most inclined to do this, which is surprising given their supposed pragmatic approach and role as negotiators of prices, wages, and production arrangements.

This tradition began even before the American Revolution.[9] In the "Stamp Act" Congress of 1765, the colonists declared that an essential *right* of British subjects was that they could only be taxed by their consent *and* this consent could only be given by colonial legislatures. In 1776, while Adam Smith was weighing up the costs and benefits of the colonial empire and Edmund Burke was pragmatically urging accommodation of colonial demands, Americans threw down the gauntlet on grounds of *moral* principle. "We hold these truths to be self-evident," began the Declaration of Independence, "that all men are created equal, that they are endowed by their Creator with certain unalienable rights, that among these are Life, Liberty, and the pursuit of Happiness. . . ." The imposition of a tax on tea (together with some other grievances) called forth this magnificent statement of principle!

In 1828, a committee of the South Carolina legislature inveighed against the tariff on the ground that it was unconstitutional, and this later served as the basis for the "Nullification Doctrine" which led to secession and Civil War in 1860. The ground on which the tariff was held to be unconstitutional was that it favored certain geographic areas with protection and, thus, it was claimed, was not authorized since tariffs could only be levied "for the general welfare." This was an early statement of the principle that any government act which interfered with an interpersonal income distribution was a confiscation of property.

In 1857, in the famous Dred Scott decision, the Chief Justice of the Supreme Court stated that Congress had no right to prohibit slavery in

---

[9]An excellent collection of documents concerned with American history has been assembled by Richard Hofstadter, *Great Issues in American History* (New York: Vintage Books, 1958), two volumes. Many of the issues treated in the present volume will be found in the documentary selections included in the collection.

certain states; "no word can be found in the Constitution which gives Congress a greater power over slave property, or which entitles property of that kind to less protection than property of any other description."[10] What kind of government would be possible if all actions had to be specifically authorized in a written constitution and if property rights could never be changed by the legislature?

In the second of the so-called "Slaughter House"[11] cases which came before the Supreme Court in 1878 Justice Stephen Field gave an eloquent defense of the natural and constitutional rights of butchers to practice their trade as they pleased:

> As in our intercourse with our fellow men certain principles of morality are assumed to exist, without which society would be impossible, so certain inherent rights lie at the foundation of all action, and upon a recognition of them alone can free institutions be maintained. These inherent rights have never been more happily expressed than in the Declaration of Independence, that new evangel of liberty to the people . . . "We hold these truths to be self-evident"—that is, so plain that their truth is recognized upon their mere statement—"that all men are endowed"—not by edicts of emperors or decrees of parliament, or acts of Congress, but "by their Creator with certain inalienable rights"—that is, rights which cannot be bartered away, or given away, or taken away except in punishment or crime—"and that among these are life, liberty, and the pursuit of happiness, and to secure these"—not grant them but secure them—"governments are instituted among men. . . ."

The Interstate Commerce Commission, established in 1887 for the control of the railroads, was brought into being in response to tremendous popular pressure resulting from the possibilities and actualities of monopoly exploitation. Even the railroads were glad to see some control brought into the industry. Yet, in 1905, when certain changes were being considered by a Congressional committee, a prominent railroad man pointed out what he thought to be a very dangerous new precedent in regard to the public regulation of private utilities:

> It is a very, very serious moment when an Anglo-Saxon government undertakes the charge of people's money and says how much they shall earn by the exercise of their constitutional rights to liberty and property. And it should be recognized that possibly we are at the parting of the ways, and that if this be done it will go on until those constitutional guaranties have but little value, and the only profession worth exercising in the country will be that of holding office in some administrative board. . . .[12]

---

[10]*Dred Scott v. Sanford*, 19 Howard 393 (1857).
[11]*Butcher's Union Co. v. Crescent City Co.*, 111 U.S. 746 (1884).
[12]58th Congress, 3rd Session, House Documents, Vol. C, p. 226.

Was the notion that the state should control the price charged by a state-created and state-protected monopoly a dangerous new notion? Or was the doctrine that the Constitution guaranteed a person the right to use economic power unhindered by public control the dangerous new idea?

In 1908, the power of Congress to regulate working conditions was denied by the Supreme Court on the grounds that it was a deprivation of liberty which violated the Fifth Amendment to the Constitution:

> The right of a person to sell his labor upon such terms as he deems proper, is, in its essence, the same as the right of the purchaser of labor to prescribe the conditions upon which he will accept such labor from the person offering to sell it. . . . In all such particulars the employer and employee have equality of right, and any legislation that disturbs that equality is an arbitrary interference with the liberty of contract, which no government can legally justify in a free land.[13]

Inequality of bargaining power was to be ignored in order to maintain an "equality of rights" even when a democratically elected legislature wished to redress the disability of one type of party to a contract.

In the presidential campaign of 1928, Herbert Hoover stated his opposition to some of the programs advocated by his Democratic opponent such as agricultural price supports, production of hydroelectricity by the government, and state control of liquor distribution. He said that this:

> . . . would be a long step toward the abandonment of our American system and a surrender to the destructive operation of government conduct of commercial business. . . . The effect of this projection of government in business . . . would impair the very basis of liberty and freedom not only for those left outside the fold of expanded bureaucracy but for those embraced within it. . . . True liberalism seeks all legitimate (economic) freedom, first in the confident belief that without such freedom the pursuit of all other blessings and benefits is vain. That belief is the foundation of all American progress, political as well as economic . . . economic freedom cannot be sacrificed if political freedom is to be preserved. Even if Governmental conduct of business could give us more efficiency instead of less efficiency, the fundamental objection to it would remain unaltered and unabated. . . . It would extinguish equality and opportunity. It would dry up the spirit of liberty and progress. *For these reasons primarily* [italics the author's] it must be resisted.[14]

In 1960, the president of American Telephone and Telegraph, the

---

[13]*Adair* v. *United States*, 208 U.S. 161, 175 (1908).
[14]*The New York Times*, October 23, 1928. Quoted in Hofstadter, *op. cit.*, Vol. II, p. 341.

largest business corporation in the United States, attempted to argue the merits of capitalism on the grounds of its unique ethical content:

> We are involved in one of the great ideological struggles of all time. We are in it so deep that it is hard to see it in perspective. But essentially it is a contest between two quite basic concepts. One is that men are capable of faith in ideas that lift their minds and hearts, ideas that raise their sights and give them hope, energy, and enthusiasm. Opposing this is the belief that the pursuit of material ends is all that life on this earth is about.[15]

Assuming that it is capitalism which is distinguished as the faith which inspires, one has difficulty seeing why private property and free markets should have much emotional appeal. Surely, it is communism which appeals to men on the grounds of a revolutionary faith and the hope of a future classless utopia rather than capitalism whose traditional justification has been the ability to "deliver the goods." Also difficult to understand is why businessmen, whose claim to status is their ability to organize, bargain, and produce, should have to justify the system they operate on the grounds of its ability to generate "faith in ideas." The justification of the system, surely, is in its ability to generate maximum output and do it with a maximum of self-interested cooperation and a minimum of coercion. To paraphrase Keynes' toast to economics, capitalism is not a civilization but the possibility of a civilization.[16]

The Modern Version
of Natural Rights

In a book published in 1962, a distinguished economist wrote that an American who could not buy a foreign-made watch because of an import quota, or a merchant who could not sell Alka-Seltzer below the fair trade price, a farmer who could not plant wheat without a quota was being deprived of an *essential* part of his freedom.[17] The same author went on to insist that historical evidence showed that societies which restricted free markets also restricted political freedom. Thus, has the long tradition of equating economic freedom with political freedom been carried down to the present.

[15]Frederick R. Kappel, *Vitality in a Business Enterprise* (New York: McGraw-Hill Book Company, 1960), p. 75. Mr. Kappel is not singled out as an individual. His speech is fairly typical of the utterances heard at businessmen's lunches.

[16]Keynes' famous toast to the Royal Economic Society, "To economics—not a civilization, but the possibility of civilization."

[17]Milton Friedman, *Capitalism and Freedom* (Chicago: University of Chicago Press, 1962), p. 9.

The eminent American economist just cited, Milton Friedman, merits further examination here both as one of the most articulate expositors of the traditional "natural rights" or "moral principles" approach and as a person of sufficient influence to be a president of the American economic association and economic advisor to the Republican presidential candidate in the 1964 election. Rather than belabor the material accomplishments of the American capitalist system, Friedman offers an argument for its *moral* superiority on the grounds of noncoercion—a modern version of the old natural law argument. He posits that "freedom in economic arrangements is itself a component of freedom broadly understood, so economic freedom is an end in itself."[18] The difficulty with his statement is that it begs the question about freedom *for whom to do what*. A society is not necessarily more free if it has less restrictions placed on individual actions by law. The critics of laissez-faire capitalism have for centuries condemned the absence of social constraints on the power of one individual economically to coerce another on moral grounds. The important question is not whether there should be freedom but *who* should have the power to do *what* things. Friedman's lack of explicitness about this question makes his explanation of the logic of capitalism on "moral" grounds unconvincing except to those who are presently very satisfied with the extent of their power and alternatives under the status quo.

Consider his application of the "moral" argument to the Fair Employment Practices Commission (FEPC) which seeks to prevent racial discrimination in employment. Friedman states:

> Such legislation clearly involves interference with the freedom of individuals to enter into voluntary contracts with one another. It subjects any such contract to approval or disapproval by the state. Thus, it is directly an interference with the freedom of the kind that we would object to in most other contexts.[19]

Friedman would rather allow racial discrimination in employment than curb the power of the discriminating employer in his freedom of contract. Preservation of the legal freedom of contract for the employer is more moral than increasing the effective freedom of the weaker party to the contract! We long ago outlawed the freedom of the employer to offer a "yellow dog" contract which made nonmembership in a labor union a condition of employment. The principle of social intervention on behalf of the weaker party to the contract is exactly the same. One can say for Friedman, however, that he is consistent in decrying that latter limitation

18*Ibid.*, p. 8.
19*Ibid.*, p. 111.

on the freedom to discriminate for the employer on grounds of the employee's union membership as well as his race.

Friedman makes an impressive apologia for capitalism in his development of a pragmatic argument for freedom, property, and minimal state intervention. Yet here, the pragmatism frequently misses the point by not enquiring into *why* capitalist institutions of freedom and property work. Thus, with regard to property, Friedman follows the usual practice of economists in taking property relationships as "given" and states: "The existence of a well-specified and generally accepted definition of property is far more important than just what the definition is."[20] Of course, social acceptance of the definition of property is the important point. Social consensus about the definition of property is the *sine qua non* of social stability. The acceptance of the definition, however, depends on what the definition is. The definition must change if the social consensus about *what people should have the power to do which things* changes.

We had a Civil War in this country a century ago because one part of the population decided that they would no longer tolerate and enforce one person having property in another in the institution of chattel slavery and because another part decided that Congress could not constitutionally impose protective tariffs. We had considerable labor strife in this country before the courts and legislatures conceded the right of employees to bargain collectively and strike in support of their demands. We are likely to have considerable civil disturbance in this country today if the courts include the right to discriminate as one of the powers of the property owner or employer. It is disagreement about what claims *ought* to be given social sanction as property which necessitates inquiry into the principles used by a capitalist society to apportion and reconcile those claims.

The Need for a
20th Century Philosophy

The author lays the blame for much of our current social malaise directly on the failure of twentieth century American society to adapt our individualist principles to the realities of a modern, interdependent, industrial society. Attempts to refurbish the old "natural rights" arguments have been rightly rejected as intellectually unsatisfactory and suspect as arguments for the privileges of the established order.

Economists, so it seems to the author, must accept part of the blame for the failure of our society to develop an acceptable social ideology.

[20]*Ibid.*, p. 27.

They have found it intellectually convenient to operate with an economic model of society in which there is a certain set of claims to productive assets and conventions about their use. Without passing judgment on the question of the empirical usefulness of the model for purposes of analyzing economic behavior *within* a given social framework, one can say that economists have been singularly uninterested in the process by which the framework was evolved and the reasons why the members of society have an interest in maintaining it. Leaving the explanation of the logic of property and freedom, the economic powers of the state, and the existing rights and liabilities of the corporation, the labor union, and the individual citizen to the lawyers, political scientists, and sociologists is not satisfactory. It is not satisfactory because economic arrangements need economic justification.

The core of the problem of a coherent capitalist ideology lies with the justification of the twin cornerstones of capitalist organization—property and freedom. A variety of noneconomic arguments have been offered over the course of centuries for the institutions of private property and economic freedom. These arguments range from natural rights to arguments for political freedom and the impossibility of maintaining it without the guarantees of certain economic rights, to arguments purely and simply against disturbing the status quo. All of these justifications beg the question about *who* is guaranteed the right to control the use of *which* productive assets. What must be justified in any existent capitalist society is the actual distribution of property and effective economic freedom.

What makes our society profoundly uneasy and alienates its dissidents is a growing belief that capitalism rests only on the coercive power of entrenched economic interests. This charge, most eloquently made by Marx a century ago, has paralyzed discussion of the nature of property and freedom in a capitalist system because it is implicitly accepted as true by many of capitalism's strongest advocates. It has bothered the philosophers of possessive individualism from John Locke to Milton Friedman.

The "practical man's" view was succinctly stated in the eighteenth century by the great English jurist, Blackstone:[21]

> There is . . . nothing which so generally . . . engages the affections of mankind [as that] sole and despotic dominion which one man claims and exercises over the external things of the world, in total exclusion of the right of any other individual in the universe. . . . And yet there are very few, that will give themselves the trouble to consider the original and foundation of this right. . . . Pleased as we are with the possession, we seem

[21]William Blackstone, *Commentaries on the Law of England* (Philadelphia: Robert Bell, 1771), Book II, p. 2.

afraid to look back to the means by which it was acquired, as if fearful of some defect in our title . . . not caring to reflect that [accurately and strictly speaking] there is no foundation in nature or in natural law, why a set of words upon parchment should convey the dominion of land: why the son should have a right to exclude his fellow-creatures from a determinate spot of ground, because his father had done so before him: or why the occupier of a particular field or of a jewel, when lying on his death-bed, and no longer able to maintain possession, should be entitled to tell the rest of the world which of them should enjoy it after him . . . [Nevertheless] it is well if the mass of mankind will obey the laws when made, without scrutinizing too nicely into the reasons of making them.

The contemporary dissatisfaction with the structure of American economic and political power stems from a rejection of Blackstone's counsel to accept the status quo without inquiring too closely into its rationale. Those who lack "sole and despotic dominion . . . over the external things of the world" are increasingly unwilling to accept the claims of others unquestioningly. And many of the possessors are profoundly uneasy about the legitimacy of their position.

Intellectual Justification of Political Power

Advocates of the use of political power to alter the status quo have usually felt obliged to adapt their arguments to their opponents' claims and cloak their demands in terms of the "rights" of individuals against the rights of property. In his criticism of capitalism even Marx found it expedient to argue that capitalism had been false to its principles in allowing certain men to alienate part of the value created by the labor of other men in the wage bargain. Marx, like John Locke, argued that every man had a natural right to what he had produced with his own labor. While Locke argued that a capitalist system was the only way to guarantee men property in their natural rights, Marx argued that a capitalist system systematically denied the masses property in life, liberty, and estate and, *therefore*, men should overthrow capitalist governments which failed to protect their property.

In the United States the advocates of changes in the status quo have practically always accepted the legitimacy and desirability of preserving a system based on the preservation of freedom and security for the individual. They have usually argued only that existing practices represented overweening claims by some members of the community which denied others their freedom and security. The opponents of slavery argued that the state could not go on sanctioning a property arrangement which denied men their freedom. The populists who complained about their treatment at the hands of the railroads denied that government-created monopolies could ask any price they wished in the absence of alternative transportation facilities. Labor unions fought to establish the principle that wages and the conditions of employment were not the exclusive prerogative of management but were established by contract. In our own day, minorities are seeking to establish that the rights of property do not include the right to discriminate.

In any society the powers or rights of individuals are defined, protected, and limited by the state. A society cannot escape making a determination of the content and distribution of the powers embodied in freedom and property. The status quo always represents some particular distribution. To follow a policy of laissez faire is to make a judgment that the present distribution is optimal.

The arguments for nonintervention by the state in existing economic arrangements have usually been of two types. The first the author has designated the "moral principles" or "natural rights" argument. The second is pragmatic. The essence of the "moral principles" argument is the proposition that freedom and property are inalienable rights with a basis in natural law or divine establishment. The argument derives from natural law theories and specifically from John Locke's theory of civil government. It acquires policy implications when a second proposition is slipped in that the existing definition and distribution of property and freedom is divinely ordained or naturally evolved. Social intervention to modify the existing distribution then becomes immoral or unwise because it interferes with the inexorable forces of nature.

Marxism, just like capitalism and every other "ism" also, has a moral justification. It is the "labor theory of value." The primary proposition is that all value is created by labor and, consequently, the social framework must be constructed to ensure that every man receives the value he has produced. The secondary proposition is that a capitalist society is unable to secure this and must, therefore, be replaced.

The pragmatic argument for nonintervention by the state with the freedom of individuals to bargain about the use of their property as they please claims to be empirical and realist. It has no illusions about the status quo being the best of all possible worlds, and it eschews judgments about morality or immorality. It merely argues that attempts by the state to regulate the affairs of private citizens inevitably are unsuccessful in achieving their objectives. The argument has its origins in responses such as that made by the seventeenth century French merchant to the Finance Minister of Louis XIV, Jean Baptiste Colbert. Colbert asked how the state could best foster and promote commercial prosperity. The merchant responded, "Nous laissez faire" (Leave us alone), and "laissez faire" has been the description of a policy of governmental non-interference in the economic process ever since. It merits emphasis that the rationale for laissez faire in the heyday of natural law was the pragmatic interest of the state in increasing economic output.

Adam Smith was the first great Anglo-Saxon protagonist of this position. He emphasized that even when social policies were intended to be "in the public interest," civil servants would be inept in administration and policies would be evaded and turned to their advantage and the disadvantage of the public by selfish interest groups. Smith concluded it was better to restrict government interference with the economy to the maintenance of law and order. He even added optimistically that an "Invisible Hand" would reconcile the pursuit of individual self-interest to serve the public interest in the most efficient manner.

An interesting note here is that the Marxist-Leninist version of the pragmatic argument likewise stresses the impossibility of reforming and controlling a capitalist system and, therefore, advocates revolution and a dictatorship in the name of the proletariat with the abolition of bargaining as the only workable system, given human nature.

Both the "moral" and the "pragmatic" arguments for nonintervention by the state in men's economic activities are attractive to the strong and a counsel of submission for the weak. The status quo can be explained in either approach by reference to natural law, historical inevitability, or human fallibility. The most important reason for examining these arguments as a rationalization for our economic institutions is that they no longer command the widespread acceptance in the United States they once did. This is because the "moral principles" argument has usually been made in a way which begs the question about the morality of capitalism by moving from a proposition that freedom and security are desirable to the second proposition that capitalism provides them.

The pragmatic argument for governmental nonintervention in economic arrangements has frequently been ignored in practice in the United States, and its relevance to the pluralistic society of huge corporations, labor unions, and government which has replaced the Jeffersonian dream of a nation of small farmers necessitates the adaptation of principles to govern a new pragmatic approach to the relationship of public interest and individual enterprise.

Intellectual Foundations for
Modern American Capitalism

At the present time, Americans are in the process of questioning and redefining their basic principles concerning the relationships between the individual and the state. This is not a unique occurrence. It is an ongoing concern in a society which is technologically dynamic and politically democratic. Problems change and the values of society do also. "The Great Depression," and "The New Deal" shattered a traditional, largely "laissez faire" definition of individualist principles and led to an acceptance by most Americans of considerable governmental participation in the economic process. The desirability of *some* state interference with individual economic freedom and an existing distribution of property was accepted. However, a clarification of individualist principles to indicate the proper limits to political power has not emerged.[22]

Our traditions have historically emphasized limitation of the power of the state in the belief that the individual should have some rights even against the majority. Acceptance by the majority of a limitation on its *de facto* power depends upon an understanding by the majority of the desirability of limitation. While those who advocate more governmental control of the economy are often insufficiently aware of the practical limits to direction and coercion and of the dangers inherent in the arbitrary use of political power, individualists are also often unaware that their rights have a social origin and are guaranteed by the majority only in the expectation that certain rights to freedom and property will produce socially acceptable results. Those who advocate less government interference with private economic power are frequently blind to the social unacceptability of certain uses of economic power by its *de facto* holders.

Much of the intellectual confusion about the "rights of the individual," "the rights of property," "the rights or power of the majority" and/or the responsibilities of the individual, the state, the corporation, the labor union, *et al* have been inherited from political and economic philosophers who have concerned themselves with the nature of a "capitalist system." Many of the confusions have originated from the attempts to carry forward the explanations and arguments appropriate to the technology and beliefs of one age to another. As John Maynard Keynes wrote in his *General Theory* in an attempt to persuade his contemporaries that traditional arguments might be inapplicable to the economic system which had evolved: "Practical men, who believe themselves to be quite exempt from any intellectual influences, are usually the slaves of some defunct economist." [23]

The preservation of myths is not without value to a society. They are, properly considered, allegories and attempts to present in simple language profound truths about human behavior. John Locke's mythical

---

[22]One perceptive observer has argued that people have rejected ideological disputation. See Daniel Bell, *The End of Ideology* (New York: The Free Press, 1960).

[23]John Maynard Keynes, *The General Theory of Employment, Interest, and Money* (London: Macmillan & Co. Ltd., 1936).

"social contract" between men to protect their "natural rights" to property points to some fundamental tendencies in human behavior and the consequent desirability of making social guarantees to provide security and incentives. Adam Smith's "Invisible Hand" points up some of the equilibrating tendencies operating in an individualistic society to check the pursuit of self-interest and make it produce good social results. Even Marx's labor theory of value was a confused protest about income distribution and alternatives in an industrial society which contained insights into real problems in an individualist society with inequalities in wealth distribution. To be useful, however, the myths must be reinterpreted in every age lest the old interpretations and policies based on them become irrelevant to the present. Neglect of a lengthy intellectual tradition would deprive us of an immense accumulation of understanding. But failure to base the arguments for capitalism on the technological and sociological needs of our own day will be summarily dismissed—not as right or wrong, true or false, but as irrelevant.

Almost thirty years ago, the distinguished economist-historian-philosopher, Joseph Schumpeter, despaired for the future of capitalism on the grounds that less privileged groups and the intellectuals would not listen to the rational arguments to be made in its defense.[24]

The author does not share Schumpeter's pessimism about the rationality of men—at least men who have had as long a tradition as Americans of freedom and property defined by the consent of the governed. The logic of our system has always rested on a cost-benefit calculation of the desirability of freedom even though it may have been frequently moralized about in terms of "inalienable rights." One need be pessimistic about the future of capitalism in the United States only if it is defended by outworn concepts subscribed to by Americans who would rather moralize than change. The justification of private property and economic freedom is its utility in producing socially acceptable results. Private enterprise has historically been sanctioned where it suited public interest. It will be in the future as long as the freedom and property are defined in a way which leads the community to accept them on a self-interested calculation of benefits and costs.

Few Americans would claim today that the present distribution of freedom and property for members of society represents some natural or inevitable result. Yet, underlying American social pragmatism there is at least a wish on the part of many individuals to look at their present freedom and property as something inviolable. Many Americans deny the legitimacy of state interference with their claims and seek to avoid bargaining with other members of society over their property claims. They

[24]Joseph A. Schumpeter, *Capitalism, Socialism and Democracy* (New York: Harper & Row, Publishers, 1942). See especially chap. xiii.

view the Constitution as a safeguard against any legislative action which they find contrary to their interests and deny the right of the government to interfere with their use of their property. This book is written in an attempt to disabuse these Americans of their illusions about the inviolability of their claims.

On the other hand, another group of Americans, finding that they have little property worth protecting and little freedom of action, believe that the existing capitalist institutions of freedom and property are structured by the existing holders of political power to suit their interests without regard for the interests of others. This book is written to explain the logic of freedom and property to those people—partly to give them increased intellectual understanding of the system they wish to reform and to aid them in pressing for legitimate changes of institutions which can no longer be said to protect either individual or public interest.

2

An Economic Theory of Institutional Development:

the argument

In order to understand the character of contemporary American capitalism it is necessary to examine both the process by which it has evolved and the logic of the rules which govern social behavior. An explanation of how we came to possess the existing set of "rights" or rules governing the behavior of individuals, corporations, labor unions, and government must be both historical and analytical.

Reading the tea leaves of history in search for an implicit dynamic process which determines the changes in economic institutions is a tricky business. What one sees in the bottom of the cup is very likely what one expects to find. Yet, we must start out with some assumptions about human behavior in order to make any sense out of the past. The author's approach to the explanation of the historical development of economic institutions is essentially functionalist. The author posits that sets of institutional arrangements are worked out by men and survive as long as they are perceived to be useful in contributing to such individual and social goals as security, provision of the material means of existence, and opportunity for individual advancement. The arrangements are changed when technological advances create new opportunities for economic improvement or when they create a demand for protection by groups who are able to exercise political power to win protection of their interests from the other members of society.

In our skeptical and empirical age it may seem unnecessary to write polemics against conceptions of economic institutions based on "natural law" or "historical inevitability." Yet a curiously unreflective attitude exists toward property rights and economic freedom in the United States. Existing claims to economic prerogatives are taken for granted, and demands for change are often greeted with reiteration of claims to those prerogatives rather than their justification in pragmatic terms. While this might be explained as the arrogance of privilege, the author thinks a more reasonable (and less damning) explanation is to be found in the peculiar historical development of the United States. We were, as Carl Sandburg rhapsodized, "born free." For generations we have been taught to believe that "life, liberty, and the pursuit of happiness" are inalienable rights and that they are secured to all Americans by the Constitution. For this reason any attempt by the Congress or the courts to interfere with an existing distribution of prerogatives is assailed by those who feel their rights are being impaired. They do not ask how they came to have those rights or why society has an interest in protecting them.

This attribution of the status quo to natural law has served to frustrate the demands of new claimants for state protection of their interests and has contributed, on their part, to overweening claims and frequently to a cynicism about the possibility of achieving reform by peaceful and pragmatic means. By failing to inquire into the logic and development of property and economic freedom, both groups of people have made rationalization of economic institutions to serve their own interests *and* those of the remainder of society more difficult. That is why the argument for freedom and property as socially created guarantees is presented in historical prospective and analytical terms in this volume.

The Social Necessity of Property Definition

Every society must have some set of generally accepted rules and conventions about the use, enjoyment, and exchange of productive assets. In our own society we subsume the particular claims of individuals and organizations with respect to certain assets under the term *property*. The term *property* is often used to designate a parcel of land because the conceptions about land use and legal terminology with respect to any asset grew up largely from ancient rules about the use of land. Property in land originally meant the socially guaranteed right of an individual to exclude others from trespass on his land and the right to exchange or enjoy the land or its produce free from the interference of others or the arbitrary power of the state. "Property," however, is also a general concept. A person's property in any type of asset gives him certain socially sanctioned powers with respect to the asset.

The assignment of property claims by a society fulfills three important economic functions: First, it determines the distribution of income by vesting the use of particular assets with particular individuals. Second, it rationalizes the use of resources by giving individuals an interest in using them at an optimal rate over time rather than consuming them all in the present before others do so.[1] Third, by vesting the control of assets with an individual and securing their enjoyment to him over time, property gives an inducement to the individual to increase the output available from those resources by the investment of capital or the improvement of technology or more efficient organization of productive activity.

Controlling the use of assets is an inevitable feature of social organization. At the most basic level, there must be a set of conventions about the legitimacy of possession and shares of consumption to avoid anarchy. However, no inevitability exists about the particular configuration of property rights. The organization of production and consumption has been accomplished by a variety of methods in the past and the present by different societies. Our own conventions with regard to the assignment of property claims have evolved from the modification and adaptation of Roman law and the practices evolved in the day-to-day practices of merchants, agriculturalists, and workmen. They were not discovered on tablets of stone or invented *de novo* by the American founding fathers or their successors in legislative assemblies.

The Evolution of
Property Assignment

The argument developed with regard to the evolution of property rights in subsequent chapters emphasizes the progressive realization by the rulers of society of the utility of granting security to the claims to assets worked out by individual members of society in bargaining between themselves as opposed to the claims settled on members of society by tradition or physical coercion. The first step in this process was the change from the chattel slavery of the Roman Empire to the feudal arrangements of the Middle Ages where men were still not free to leave their inherited status but at least had certain privileges and the opportunity to bargain about them. The second step was the substitution of legal freedom of opportunity to use or sell one's labor or the products

---

[1]The allocatory function of property in production is discussed at length with some interesting examples taken from the work of social anthropologists in, Harold Demsetz, "Toward a Theory of Property Rights," *American Economic Review*, May 1967.

of one's labor as one wished and was able. The third step, which we are presently making, is the alteration of social arrangements to increase the effective bargaining power of all members of society so that their legal freedom may be effectively utilized.

The traditional arguments for private property and economic freedom have largely been made in the past by deriving the "right" to freedom from the nature of man and the right to property from man's exercise of his freedom.[2] These rights have been coupled with the "Golden Rule" —the ethical imperative of treating others as one would be treated. They have also been linked with such a system of behavior as Kant's "categorical imperative." The author prefers to abandon this ontological approach in favor of one which emphasizes the self-interest of granting freedom and property to individual members of society by other members on the rationale that those granting and guaranteeing the rights of other individuals will benefit by the process. This, the author maintains, is why an increasingly large proportion of society in the capitalist countries of the West have secured progressively more freedom and property —not because of any high-flown beliefs about the rights of individuals derived from an analysis of human nature.

The Rationale of

Institutional Change

If one inspects the disintegration of feudal ideas about land use and the substitution of modern notions about freehold ownership or secure tenancy, one notes the economic rationality of those who traded the feudal system of privileges and obligations for the property rights of modern practice. If one considers the breakdown of the elaborate system of guild regulation of manufacturing and commerce one notes the practical political problems and economic disadvantages which were increasingly realized by those in political control.

The abandonment of many types of trade regulation by political authorities and the withdrawal of sanctions for the regulation of trade by private groups did not come about because of some realization of the right of men "to truck, barter, and exchange" as they pleased. It occurred when those who held political power realized that trade regulation was limiting prosperity, diminishing government revenue, and creating political disaffection amongst those placed at a disadvantage by

[2]See, for example, Otto von Gierke, *Political Theories of the Middle Age*, translated with an introduction by F. W. Maitland (Cambridge: Cambridge University Press, 1900). A more compact discussion for the more casual reader may be found in G. H. Sabine, *A History of Political Theory* (New York: Holt, Rinehart & Winston, Inc., 1937), chap. xxi.

regulation.[3] A similar realization has been taking place in the Soviet economy since the death of Stalin.[4]

The legalization of interest taking, political enforcement of debt contracts and guarantees of their negotiability, provision of freedom of market access, and granting patents and copyrights to encourage the production of knowledge were all cases of social acceptance of practices worked out by individual members of society. They were initially resisted in every case on grounds of principle and (usually) reluctantly accepted because those who advocated them were able to win recognition of the social utility of the arrangements.

The United States started out with extremely individualistic views about the rights of individuals to unregulated possession and use of their assets. The absence of guild organization of trade or a feudal past in agriculture and the conscious rejection of mercantilist policies in the regulation of commerce coupled with the opportunities afforded by the frontier lent practically universal credence to the doctrine that what an individual possessed was the result entirely of his unaided efforts and that interference by the state or by others with his use of his assets was morally wrong. The social character of the definition of freedom and property, however, soon began to present problems and conflicts of interest which had to be resolved politically, and, in 1860, by a bloody civil war.

One of the thorniest problems which had to be worked out was the power of the state to interfere with an existing distribution of property rights. Before the Civil War, the South contended that the Federal government lacked the constitutional power to levy protective tariffs, carry on public works, or interfere with the extension or practice of chattel slavery. After the Civil War and up until the 1930's, opponents of government regulation of business, who were supported by the courts, frequently alleged that the "due process" clauses of the Fifth and Fourteenth Amendments protected private property from legislative control of their use. At the root of much of the disagreement about the proper role of the state in the regulation of men's economic transactions was an inadequate recognition of the inevitable conflicts arising from the state's need to provide both freedom of action and freedom from the coercive action of others in order to maintain the support of its constituents.

Market Freedom and Market Control. The argument with respect to freedom to bargain and exchange presented in subsequent chapters emphasizes the recognition by society of the social utility of individual

---

[3]For an account of the process in France at the end of the Middle Ages, see Martin Wolfe, "French Views on Wealth and Taxes from the Middle Ages to the Old Regime," *Journal of Economic History*, Vol. xxvi, No. 4, (Dec. 1966) pp. 466–483.

[4]See Chapter XI.

freedom in certain circumstances. The state can afford to allow parties to the exchange of goods or factor services freedom to bargain within the limits of voluntarism only as long as both parties to the exchange are protected from the power of the other by the existence of alternative exchange possibilities. It was the absence of alternatives which led medieval society to the protection of consumers from the powers of suppliers. It was the existence of alternatives which contributed to the breakdown of the guild laws designed to give protection through status to labor. It was the increasing limitation of effective alternatives for labor and for consumers after the development of the modern industrial state which led to demands for protection of the former by unions and by law and for the latter by anti-trust legislation.

Growth and Control of Surplus. The process of economic growth leads to increasing gains from exchange of labor and goods by the parties and, at the same time, may increase the indeterminacy of the exchange bargain when the parties lack alternatives. The author has resurrected at many points in the argument the notion of a "surplus," the difference between what a seller would be willing to accept and what a buyer would be willing to give in an exchange.

For an unconscionable period of time, intelligent discussion of the function of markets and the proper role of the state in ordering exchange transactions has been confused by ideological commitments concerning the existence and distribution of a "surplus." On the one hand, Marxists and their intellectual cousins have contended that the markets for labor and goods would always be "rigged" by the capitalists to allocate the largest part of social production to a small proportion of society which continued to control political power. On the other hand, supporters of the status quo and evolutionary change in economic institutions have been prone to emphasize the theoretical results and inevitability of perfect competition in which all goods would be exchanged in terms of their cost of production and all owners of factor services would receive the value of the marginal product produced by those factors. Both have ignored the change in institutional arrangements which have been made in the United States and other capitalist countries to secure a socially acceptable division of income by altering the distribution of "surplus."

Disagreements between defenders and critics of evolutionary capitalism over what actually happens to income distribution in the course of capitalist development have been further befuddled by the confusion of positive and normative judgments. Marxists have argued that goods *ought* to exchange at prices equal to their relative labor content and members of society *ought* to receive a share of output equal to their contribution of labor. Insofar as defenders of "free" markets have developed any ethical (as opposed to efficient allocation) argument, they have tended to argue that the owners of the factors of production *ought* to receive the value of the marginal social output of the factor services which they own. Questions about the legitimacy of ownership are usually pushed conveniently into the background as are questions about the determinants of marginal productivity.

In the United States the problems arising from the use of markets in regard to income distribution have been countered by anti-trust legislation to preserve competition in goods markets, by labor legislation to encourage the formation of strong unions, and by progressive taxation and the redistribution of income through the provision of social services and, especially, education. These measures, which have helped to limit the share of national income going to the owners of physical capital, have been acquiesced in by them because of a realization that they had less to lose from the progressive modification of an existing system than from the repression or revolution which would have ensued if they attempted to maintain their claims by force or appeals to the inviolability of an existing distribution of property from change by constitutional means.

Marx prophesied that revolution was inevitable because the rulers of a capitalist society would never peacefully accept the modification of their property rights and the circumscription of their bargaining power. He was wrong. At least he was wrong in the United States and the industrialized countries of Western Europe.

Individual Freedom and Collective Action. In the United States, one of the most difficult problems of adjusting the social structure to the realities of technology in a modern industrial state has been that of resolving the relationship between collective action by individuals and the interests of the public and individual members of those groups. The creation of the modern industrial corporation by individuals pooling their capital necessitated legal changes to allow them to limit their liability by contract. The legitimation of the powers of the modern labor union required the abandonment of older doctrines about the danger of conspiratorial action to the public at large and to individuals coerced by the power of conspiratorial activity. The resolution of conflicting interests has frequently been unsatisfactory because of a tendency of individual citizens, the legislatures, and the courts to think in terms of legal freedom rather than economic power.

Giant business corporations may be entitled to some safeguards from arbitrary action by the state in their capacity as artificial persons just as the real persons who own them enjoy certain immunities. Their size and *de facto* power to affect the interests of large numbers of people by their actions, and public control and/or the acceptance of particular responsibilities by corporations has been increasingly recognized in our society by those who have noted the evolution of capitalism from a society of small, independent individuals to one of large interdependent groups.[5]

The progressive acceptance of collective action by labor in unions came about slowly in the United States as it was recognized that imperfect labor markets and inequalities in bargaining power made collective bargaining a necessity. The traditional arguments against conspiracy, however—protection of the consuming public and of individual workers affected by the power of the union to control the conditions of employment—have not been adequately answered. In large part this has been the result of neglect of the realities of power and concentration on the theoretical freedom of individuals to turn to other alternatives which do not exist.

The economic security of the individual in a capitalist society was to be provided by the opportunity for the individual to make provisions for his own welfare during times of adverse economic conditions, sickness, or old age. This solution has not proved to be viable or socially acceptable and has led to arrangements for government insurance schemes to force individuals to make provision for themselves. The appropriateness of these schemes (in the United States such programs as Social Security, Unemployment Compensation, and Medicare) has frequently been questioned on the grounds of efficiency and interpersonal equity. In this volume they are explained as another specification of the operation of the market designed to alter income distribution by political means because of the failure of the market to work acceptably.

Capitalism and

Economic Rationality

Insofar as "capitalism" can be distinguished as a particular kind of socio-economic system, this author feels that it can be identified with a type of calculating, benefit-cost analysis of social institutions and adaptation of those institutions to changes in costs and benefits. Let us be specific. In medieval society, the conception of social order emphasized its structuring from the top down. The powers of government were derived in theory from divine ordinance or force, and the governed had privileges and obligations which they were to accept without question. To bargain about those privileges and responsibilities was to confront divine preroga-

[5]See, for example, Adolph A. Berle and Gardiner C. Means, *The Modern Corporation and Private Property* (New York: Macmillan, 1932), and subsequent writings by Berle.

tive or the threat of physical coercion. The theory was that the rulers would protect the governed in the possession of privileges appropriate to their status. That was their responsibility and the basis of social order. Various revolutionary governments in the modern world justify autocratic government in terms of rule in the interests of the people but the governed are denied effective choices and bargaining power against the state by every means possible. Bargaining and criticism is viewed as subversive of the social order.

Capitalism differs from more corporate, authoritarian views of society in accepting and strengthening the powers of individuals in the society, even *against* the government in power. A capitalist society does this because of a belief that the members of society will be able to protect themselves against other members of society in making economic arrangements. Bilateral exchange contracts arrived at voluntarily are sanctioned because of a belief that the resulting division of the gains from exchange will be acceptable to the parties concerned. Individually bargained claims to property are sanctioned because of a calculation that this will lead to behavior which will enrich society as well as the individual to whom property rights are guaranteed. This, in fact, is the principle which claimants to freedom and property have historically made to justify the social recognition of individual claims. The justification of capitalism, as an economic system, has been its tendency to increase social output through the ordering of incentives which induce appropriate individual responses.

Viewing claims of individuals to property and freedom as being granted by society in order to induce asset creation and efficient utilization of existing resources points up the origin of these rights in a social contract. Society sanctions individual claims to do certain things and undertakes to guarantee individuals security in the exercise of certain powers. The individual does not have a *carte blanche* to use his assets in any way he wishes. On the other hand, the origin of rights in the state does not mean that the state can rescind or deny the powers granted arbitrarily. It cannot because this would destroy the credibility of the guarantee which is necessary to induce asset creation by individual members of society.

The argument about the logic and development of capitalism presented in this book, then, is one which emphasizes the social utility of capitalist arrangements for a society interested in maximizing economic growth while retaining the security of the individual. It does not depend on any belief in the "natural" or "moral" rights of men to property in assets, or freedom from social control of their use. It emphasizes that institutions have been changed as individuals have been able to convince the rest of society that the rest of society would be better off by recognizing certain rights to freedom and property than it would be if it did not recognize them.

In the last analysis, society's response to individual demands depends upon a calculation as to what the individual's contribution is worth in terms of social output and, also, the costs of denying the individual what he demands if society feels that the individual's contribution to social output is less than he demands.

The author asks the reader not to shudder at this portrayal of the calculated character of the social contract which defines the distribution of social output. The author does not mean to suggest that members of a society are not motivated by regard for their fellows and a willingness to sacrifice their own short-term interests for the benefit of others. In the absence of a fairly broad view of "self-interest" which results in a sense of social responsibility, a "civil" society is impossible. The author merely wishes to point out that, *in extremis*, individual demands and social response are based on a calculation of the costs of violence, coercion, and revolution as well as the benefits of cooperation.

Income Distribution and

Rationality

The distinguishing characteristic of a capitalist system of economic organization with respect to the distribution of the "surplus" between what an individual produces and what he actually receives is that capitalism allows the "surplus" to be distributed among the population according to their economic bargaining power. This is a rather difficult point and may best be explained by some comparison of alternative economic organizations.

In a slave system such as existed in classical antiquity or in the United States between the seventeenth century and 1860, the difference between what the slave produced and what it cost to maintain him was appropriated by the slave owner. In Rome, a great deal of this surplus was taken by the Imperial Administration for the support of the Empire. In the United States, a great deal of the surplus was left by the state to the slave owner for reinvestment in the clearing and cultivation of new land.

In medieval feudalism, the serf was able to produce very little above his own subsistence. What little extra he did produce, his lord attempted to take from him in the form of feudal dues. While in theory these were fixed by the lord in accordance with custom, in practice some bargaining took place regarding how much of his output the serf would retain. The serf's bargaining power was limited, however, by his lack of freedom to take alternative employment.

In Russian socialism, the state decides how much of current output will be devoted to investment and defense and how much of the remainder will be devoted to consumption and by whom. The power of the individual to increase his own share is extremely limited because the state is practically the sole employer. Thus, the state can allow the individual to consume a relatively small share of what he produces and use the "surplus" for various purposes.

In a capitalist society, the presence of alternatives for individuals in employment and in the sale of capital services allows them to bargain for their share of output. The size of the surplus they can acquire over what they would be willing to accept from society *in the absence of alternatives* has a maximum in the difference between the acceptable minimum remuneration and the social estimation of the value of their marginal output. In a capitalist society, the distribution of this surplus is bargained for by individuals. Critics of capitalism have frequently alleged that this allowed a small group of individuals to acquire the largest part of a growing social surplus through their superior bargaining position and control of political power. The state, we should note, sanctions the distribution which results from bargaining through its definition and enforcement of property and the limits of bargaining. We should also note that it confiscates part of the "surplus" by taxation.

"Real" Costs and Economic Rationality. This book attempts to explain social organization in terms of "real" costs. A "real-cost" basis for the individual in his sale of productive services has its usefulness in the comparison of different systems of economic organization. (It is also useful in attempting to determine the supply of factor services to a society when they are not to be taken as "given" in static analysis.) In a socio-economic system such as capitalism where the individual has legal freedom to sell his factor services, the "alternative-cost" theory on which neo-classical economic analysis is based allows the identification of the effective limits which govern the bargaining of individuals over the distribution of the before-tax surplus but it does not explain the establishment of those limits.

The attempt in this volume to reimpose an older "real-cost" conceptual apparatus into an analysis of the development of capitalism is necessary because of the author's emphasis on the limits specified by a particular definition of property rights and economic freedom as being social contracts between individuals and society. The author believes that the only way in which the particulars of these contracts can be understood is by focussing on the way in which changing technology and social priorities have led to a redistribution of bargaining power and, hence, the distribution of property claims and freedom to bargain over the conditions of their exchange.

Social Allocation of Surplus. The "alternative-cost" conceptual apparatus of neo-classical economics tends to obscure the character of the "surplus" which the individual retains when he sells his services in "free" markets. It does this by making the cost of factor services equal to the value of production foregone by society in using productive factors in one employment rather than in alternative uses. This tends to conceal (as Marx pointed out) that the retention of a surplus by private individuals was made possible by a system of economic organization which assigned private property claims and economic freedom to individuals. Insofar as economics is restricted to a study of market behavior, it can explain the production and distribution of income which proceeds from the existence of property claims and freedom in their exchange. But taking the definition of property and economic freedom as "given," neo-classical economics ignores the ultimate determinants of economic organization— political power.[6]

The way in which political power is used depends upon the priorities of a society and the technology available to fulfill those priorities. Therefore, one can say that the institutions of a society used to organize production and distribute the "surplus" between its members and various uses depends upon a society's perception of its needs and its technology. Let us illustrate this sweeping generalization by passing reference to several different types of society: Low productivity societies have little surplus to extract from the individual because most social output must be allocated to maintain a minimum level of biological existence. What little surplus is available may be channeled to military purposes and religious observances since these constitute priorities for static societies.

In a society undergoing economic development through the application of improved technology to the problems of production, an attempt may be made to maximize growth subject to a minimal set of other constraints. This may be accomplished by offering large incentives to entrepreneurs in the form of property rights which allow retention of a large part of social output. Their retention of "surplus" may be conditional on the assumption that the largest part of the surplus will be privately allocated to investment rather than consumption. Or a developing society may annex a large part of the "surplus" and direct its investment centrally

---

[6]Failure to deal with the basic question of property distribution is a long-standing omission in Western political economy. An excellent example of this is a recent brilliant study of the economic rationality of the constitutional checks placed on the political use of economic power in the United States: James Buchanan and Gordon Tullock, *The Calculus of Consent* (Ann Arbor: University of Michigan Press, 1962).

while relying on inelastic supply functions for entrepreneurial talent and labor and on appeals to patriotism to forestall any curtailment of effort by the population.

An advanced society in which growth is given a somewhat lower priority may redefine property claims in order to make a more equal distribution of the "surplus" among the population. Or it may devote more resources to culture, science, or helping other societies than would be forthcoming in a system which allowed for more private retention of surplus and consumer sovereignty.

The one constraint on an open society in reducing the inducements and, hence, the surplus accruing to individuals is that with an elastic supply function for labor, capital, and entrepreneurial talent, a reduction in the inducements offered by society in terms of private retention of part of the "surplus" may lead to a diminution in the provision of socially productive services. The constraint is the more powerful as the individual members of the society are free to withdraw their labor and capital services by migration to other societies or devotion to production or leisure, over which there is ineffective social control. The author believes that the lack of success of the British economy in the last two decades may be explained by the lack of attention to the "real" constraints on political control.

One may object to the argument as developed in that it attributes to society a consciousness and ability to act which it lacks—the same sort of objection as made by those who have taken the mythical "social-contract" arguments of Hobbes, Locke, and Rousseau in too literal terms. The thrust of the author's argument is that the definition of freedom and property and allocation of "surplus" by the *de facto* rulers of a society must have the implicit assent of its members or a stagnation of production or a revolutionary situation will occur which can only be dealt with by coercion. But coercion is self-defeating because it consumes and dissipates the "surplus" which the rulers of society are attempting to wrest from the governed.

In a rapidly growing, open society, the self-interest of the ruling classes motivates a definition of property and economic freedom which will stimulate the growth of production and bind the rising and aggressive members of the population who possess limited property claims to the existing power structure. This has been accomplished in the "capitalist" states of the Western world with greater or lesser degrees of success and, by and large, with the avoidance of either revolution or ruthless repression. Property has been redefined and redistributed to allow for a peaceful evolution toward more egalitarian societies. One might very well compare the process to the market situation designated by economists as "oligopoly with low barriers to entry." The existing oligopolists (the wealthy and powerful) have had to recognize the existence of more and more entrants because it was not economically rational to incur the losses which would be necessary to keep them out. As a consequence, oligopoly power and profits (political and economic power) have been progressively distributed to more and more individuals with the eventual result of perfect competition (economic and political equality).

Income Creation and

Income Redistribution

The less affluent members of an economically progressive society must always consult their own self-interests in agitating for greater equality of income distribution. The acceptance by populations of even highly democratic societies of considerable inequality of income distribution may be economically rational. *If* the equalization of income slowed down the rate of growth by lessening the incentives offered to exceptional members of society with a consequent diminution in their contribution to social output, or *if* the reallocation of income from rich to poor diminished the aggregate amount of saving and capital formation, *then* at some time in the future the real incomes of even the poorer members of a society would be absolutely less than they would be under a system of arrangements which sanctioned greater inequality. This is illustrated graphically in Fig. 2–1 below.

At time t_1, aggregate income *OB* is unequally distributed with one

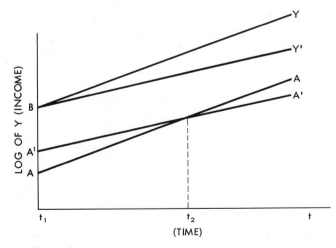

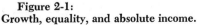

Figure 2-1:
Growth, equality, and absolute income.

(large) segment of society receiving OA and the other (smaller) segment receiving AB. This set of institutional arrangements produces a growth rate of income shown by $Y = f_1(t)$. (Using the log of Y allows a constant percentage rate of growth to be shown as a linear function.) An institutional change which alters the distribution of income at t_1 to increase the share of income going to the poorer segment of the population from OA to OA' leads to a lower growth rate $Y' = f_2(t)$. After time t_2, the absolute income OA' is less than OA—the smaller share of an absolutely larger national income.

If *homo economicus* always strives to maximize the present value of a future stream of income subject to uncertainty and given time preferences, *homo politicus* might rationally vote for institutional arrangements which restrict his present income. The preceding illustration assumes that greater inequality of income will be associated with a higher rate of growth. This is not a necessary assumption.[7]

The real weakness of the argument sketched out above for the prudential obligation of the less "well-off" members of society to support a social framework which countenances considerable inequality is that it is incompletely specified.[8] It provides neither an explanation of specific historical changes in the economic "rights" given to individuals nor a guide to rational policy in the determination of *how* much in the way of incentives should be given to *which* individuals. What must be explained by a historical account of capitalist development is why specific changes were made in economic institutions at the times the changes were made.

The theory of prudential obligation used in the analysis of this volume is concerned with a historically more important question than why the mass of the population has not overthrown regimes which relegated them to an inferior position. It deals with the process by which individuals have bargained for economic and political power and established the institutions which we presently use to organize social production and distribution.

---

[7]One might argue, for example, that the supply of capital is inelastic with respect to interest rates while the supply of labor is highly elastic with respect to wages so that decreasing the return to capital and increasing the return to labor would increase the supply of productive factors and increase output.

[8]Another problem is that it assumes the rationality of cohesive class action. An economic explanation of the lack of class cohesion is made with considerable elegance in Mancur Olsen, *The Logic of Collective Action* (Cambridge: Harvard University Press, 1965).

3

Intellectual

Origins:

political

Social institutions are appropriate to the values and technology of an age. So are the tracts in political economy written to support or attack them. Because "explanations" of social institutions are usually written to attack or defend existing institutions or in support of proposed changes, they tend to appear at junctures in history when societies are experiencing social revolution or accelerated technological change. Both the social institutions and the tracts written about them must be judged in terms of their age. The universality of social arrangements and social theory stems only from certain constancies in human behavior and the continuance of such problems as the provision of defense against external aggression, the maintenance of internal security, the organization of economic production, and distribution of economic output.

Chapter I argued that a clarification of principles to indicate the proper limits of the powers of individuals, organizations, and the government had not emerged in our own society to accord with the realities of modern values and technology. The suggestion was made that part of the reason for this was that we were still conditioned by the myths, concepts, and solutions of the past. Examination of antecedent political and economic philosophy is undertaken in the succeeding pages of this chapter and the next in an attempt to put the argument of this book in intellectual perspective.

John Locke and

American Constitutionalism

The belief that the rights of the individual are natural rather than negotiated and that governments are instituted to protect rather than create and define them, stems from the political tracts of the seventeenth century British philosopher, John Locke.[1] Locke wrote to justify the creation of a constitutional monarchy with limited powers by a Parliament representative of the substantial economic and religious interests of his own time. His arguments were adopted in the American Declaration of Independence as an intellectual justification of revolution against established order and have subsequently been invoked in various forms to support a particular narrow interpretation of the Constitution.

In order to understand what Locke was arguing for, we must understand what he was arguing against. Seventeenth century England experienced religious schism, assertions of divine right absolutism by the Stuart monarchs, and the replacement of older feudal forms of economic organization. Between 1642 and 1660, the country was ravaged by a long, bloody civil war between the adherents of Parliament and supporters of the King. A Stuart monarch was restored to the throne in 1660 in reaction to all the violence in an attempt to regain national unity and establish civil order. Another Stuart king was replaced by Parliament in 1688 in what the English euphemistically refer to as "The Glorious Revolution," which established a government with constitutional limitations and procedural safeguards on its power.

Locke was writing as an apologist for "The Glorious Revolution," and his arguments were designed to secure the support of conservative economic, political, and ecclesiastical elements for the new order. His views on the contractual character of government and the rights of individuals to freedom in the use of their property were widely, if not universally, held by the modernizing landlords and aggressive merchants who formed the support of the Whig Party in Parliament. Locke was writing against a paternalistic view of government with its divinely assigned patterns of privileges and responsibilities for each class of society. At the same time, Locke sought to justify an existing pattern of wealth claims, and this he did by substituting the doctrine of "natural rights" in all wealth created by a man's own labor for the medieval notion of divinely assigned status.

[1] Locke's most important writing in political theory is his *Second Treatise on Civil Government* (London, 1690). A number of editions of this were published but the original manuscript was lost. The best modern scholarship edition is by Peter Laslett, *Two Treatises of Government* (Cambridge: Cambridge University Press, 1960).

Locke and Possessive Individualism. The core of Locke's argument is the existence of individual human rights independent of the powers of the state. Locke couched his argument in terms of the "natural right" of every man in his life, liberty, and rightfully acquired material possessions. The significance of Locke's political philosophy, however, is not the introduction of the notion of natural right to the possession of property and the pursuit of self-interest. He made an attempt to put his argument in the conceptual apparatus of natural law because it enjoyed great currency in his day.

The importance of Locke's writing was the introduction of the idea that man has a right to certain things *independent* of society. This was a rejection of the medieval notion that the enjoyment of life, liberty, or material possessions was a *privilege* which entailed the acceptance of certain corresponding responsibilities to society.

Medieval society did not morally sanction the unbridled pursuit of self-interest. The individual was under obligation to use his privileged prerogatives in the service of society. This was particularly true with regard to the use of land, the most important physical asset in an agricultural society. It was also true with regard to industry and commerce which was rigidly controlled to achieve certain social objectives. The revolutionary idea which Locke introduced was the morality of the pursuit of self-interest which he sought to justify in terms of "natural rights."

Locke's basic premise concerning civil society was that it is created and sustained by a voluntary compact entered into by men to protect their property. By *property* Locke meant socially guaranteed rights to personal liberty as well as security in the possession of assets. The radical and modern character of this premise does not bear in upon the twentieth century with the same force that it did in Locke's time. This was a rejection of the most basic postulates of a traditional society in which the liberty and assets of the subjects of the sovereign were held at his pleasure. Locke was proclaiming an atomistic view of society in which no man owes anything to society other than the prudential obligation to honor contractual arrangements between himself and his fellow men.

In his rejection of a corporate society, Locke was laying to rest the traditional feudal idea that every man had a status-defined role in society and was not free to leave it for the pursuit of his own interests. This no longer had much force, at any event, in seventeenth century England. What was far more important in the context of his times was his claim that the possession of assets was absolute and laid no social obligations on the possessor for their use. In theory at least, the medieval lord held land in trust and was obliged as a condition of his trusteeship to render certain things to the sovereign and to the serfs in his care. The medieval merchant was responsible to his town corporation for his actions since his privileged access to markets depended upon its grant of privilege. The medieval workman was responsible to his craft guild for price and quality because his privilege to practice his trade depended upon permission of the guild.

Natural Rights to Property. Locke's doctrine of property was founded on his assertion of the inalienable right of all men to be free. Part of this freedom is the right of all men to sell their labor power to others on whatever terms they can secure without the interference of society. The other part of the freedom is absolute ownership in the commodities created by their own labor.

Locke's assertion about man's right to absolute control of the use of his assets grows out of his analysis of their source. This is particularly crucial with respect to the control of land. In medieval society the use of land was held to be a trust because of the belief that it had been created by God to serve as the support of his creatures. Locke's argument was that the *increase* in the productive powers of land which give it an economic value has its source in human labor. Labor is the property of the man who renders it, and, consequently, the use and enjoyment of the productive powers created in land by the expenditure of human labor upon it rightly belonged to the man who had "mixed his labor with it."

If one starts with the proposition that man has a right to be free and secure in his control of himself, it is difficult to deny that he should not be free to dispose of the assets he has created by the use of his freedom and security. Locke was trying to emphasize that a moral right is established by the labor which creates productive potential.

This is a very different argument than that of the establishment of property in land by the state through occupation with the assignment of privilege in use in return for the fulfillment of certain obligations. This was the medieval theory with its origins in Roman law.[2] Pre-Lockean conceptions of property assumed that asset possession was a privilege revocable by the state. Assets were held to be created by the use of political power over men and not by individual effort. The confirmation in possession of those in occupation of assets by the state was made to preserve civil peace. The legitimacy of occupation was not an issue. Ownership of land was confirmed by making a trespass on the land a trespass against the person in *de facto* possession of the land. Protection of *de facto* possession was the role of the state to prevent violence erupting between conflicting claimants.

The problem which Locke faced when he wrote was the necessity of justifying the existing distribution of assets on other grounds than divine

[2]For a concise and far-reaching essay on the development of legal concepts with respect to property, see the essay on "Property" in Roscoe Pound, *An Introduction to Philosophy of Law* (New Haven: Yale University Press, 1954).

right, social stability, or the inevitability of the status quo. The problem was particularly severe with regard to land ownership. Land had changed hands frequently during the English Civil War of the seventeenth century, and many of the lands in the kingdom had been seized from their traditional tenants in the two centuries preceding Locke's treatise. Because land had changed title so many times and because the large land owners never "mixed their labor" with the land in any literal sense, one has difficulty taking Locke's argument seriously as a moral justification of existing patterns of land ownership.

The Origin of Property in Social Contract: A New Interpretation of Locke. This author feels that in addition to assertions of natural rights Locke is groping toward an explanation of property analogous to that which he makes for civil government. He argued that civil government was created by consent among men to secure their interests. Likewise, he also seems to be moving toward an argument that property is a contract between men to allow those who create assets to have the enjoyment and use of them. He might be interpreted as arguing that property is an incentive offered by society to induce asset creation.

The whole burden of Locke's argument, of course, is that property does *not* arise from social contract but from natural right to what is created by one's own labor. He argued that the natural right of property is only *enforced* by the civil government which is created by social contract.

Nevertheless, Locke expends a great amount of effort attempting to demonstrate the reasonableness of property in land in order to justify the necessity for the state upholding it. This may be interpreted as an attempt to demonstrate the reasonableness of natural law. On the other hand, the argument could be construed as an attempt to demonstrate the mutual advantage of a social contract to create property in terms analogous to the argument about the utility to all men of a social contract to create a sovereign state. This interpretation would make *both* property and the state the creation of a social contract based on calculations of self-interest by the contracting parties.

Locke's argument about the property that men have in food that comes from land or in animals that graze on it emphasizes that alienation from common possession takes place as a result of human effort. The argument about individual property in land, itself, depends upon labor having been incorporated into improvements on the land. This is an important distinction. The alternative theory of property depends only on prior occupation and the preservation of an existing pattern of ownership which has its only justification in the maintenance of production and preservation of civil peace. Yet, this was not Locke's concern since he wished to justify a revolution to overthrow an order which did not preserve a distribution of interests which he considered fundamental.

The social-contract character of Locke's argument for property can be seen most clearly in the following passage:

> To which let me add, that he who appropriates land to himself by his labor does not lessen but increases the common stock of mankind. For the provisions serving to the support of human life produced by one acre of enclosed and cultivated land are (to speak much within compass) ten times more than those which are yielded by an acre of land of an equal richness lying waste in common. And therefore he that encloses land, and has a greater of the conveniences of life from ten acres than he could have from a hundred left to nature, *may truly be said to give ninety acres to mankind*: [Italics the author's] for his labour now supplies him with provisions out of ten acres, which were but the product of a hundred lying in common.[3]

This passage was added by Locke in a later edition of his work, and one can easily supply the argument against which it was directed. The improvement of agricultural technique in England, coupled with the growth of the population and the breakdown of feudal agriculture, led to the enclosure of land which had traditionally been held in rough pasture or woodland. The population had "common rights" on this land before it was enclosed to pasture animals and gather nuts, berries, and wood. Locke is merely pointing out that its enclosure for field crops greatly increases the productive potential of society, from which one could infer that society has an interest in granting property to individuals.

The justification of private ownership in land is to be found in its benefit for society *as a whole*. Alienation of land from common possession to private ownership does *not* make society "worse off" as alleged by the opponents of enclosure but "better off." If improvement of ten acres of land increases the output from that land tenfold, then mankind *as a whole* has enjoyed an increase in productive resources. Further, the man who improved the ten acres can now live as well from them as he formerly did from a hundred, and society, *ex encloser*, can use the ninety unimproved acres formerly used by him to improve their standard of life. The logic of this argument will be considered more closely in the discussion on Social Gains from Property in Chapter 5. Suffice it to say here that Locke is not really offering a justification of property based on some system of natural rights—he is offering a self-interest justification of property, and this is what makes him the intellectual precursor of modern capitalistic, individualistic society.

Locke advanced his arguments about the *source* of property to make property prior to the state which he wished to make dependent on prop-

---

[3]Laslett, *op. cit.*, Sect. 37, p. 312.

erty. The author's interpretation of Locke's argument makes the institution of property the same sort of social-contract institution as the state. This creates the dilemma which Locke sought to avoid. *If* the argument for property is based on a contract growing out of the self-interest of all members of a society, then it is exactly the same kind of institution as the state. Just as the state can be dissolved or changed when it no longer safeguards the interests of some members of society, property rights can be altered or confiscated by members of a society when they no longer serve and safeguard their interests. If the state does not protect the "life, liberty, and estate" of an individual, Locke argued that the individual has no obligation growing out of self-interest to support it. On the other hand, Locke, and his successors who have advocated constitutional government, have wanted to avoid admitting that if an individual gets no benefit from supporting a guarantee of property to another person, he has no interest in supporting existing property relationships or the civil authority which defines, guarantees, and enforces them.

Locke was anxious about the state taking the property of an individual without his consent. This was the greatest fear which an individual had in seventeenth century England, and it was a constant threat from any government which claimed to rest on any other basis than the consent of its subjects. Locke's argument about the impropriety of the state confiscating property through taxation without consent or seizure without compensation is partially responsible, in the author's opinion, for the development of his argument along "natural-right" lines. (It was also much more in keeping with the intellectual currents of his age and would not offend the more traditional thinkers who would find self-interest an immoral basis for a social system.) Safeguarding the natural rights of property is made the basis of the state in Locke's system to avoid the power of the state being used against an existing distribution of property.

Locke was in a dilemma in basing the state on property as soon as the power to tax was considered. If the state could compel a member to pay taxes without his consent, then it could confiscate part of a man's property. Locke escaped the logical difficulty by arguing that if a man did not wish to consent to the payment of taxes he could leave the state which levied them, but, of course, this was no more a real possibility in the seventeenth century than it is today. Locke's solution to his dilemma was the traditional Anglo-Saxon practice of regarding taxes as a "gift" voted by Parliament as the representatives of the people for the necessary support of government. In pragmatic terms, the danger of taxation to property was checked by having the parliament composed of men of substantial property who were subject to periodic reelection and the same taxes that they voted on their constituents.

The power of the state to control the use of property, even though it is not the source of assets, was admitted by Locke in a paradoxical passage in which he argues that a superior officer can order a soldier to perform an action which may result in his death but may not take part of his pay away from him. This is preceded by the assertion that: "The prince, or senate . . . may have power to make laws for the regulating of property between subjects one amongst another, yet can never have a power to take to themselves the whole or any part of the subjects' property without their consent."[4] The regulation of the use of property between the members of a society must be a legitimate political function since it is necessary to the peace of the society. Locke is perfectly willing to see this control exercised by the properly constituted legislative and administrative authority. He failed to realize, partly because his argument was made largely in terms of agricultural land, that regulation of the use of assets could confiscate part of their exchange value.

Natural Rights and Practical Power. Locke's argument is closely related to the author's in that what Locke considered to be the "natural rights" of man the author would consider to be the *de facto* power of men. The state cannot take away men's property in "life, liberty, and estate" because if they did there would be: (a) civil violence, and (b) a diminution of productive labor and asset formation as men would no longer find it a matter of self-interest to work and create capital assets if they were denied their enjoyment and use.

The "natural right" of man to the fruits of his labor could be behaviorally interpreted as the necessity for men to receive the fruits of their labor in order to induce them to produce. The claim to property in land or capital assets is a claim to a stream of income created by labor. The absence of a guarantee that the stream of income will be the property of its creator lessens the incentive to abstain from current consumption in order to create the asset.

As it seems to the author, the introduction of the notion of "natural right" has been a long-run liability for Western political economy insofar as it has deflected attention from the character of the state and property as a social contract based on consent. Further, while Locke's radical individualism might have been a useful antidote in its time, there has been a recurrent tendency for individuals in Western societies to make property claims far in excess of what could be justified in terms of their own creation of productive assets.

As will be argued subsequently,[5] a considerable part of the income in our society accrues to individuals as "an economic surplus"—payments

---

[4]*Ibid.*, Sect. 139, pp. 379–80.
[5]See the section on Property and Resource Allocation in Chapter 5.

for the services of factors of production in excess of the cost of inducing production. Good arguments exist for allowing the private receipt of these surplus payments, but the arguments are all based on the recipients being fiduciary agents of society. They entail social responsibility and the oft-heard claim of individuals to use their property or the income from it *as they please* is a species of individualism completely unjustified by the logic of the argument which finds the basis of private rights in the creation of assets.

Property and Political Power:
The Dilemma

The danger of making the distribution of property claims a matter of legislative control has always been recognized by men of property. If property is created by social contract, the contract may be open to continual renegotiation, and factions may use the power of the legislature to renegotiate or redefine the powers of individuals in society with respect to income streams from land, labor, and capital. For Locke, the threat to property posed by the government was mitigated by his expectation that the legislature would be controlled by a cohesive class of men of substantial wealth who would recognize their self-interest in respecting the property of their peers.

We should note that the drafters of the American Constitution were not as sanguine as Locke in relying on natural rights or class cohesion to safeguard the rights of property from legislative control. The power of the legislature was at the root of the Constitutional struggles to establish the American republic. (The revolt against English rule, after all, had its source primarily in objections raised by various economic interests to the methods and incidence of taxation and trade regulation by the English Parliament.) The problem of protecting the interests of the various wealthy classes from legislative control was clearly perceived and elegantly stated by James Madison, the primary architect of the Constitution. In *The Federalist Papers*, he noted that the freedom to engage in economic enterprise coupled with diversities of talents would inevitably lead to conflicts of interest between various economic interests as well as inequality of income distribution:

> Those who hold and those who are without property have ever formed distinct interests in society. . . . A landed interest, a manufacturing interest, a mercantile interest, a moneyed interest, with many lesser interests, grow up of necessity in civilized nations, and divide themselves into different classes, actuated by different sentiments and views. The regulation of these various and interfering interests involves the spirit of

party and faction in the necessary and ordinary operations of government.[6]

Madison realized that popular government would inevitably be subject to factional interests. Thomas Hobbes, another seventeenth century English political philosopher, had argued before Locke that representative government was inherently unstable on these grounds and that the only escape was the creation of an absolute ruler.[7] Madison conceded the dangers of factionalism but argued that they could be balanced and controlled by procedural safeguards. Unlike Locke, who counted on propertied classes to maintain a community of interest in the affairs of state, Madison realized that the conflicts of interest between various propertied interests would be a serious source of strain. Locke's answer to the abuse of legislative power—revolution and withdrawal from society—was scarcely practical, while Hobbes' solution—subserviance to a benevolent despot—was completely unacceptable.

Madison faced the problem. He was frank in saying that it was not a matter of enlightened statesmanship because the conflicts of interest were real and had to be resolved by the elected representatives of the various factional interests. He conceded that with popular governments:

> . . . the public good is disregarded in the conflicts of rival parties, and . . . measures are often decided, not according to the rules of justice and the rights of the minor party, but by the superior force of an interested and overbearing majority. However anxiously we may wish that these complaints had no foundation, the evidence of known facts will not permit us to deny that they are in some degree true.[8]

Madison found the source of faction in popular governments in the unequal possession of property which resulted from men's use of their economic freedom. He further noted that men would seek to use the powers of government to advance the interests of specific producers' groups at the expense of others. Representative government could not prevent this because the legislators owed their offices to their constituents who expected them to pass legislation in their interests.

American Resolution of the Dilemma. Madison argued that there was no escape from the problem of the majority or interested minorities using the power of government to advance their own interests except by a division of powers and "obstacles opposed to the concert and accomplish-

[6]*The Federalist Papers*, ed. Jacob E. Cooke. Middletown, Conn.: Wesleyan University Press, 1961. Paper Number X by James Madison.

[7]Thomas Hobbes, *Leviathan* (London: 1651). For an account of Hobbes' political philosophy, see Sabine, pp. 455–75.

[8]Madison, *Federalist Papers, op. cit.*, Section X.

ment of the secret wishes of an unjust and interested majority."[9] The Constitution of the United States embodied Madison's solution of division of powers and procedural safeguards. The power of the Federal government was divided between three branches, of which the legislative branch had two parts while the judiciary was appointed for life. States were allowed to determine the electoral franchise. Any changes in the Constitution necessitated a vote by two-thirds of the States.

"Natural rights" are not mentioned in the Constitution. The checks on the powers of a majority in the United States are procedural rather than substantive. The majority or interested minorities have always been frustrated in their attempts to redistribute freedom and property only by procedural obstacles. Even so this has been a powerful conservative influence whose beneficent or deleterious effect is not at issue here. It has tended to reenforce the property claims of the status quo and frustrate change by legislative and judicial means even when there has been substantial majority sentiment for changes.

Constitutional History and Limitation of Power. The constitutional history of the United States is partly responsible for present-day limits of power. An early Chief Justice of the Supreme Court, John Marshall, established the right of the Supreme Court to void legislation of the Congress which offended the constitutional contract. As Marshall stated in 1803:

> That the people have an original right to establish for their future government such principles as, in their opinion, shall most conduce to their own happiness, is the basis on which the whole American fabric has been erected. The exercise of this original right is a very great exertion, nor can it, nor ought it to be frequently repeated. The principles therefore so established are deemed fundamental. The powers of the legislature are defined and limited; and that those limits may not be mistaken or forgotten, the constitution is written. To what purpose are powers limited, and to what purpose is that limitation committed to writing, if these limits may, at any time, be passed by those intended to be restrained? The distinction between a government with limited and unlimited powers is abolished if those limits do not confine the persons on whom they are imposed.[10]

Marshall also affirmed, however, that the Constitution was not to be considered as a straightjacket confining the legislature in its attempts to put into practice the powers with which it was invested. In *McCulloch* v. *Maryland* he enunciated the rule which he thought should govern the determination of constitutionality:

[9]*Ibid.*
[10]*Marbury* v. *Madison*, 1 Branch, 137 (1803).

> The sound construction of the Constitution must allow to the national legislature the discretion with respect to the means by which the powers it confers are to be carried into execution, which will enable that body to perform the high duties assigned to it in the manner most beneficial to the people. Let the end be legitimate, let it be within the scope of the Constitution, and all means which are appropriate, which are plainly adapted to that end, which are not prohibited, but consistent with the letter and spirit of the Constitution, are constitutional.[11]

In the period from 1870 to 1935 the courts of the United States under the leadership of the Supreme Court did attempt to place substantive checks on legislative power. The essence of the judicial argument was that it was improper for legislatures to pass legislation which would tend to confiscate part of the exchange value of property or to interfere in the bargaining process between individuals and groups. The argument had its roots in John Locke and Adam Smith or at least the jurists' understanding of these writers. An underlying assumption was that economic freedom and property were "natural rights" guaranteed by the Constitution and that the existing distribution of property and freedom were the results of a natural process with which it was unconstitutional and unwise for government to interfere. While this author thinks their concepts of freedom and property were biased and incomplete, the author heartily agrees with the attempt to limit power in the name of principle, only noting that the principle must be democratically defined.

Since the "New Deal" of the 1930's, a majority of the American people and the Supreme Court justices have accepted the desirability and constitutionality of extensive governmental participation in the economic life of the United States. Labor-management relations have been greatly affected by a succession of acts affecting the status of labor unions and the conduct of collective bargaining. Capital markets have been regulated by the Securities Exchange Commission, the Federal Reserve Bank, and government fiscal and monetary policies, farmers are subjected to production controls in conjunction with agricultural support prices, and many large corporations are harrassed by the anti-trust division of the Attorney General's staff.

The constitutionality of government intervention in the economy is seldom questioned any longer. In fact, anyone who ventured a criticism of government control on the grounds of constitutionality would probably be considered a crank. This is unfortunate. Unquestioned legitimacy of government control of the economic relations is not appropriate to a society based on the constitutional limitation of power of government over private citizens. The failure to affirm the necessity of constitutional guarantee of the liberty and property of individual citizens would leave

---

[11]*McCulloch* v. *Maryland*, 17, Wheaton, 4 (1819).

the citizen of the United States no more security against coercion than the citizen of a communist state.

The Recurrent Dilemma. We now live in an age in which we recognize that there are no substantive restrictions on the collective power of the state over the life, liberty, and property of the individual citizen. This should not alarm us. Procedural restrictions are still there, and they are the only restrictions on the power of the state which have ever existed. The Fifth Amendment to the Constitution, after all, states only that no person shall be deprived of life, liberty, or property "without due process of law." What is of paramount importance is that the working rules of our society be guided by a set of principles which have a wide consensus.

The central problem of a society which is both democratic and individualist is that all members must be made to realize a self-interest in preserving the rights of others. The Lockean concept of society as a voluntary compact between free men to preserve their liberties and property necessitates that all men subject to the civil government of that society believe that their liberty and property are protected. They must also believe that an existing definition of property and economic freedom accords with their interests.

Abandonment of a "natural-rights" justification for the private-property —economic-freedom foundations of a capitalist system allows it to be placed on the more acceptable, if infinitely more complicated, basis of individual self-interest and social contract. While this lacks the more heroic characteristics of a supernatural ethical system, an examination of the process of historical development will show it to be the real reason why capitalism has won increasing acceptance.

The institutions of economic freedom and private property were instigated by civil society to promote economic welfare. Economic growth has vastly increased their importance and necessitated continual change in their definition. The idea that there is some metaphysical absolute of "freedom" or "property" and that particular historical forms are imperfect embodiments of an ideal form is not an idea which can be dispelled by empirical analysis since it has no basis in fact. Freedom and property as actual institutions are what the state says they are and "the state" is no more than the administrative and judicial agent of the particular interests who succeed in controlling it for their own benefit and protection.

When modern notions about property and economic freedom first began to take form and embodiment in the practices of seventeenth century Britain, they were attacked, on one hand, as an attack on the prerogatives of the monarch who was the state and, on the other hand, as means by which the classes in economic ascendancy could oppress the lower classes and deprive them of protection in the status system of a primitive society. Both charges were true. Individual freedom and property are derogations of sovereignty from "the state." Property and freedom are always defined to protect the interests of a particular class. Fortunately, however, the process of economic growth in the Anglo-American experience has led to the progressive enfranchisement of the largest part of the population and consequently to an implementation of freedom and property which has protected both private and public interests.

4

Intellectual

Origins:

economic

The belief that markets are naturally self-regulated to produce the greatest social good and that government interference in the economic transactions of private individuals is as immoral as it is unwise was first made in an articulate and comprehensive manner by that patron saint of political economists, Adam Smith.[1] In his own day, Smith was overwhelmingly correct in his analysis. The interferences and restrictions laid on economic activity by what he called "the system of Europe" enforced iniquitous monopolies, created poverty and unemployment by restricting the mobility of labor, and retarded economic growth by discouraging technological progress. To counter the paternalistic conceptions used to justify the old system, Smith advanced (in one isolated passage) the idea that state control of economic activity was unnecessary since each individual pursuing his own self-interest would be guided by an "Invisible Hand" to produce the greatest social good.[2]

The moral aspect of Smith's argument is basically Lockean: "The property which every man has in his own labour, as it is the original foundation of all other property, so it is the most sacred and inviolable."[3] In the absence of social interference, the interaction of individuals in the market would assure that every man received the value he produces in the exchange of goods. The attempt of the state to impose different conditions of bargaining and exchange on society than those which would result from a "free market" would be both inefficient and destructive of the freedom of

49

men to realize the value of the property they have in their labor in exchange. Smith's underlying assumption is that there will be numerous alternatives open to every buyer and seller of goods, labor, or capital in the absence of state interference with markets, including the alternative of self-employment in household production or subsistence agriculture.

The Relevance of Smith's Ideas to His Time. For the economic structure of which Smith wrote, his assumptions largely corresponded with reality. In the first place, agricultural employment was an alternative open to most of the British and American labor force at wages substantially equal to those offered in industrial or commercial employment. In the second place, the industrial revolution was just getting under way in Britain, and most manufacturing was still organized on the "putting-out system." Instead of being employed on the factory floor, the average worker worked as an independent artisan in the fabrication of raw materials or unfinished goods. Theoretically, at least, each worker was free to bargain with a number of entrepreneurs who were competing for his services on a contract basis for the fabrication of goods. Since the organization of the "putting-out" system required a small amount of working capital and practically no fixed capital, the ranks of the entrepreneurs were substantially open to entry by any man willing to undertake the risks and supply the organizational ability. Smith thought that legal freedom to sell labor, capital, and goods on the best terms the parties could secure in unhampered bargaining would secure to every man a return equal to his contribution to social output at the same time that social output was maximized.

The fault with the system which Smith attacked was that under the guise of protecting "the public interest," it advancd the fortunes of certain wealthy classes, allowed the subjection of the working classes through limiting employment opportunities by an apprenticeship system, and exploited consumers through guild monopolies. In medieval times (as will be discussed in later chapters) the system had considerable logic, but it had been rendered obsolete by technological change. At the beginning of the Industrial Revolution the medieval restrictions hampered the owners of factories in securing labor, and the mercantile restrictions on foreign trade restricted their markets. Smith's appeal for "laissez faire" fitted well with the interests of the rising manufacturing interests and merchants who found themselves excluded from profitable trade by state-enforced monopolies.

Smith's Objectives. Adam Smith was not concerned with income distribution in the *Wealth of Nations* but with economic growth. He argued

---

[1] Adam Smith, *The Wealth of Nations*, Edwin Canaan, ed. (New York: Modern Library, Inc., 1939).

[2] *Ibid.*, p. 423.

[3] *Ibid.*, p. 121.

for "laissez faire" in order to promote efficiency and allow the incentives of self-interest to operate. Smith argued that the level of wages would be determined by the rate of growth and could not be controlled by the government directly. When the economy was growing rapidly, the demand for labor would increase faster than the supply and temporarily force wages upward. Increasing wages would stimulate the growth of population, thus increasing the supply. At the same time they would cause a fall in profits, which would limit the accumulation of capital and lead to a slackening in demand for labor. Thus, the labor market, like other markets, was "self-regulating" and any attempts to increase the wage level would be self-defeating since they would simultaneously increase the supply of labor and limit the rate of capital formation which controlled the demand for labor.[4]

Smith's theory of population response to rising wages was transformed by Malthus into the "iron law of population." Smith, in fact, argued that the standard of living of the working classes might rise in a ratchet fashion if they would treat temporary improvements as necessary and refuse to use them to increase family size. The theory that profits, capital accumulation, and hence employment were determined by the wage level was Smith's statement of the "wages-fund" doctrine which lives on in various forms to our own day as an argument against any attempts to limit the proportion of the national income going to capital.

Survival of the "Wages-fund" Theory. The charitable view of the continuing existence of variants of the "iron law of population" and the "wages fund," the continuing belief that no point is served in trying to affect income distribution since it is controlled by "natural laws of social behavior," is that the propagators of this gospel are prisoners of their own conceptual apparatus. If one believed that every man followed his own self-interest, the tenacity with which the views are held might be explained by reference to the fact that the conclusions have policy implications congenial to the upper-income groups who hold them.

One can be charitable to Smith and concede that his generalizations were congruent with the world as he knew it. Population did increase with rising wages in Smith's England since the infant mortality rate would fall with improved nutrition.[5] Smith could not have known that this would be followed by declining birth rates. It is more difficult to forgive the fallacies of composition implicit in the "wages-fund" doctrine for as good an economist as Smith, but similar problems plagued liberal political economy until John Maynard Keynes's *General Theory of Employment, Interest, and Money*, which is even now only thirty years old.

[4]*Ibid.*, pp. 64–86.
[5]For a discussion of demographic developments in eighteenth century England, see H. J. Habakkuk, "English Population in the Eighteenth Century," *Economic History Review*, Second Series, Vol. VI, no. 2 (1953), pp. 117–33.

Laissez Faire and Social Welfare. At any event, the optimistic, pragmatic Adam Smith who polemicized the anachronistic political economy
of his age was followed by disciples who elevated self-regulating markets
into the most fundamental tenet of "the dismal science." Not content with
positing the futility of trying to interfere with the income distribution
resulting from the interplay of market forces, Smith's "Invisible Hand"
was also credited with producing the maximum attainable social utility.
Sometimes the proviso would be inserted that maximum social utility
would be secured in free markets *provided* that the initial distribution of
income equated the marginal utility of money for all individuals. But in
policy terms this tended to be relegated to secondary consideration as it
was urged that even if this could not be secured, society could move
toward maximum social satisfaction by ensuring that exchange was bilaterally voluntary between individuals in all exchange transactions.

In the latter half of the nineteenth century, the laissez-faire economic
principles which had their first cohesive policy statement in Adam Smith
were given the support of biology by Herbert Spencer. Attempting to
apply to human society the principles of natural selection found by Dar-
win in his *Origin of the Species,* Spencer argued that any interference by
the state would interfere with natural selection through the survival of
the fittest. Even state support of education was held to be an unwise
interference with man's evolutionary process! In the United States, social
Darwinism had its most articulate prophet in Professor William Graham
Sumner of Yale whose lectures and books profoundly affected several
generations of businessmen, jurists, and politicians at the turn of the
century.[6]

Smith and His Modern Disciples. In the twentieth century, Adam
Smith's pragmatic attacks on the iniquity of government "interference"
with the operation of markets have been supplemented, one might even
say, replaced by arguments against government regulation of economic
activity as subversive of liberty. The hallmark of these arguments is the
assumption that the range of personal freedom for the individual is in
inverse proportion to the amount of government participation or control
in the marketplace. A second distinguishing characteristic of these arguments is the assumption that as long as an individual has alternatives to
any exchange transaction (even if the alternative is not accepting any
exchange offer) that he is free and uncoerced. Under these criteria, com-

---

[6]An excellent discussion of the impact of social Darwinism on political and social
thought in the United States will be found in Richard Hofstadter, *Social Darwinism
in American Thought* (Boston: Beacon Press, 1955). See also Robert G. McCloskey,
American Conservations in the Age of Enterprise (Cambridge: Harvard University
Press, 1951).

pulsory Social Security payments, minimum wage or hour legislation, or a government post-office monopoly all represent significant limitations of freedom.[7]

Arguing that specific legislation to control economic behavior is misguided, inefficient, or unnecessary is one thing. Arguing that control of economic activity is a limitation of freedom and, *therefore,* to be avoided is another. One man can limit the freedom of another as effectively as the state in some circumstances. In any transaction a certain set of alternatives exists for the parties, and social intervention to restructure the bargaining situation is not a curtailment of freedom but a redistribution of alternatives to the parties.

The first ironic feature of the transmutation of Smith's argument about the desirability of laissez faire into the modern "libertarian" position is that Smith originally argued against state intervention on the ground that it created and confirmed excessive power for certain private interests. Modern libertarians want to allow these private interests freedom from state control.

The second ironic feature of the modern libertarian position is that economic freedom is transformed into an end rather than a means. One certainly can argue that economic freedom is a means of obtaining the most efficient use of resources through offering maximum inducements and competition to eliminate misallocation. Yet this argument tends to be downgraded. It is almost as if the modern libertarians had turned Marx on his head and argued that the performance of a capitalist economic system could be relegated to secondary importance because it was a more ethical and humane system than some collectivist alternative.

Surplus Value and the
Operation of Markets

Modern economic analysis dispenses with notions of an "economic surplus" or "surplus value" because of a conceptual framework which emphasizes alternative costs. Even the notion of a "rent" has been dealt with as the difference between the return to a factor of production in its most valuable use and its next most remunerative alternative. Notions about the "real" cost of securing the services of a factor of production have been abandoned in favor of a system of relative prices in which the cost of a factor service is the amount of other commodities which would have to be foregone to release the factor for production. The argument presented

[7]Professor Milton Friedman, cited extensively in the first chapter, is one of the intellectual leaders of the modern laissez-faire school of political economists. For an interesting and perceptive critique, see Paul A. Samuelson, "Personal Freedoms and Economic Freedoms in the Mixed Economy" in E. F. Cheit, ed. *The Business Establishment* (New York: John Wiley & Sons, Inc. 1964), pp. 214–20.

in this volume reintroduces the notion of an "economic surplus" as the difference between the price necessary to secure the services of a factor of production *in the absence of alternative employment* and the price actually received (which does depend upon the alternative uses for the factor and the relative value placed by the society on the services rendered by the factor of production).

Classical Origins. The analytic distinction between the price of a factor of production necessary to furnish its use to society and the price actually received is present in Adam Smith's work, both in his discussion of wages and the rent on land. Both Malthus and Marx drew on Smith's generalization about wages tending in the long run toward a level sufficient to ensure the reproduction and maintenance of labor. David Ricardo combined propositions about the increase in population and a fixed quantity of agricultural land to derive a conclusion that the share of national income going to landlords would increase as wages and profits on capital were driven to a minimum level.

Ricardo developed the theory of intramarginal rent to explain the distribution of income in his own society and drew policy conclusions with respect to repeal of the Corn Laws. He argued that as population increased, the demand for food would increase and cultivation would be extended to the less fertile land in Britain. The landlords who owned superior land would be able to collect a "rent" for its use equal to the difference between the total revenue from the sale of produce from the land and the costs of production incurred in the payment of labor and capital. Since the long-run price of labor and capital would be constant and equal to their "real cost," the ever-increasing demand for food would raise the rent accruing to landlords. An increasing share of national income would be diverted to landlords, the accumulation of capital would cease, and a static equilibrium would be reached. In order to forestall these consequences, free trade in foodstuffs should be established, Ricardo argued, to allow the supplementation of the limited agricultural land of Britain by lands overseas which would, in effect, be annexed to the British economy.

The American, Henry George, writing in the last half of the nineteenth century used Ricardian rent analysis to argue that all pure rents should be confiscated by taxation to prevent the progress of mankind from diverting an ever-increasing share of national income to the holders of land.[8]

Alfred Marshall, the great neo-classicist economist, generalized the Ricardian analysis of rent on land in pointing out that a rent accrued to

[8]Henry George, *Progress and Poverty* (New York: 1883). The Modern Library ed. 1940.

the owner of any factor of production that was in temporary short supply when the price received for its use exceeded its cost of production.[9] The Marshallian concept of "producer's surplus" was the generalized counterpart of Ricardo's rent. It was a payment accruing to the owner of a factor of production over and above the cost of production.

Rent, Surplus, and
Property

The concept of rent, the difference between the return to a factor of production and the price necessary for its provision by the owner to society, has been neglected by recent writers in political economy. It is resurrected as "surplus" in the author's argument, because a conception of private property as a "social contract" rather than a "natural right" necessitates a distinction between that return to the property holder necessary to secure performance and that which remains with him by implicit or explicit social decision to allow private retention of the "surplus." As John Stuart Mill pointed out in his *Principles of Political Economy*:

> The laws of property have never yet conformed to the principles on which the justification of private property rests. They have made property out of things which never ought to be property, and absolute property where only a qualified property ought to exist. . . . The guarantee [of property when it does not stem from the individual's creation and abstinence] does not promote but conflicts with the ends which render private property legitimate.[10]

There is no sound economic reason for the establishment of absolute property in rents. The argument for private property in "economic surplus" is political and rests on a conception of what constitutes a good society.

A Reinterpretation of Marx. At the root of Marx's voluminous criticisms of a capitalist system was his recognition that growth of productivity in a private-property system could lead to certain members of the population appropriating all the growing "surplus" through the mechanisms of market exchange. Where John Locke found the origin and necessity of the state in men's desire to protect their property and Adam Smith found the desirability of laissez faire by the state in allowing every man the oppor-

[9]Alfred Marshall, *Principles of Economics*, 8th ed. (London: Macmillan & Co. Ltd., 1920).

[10]John Stuart Mill, *Principles of Political Economy* (London: John Parker, 1848), Book II, Chapter 1, Section 3.

tunity to realize the value of the property in his labor, Karl Marx found a capitalist state the instrument for expropriation of property of the masses and "laissez faire" the best policy for accomplishing it. Marx's *predictions* about the ultimate self-destroying logic of a capitalist society turned out to be erroneous because he made some extrapolations based on limited observations. However, his predictive errors do not detract from his insight into some of the characteristics and problems of a society based on private property and economic freedom. Marx saw clearly that certain configurations of property and freedom could lead to a society which was basically unstable.

The most basic Marxian critique of the bourgeois state is a rejection of the notion that distribution of goods should be based on their production. Marx argued in his *Critique of the Gotha Program*[11] that in a communist society the distribution of goods in accordance with the labor contribution of each member is *not* the ultimate goal. This would be a hangover of the bourgeois morality of possessive individualism. Output in the communist utopia would be according to need rather than contribution— "from each according to his abilities, to each according to his need." This is the philosophy of a utopian welfare state. It rejects the necessity of offering members of a society rewards proportioned to their contribution to output and relies on appeals to "public interest" and man's cooperative urges.

Markets and Surplus: Marx's Critique of Laissez Faire.[12] In his critique of capitalism, Marx does not start from the basic postulate discussed above. Rather he adopts the morality of Locke that every man has a natural right to the value of his own labor. Capitalism becomes possible in a postfeudal society because only in a postfeudal society are the laborers legally proprietors of their own labor power. Further, the breakdown of feudalism leaves them landless, and, therefore, they are under the economic necessity of selling their labor to the owners of capital on whatever terms they can bargain.

With Marx the doctrine of a labor theory of value is not primarily an empirical generalization as it is in Adam Smith. It is an *a priori* philosophical argument. All commodities exchange at some ratio. They exchange at that ratio because of their value in terms of something else. The something else is labor content. The labor theory of value is "proved" by its inclusion in the definition.

In Marx's system in equilibrium all commodities, including labor, exchange at relative prices which express their labor content. The labor

[11]See Robert Freedman, *Marx on Economics* (New York: Harcourt, Brace, & World, Inc., 1961).

[12]The relevant passages summarized in the section following are found in pp. 41–70, 197–243, 619–710 of the Modern Library edition. The author has attempted to adapt and interpret them in contemporary idiom.

content of labor, itself, is the quantity of labor required to produce the commodities necessary for the reproduction and maintenance of man.

Increases in per capita output (with which Marx equated the industrial revolution) have a disequilibrating effect on the market system which grows progressively more unstable with higher levels of productivity. Labor continues to be paid the value of its labor content. However, output per worker increases and the employer keeps the ever-increasing margin between the price (equal to labor value) of output and cost of production (equal to the labor cost). The effect of the operation of competition in factor and product markets is to cause ever-increasing inequality in the distribution of income and wealth as the laboring classes get none of the gains from economic growth but remain at the level of subsistence misery while the capitalists get progressively richer.

The growing inequality in the distribution of income creates macro-economic instability in the system. Total income is equal to total output but is divided very unequally between the workers and the capitalists. The former spend all their income on consumption, but the latter spend a decreasing proportion on consumption as they grow richer. The result is periodic crises of increasing intensity as the demand for goods at prices reflecting their labor value falls short of the supply of goods priced at their labor value. In every crisis there is a "slaughtering" of commodity prices and capital values as the capitalist lowers the prices of goods below their labor value in order to clear a market with deficient demand.

Marx conceded that in disequilibrium situations the level of wages may be pushed above the level of subsistence by temporarily excessive demand for labor. This situation will lead to a fall in the rate of exploitation, however, checking accumulation of capital and the demand for labor. The wages of labor will be driven back to their long-run equilibrium price. Further, any increase in wages above the subsistence level will cause an increase in the labor force through natural increase.

In the long run an additional factor will accelerate the rate of growth of the labor force while tending to slow down the increase in the demand for labor. This is the increasing ratio of fixed to working capital. Increasing productivity in the production of capital goods will lower their price relative to labor and result in the substitution of fixed capital for labor. This will displace labor from existing jobs and limit the growth of new jobs which are dependent on the expenditure of variable capital (the wages fund).

The forces of natural increase of population and the increase in the ratio of fixed to variable capital will result in the creation and expansion of the "reserve army of the unemployed." This will enable the employers to withstand pressure to raise wages arising from cyclical increases in the demand for labor or demands for higher wages by workers' organizations. Additionally, the increasing organic composition of capital will lower the rate of surplus value by decreasing the ratio of workers to total capital. The increasing fixed capital will also help the larger capitalists drive out the smaller producers who lack sufficient capital resources to compete. Thus, capitalism will finally be brought to dissolution by its increasing macro-economic instability and the progressive swelling of the proletarian ranks with the ruined small capitalists.

Liberal economists have exposed many difficulties and internal contradictions in Marx's arguments. The basic flaw in the argument, however, is the assumption that labor will receive a wage equal to its labor cost of production. The assumption has proved to be inaccurate and consequently Marx's elegant theory has not proved to be an accurate description of the process of capitalist development in advanced Western countries.

The core of Marx's argument about the injustice and self-defeating character of a capitalist system is the wage bargain. The inequalities in income distribution arise from the employer paying the worker less than the value of the goods created by the worker. This is possible because the worker will work for less than the employer would be willing to pay if forced by "the market" or the state. Marx was squarely in the tradition of Locke when he argued that the workers should overthrow a government which did not safeguard their "life, liberty, and property." Paying labor less than the value of their output was a confiscation of their property, and a state which encouraged or condoned this was undeserving of any support.

Marx's analysis of the wage bargain is a compound of confusions. This is no place to disentangle the labor theory of value. Unfortunately, Marx felt compelled to "demonstrate" the inconsistencies of a capitalist system when he, in fact, believed that distribution in accordance with contribution to output was not an ethical basis for distribution, in any event. Marx would have had as little use for the marginal-productivity theory of distribution of neo-classical economics as for the formulations of the classical tradition.

Marx's real intention in his economic analysis was to explain how the bourgeois class in a capitalist society accomplished the "exploitation" of the proletariat through "the market" when previous ruling classes had done it by more overt means. He argued that it was possible through "free exchange" only when the growth in productivity created a sizeable difference between per capita output and the necessary per capita input to maintain and reproduce the labor force. Here is the theory of an "economic surplus." Appropriate market behavior is hypothesized to predict its method of expropriation by the capitalist employers who constitute the new ruling classes. Marx's predictions about capitalism have failed to come true in developed countries because workers have succeeded in bargaining away a large part of their "surplus" and because much of the rest of it has been redistributed by government fiscal policies.

Marx's Critique and Social Reform. The viability of markets for handling income distribution satisfactorily depends on the existence of alternatives for all participants. A charitable interpretation of Marx would credit him with recognizing that the division of labor and specialization of production which accompanies economic growth might drastically limit the acceptable alternatives open to some individuals—particularly in labor markets. A charitable interpretation would also admit that variations in the level of aggregate demand owing to a large proportion of savings and investment in the national income might lead to serious problems of cyclical unemployment. Much of the "underconsumption" argument in Marx foreshadows the analysis of the problem by Keynes.

Marx's great mistake was his failure to allow for change in the institutional arrangements of a capitalist society. In the United States and other countries, workers have organized to bring economic and political pressure for higher wages and the redistribution of income and wealth through taxation, public education, and other welfare services. The rights of property and freedom of contract have been redefined. "Laissez faire" has been progressively abandoned as an ideology while an attempt has been made to retain the advantages of markets for allocation and the stimulation of dynamic efficiency in production.

The argument of this book is "Marxian" insofar as it stresses the historical relativity of such institutions as property and market freedom. It is also "Marxian" in the conceptual framework which emphasizes that the proportion of national income which is a "surplus" increases as a consequence of economic growth and can be allocated by political decision between the members of a society and to various uses.

It is unfortunate that the argument has been appropriated by the Marxists because much of it is to be found in such liberals in the Western tradition as John Stuart Mill, Thorstein Veblen, Oliver Wendell Holmes, John R. Commons, John Maynard Keynes, Adolph Berle, and John Galbraith. Acceptance of the argument underlies such programs and legislation in the United States as free public education, progressive income and inheritance taxes, anti-trust laws and public utility regulation, compulsory Social Security and unemployment insurance, legislation controlling collective bargaining and securities trading, and measures to outlaw private discrimination on grounds of race, religion, sex, or age.

Social Allocation of "Surplus":

The Dilemma of a Liberal Society

Since the end of World War II most Americans have not thought seriously about the character and quality of their rapidly changing society. The commitment of the Federal government to a policy of full employment by the Employment Act of 1946 coupled with a healthy rate of growth in per capita income has led many to think that the problems of unequal distribution of income and opportunity would be solved by the "New Economics" of John Maynard Keynes and that concentration of economic power held by government, corporations, and labor unions was not dangerous since their leaders were "responsible." Too little serious examination has been made of both the place of the individual in a pluralist society and the ends to which the enormous increase in productive potential was to be applied.

The avoidance of mass unemployment by government counter-cyclical fiscal policy removed a large source of class antagonism and side-stepped the dangers to a capitalist system from the business cycle which Marx called attention to in the nineteenth century. As a consequence, many businessmen who have accepted Keynesian policies now feel that labor markets will work to ensure opportunity and bargaining power for all members of the working population. However, even in a fully employed economy interferences are needed in labor markets because of the immobility of workers. An equally serious problem in a fully employed economy (not readily admitted by labor-union leaders) is inflation and the ability of certain men whose skills are in short supply to "exploit" society by threatening to withdraw their labor and disrupt the entire productive process. Most important, some political decisions must be made as to what goods and services a fully employed economy will produce and for whom.

Social Controls and Individual Freedom. The essential character of the Western liberal philosophy has always been inimical to any power concentration on the grounds that it *might* be misused. Today we live in a society in which a large degree of government intervention in micro- and macro-economic processes is admitted to be necessary and desirable. The great consensus of the 1960's is that we do not wish to return to the philosophies of the 1870's in regard to the self-regulating market and the absolute inviolability of private property from social control. The consensus that we do *not* want a particular philosophy of society, however, is not a sufficient basis on which to base a great society. If there is to be social control of an individual's liberty and property by society, what are the proper limits of that control? It is one thing to agree that every American should be properly fed, clothed, housed, and educated. It is another to choose the means by which this is to be accomplished. The alternative of the welfare state in which income is systematically redistributed according to need rather than contribution to production is a complete rejection of the individualist philosophy on which our system has been based since the Middle Ages. Yet, the alternative of individualism requires an extensive rethinking of our assumptions about private property and economic freedom to make them produce a distribution of income which is socially acceptable in a democratic society.

Full Employment and Allocation of Output and Income. The threat of macro-economic instability in our society has largely been overcome by the systematic application of the ideas of John Maynard Keynes. His basic contribution was to point out that the volume of planned expenditures in a society could fall below the productive capacity of the economy. This could be remedied by governmental spending exceeding governmental revenues by the difference between planned expenditure and the level of expenditures which would keep the economy at full employment. At full employment, government tax receipts and expenditures would have to be brought back into equality to prevent inflation from excessive demand creation.

Keynesian fiscal policies have been easy to carry out since the Second World War because of the very large amount of governmental spending on defense and the space program. In 1962 rather than increase governmental expenditures still further, taxes were cut to increase the gap between government receipts and expenditures. This injected additional consumer spending into the economy and has helped to prolong the lengthiest continual boom in peacetime history. Still, this represented a value judgment as to ends. The tax cuts went largely to upper income groups. "Surplus" taken in taxes by the government could have been used to increase the space program, to increase expenditures in Viet Nam, to improve the quality of education, or to carry out a massive program of urban redevelopment. A different decision in 1962 about the disposition of the "surplus" might have changed the course of events in Southeast Asia, put men on the moon months earlier, affected the growth rate in the 1970's, or lessened the tensions and racial violence which seem to mark every "long hot summer."

While Keynesian policies are a remedy to deal with the symptoms of macro-economic disequilibrium, they do not really deal with a major underlying cause of the social instability, namely the distribution of income. Controlling the level of *aggregate* demand has been treated as a separate problem from the distribution of demand. We have been so preoccupied with the problem of production that we have ignored the question of production of what and for whom. This is certainly an important reason for our present social instability and restiveness.

This situation poses a real dilemma for a democratic society. On the one hand, the level of savings must be high in order to finance the investment necessary for economic growth. Inequality in the distribution of income is thought to lead to a higher level of savings. On the other hand, a free society entails the right of individual members of that society to decide both the interpersonal and intertemporal distribution of income. The micro-economic structure of the American economy has allowed many large corporations to finance their investment out of profits extracted from consumers who have little choice other than to pay prices above the cost of production including a normal rate of return on capital. Thus, even capital accumulation does not proceed only by a voluntary decision by the individual citizen to save part of his income. It comes from the decision of a large corporation to finance investment through retained earnings artificially inflated by the failure of the market to work competitively. It is a situation analogous to the Russian practice of financing capital formation through the imposition of a turnover tax on output. Yet, the alternative of increasing the share of the "surplus" allocated by the government is also fraught with many dangers and undesirable features.

The difficulty with admitting that social control of markets *is* legitimate is that when they do not produce a socially acceptable rate of growth, stability, equity, and the like, this opens the way for a government to interfere with markets to produce a different set of results. This is the dilemma which has faced the propertied classes in the United States since the adoption of the Constitution.

The writers of the Constitution recognized that there would be inevitable conflicts of interest which would arise in a society in which citizens were given both political power and a large measure of economic freedom. Madison wrote in Number Ten of the *Federalist Papers*:

> The diversity in the faculties of men from which the rights of property originate, is not less an insuperable obstacle to a uniformity of interests. The protection of different and unequal faculties of acquiring property, the possession of different degrees and kinds of property immediately results; and from the influence of these on the sentiments and views of the respective proprietors, ensues a division of the society into different interests and parties.[13]

The distribution of property, not the rights of property, arises from the diversities in the faculties of men. The rights of property are guaranteed by the state. If the state consists of a large number of men of "different degrees and kinds of property," they may be unwilling to protect the status quo.

Noting that faction in a representative government was inevitable, Madison argued that there were but two alternatives. One was to do away with liberty, which was the origin of differences in wealth and, therefore,

---

[13]*The Federalist Papers*, ed. Jacob E. Cooke, (Middletown, Conn.: Wesleyan University Press, 1961).

the source of faction. The other was to seek to control faction by the balancing of power. This solution was adopted in a government with constitutionally limited powers and the further separation of those powers between the Federal and State governments and between the various branches of government. The founding fathers never intended that the government be powerless to deal with the "natural rights of property" or the "self-regulating market." They intended only that governmental power be subject to procedural checks.

The abandonment of beliefs in the "natural rights of property" and the "self-regulating market" does not interfere with the basic conceptual framework of a capitalist society. It does away only with an accretion of myth, well-intended and valuable in its time, but unnecessary and potentially dangerous to an understanding of the logic and development of a system of political and economic organization founded on the freely given consent of individuals who are members of it.

5

The Logic
of Property

The peculiar characteristic of capitalism is not the vesting of property rights to the use of productive assets with individuals, as Marx contended, but the rationale for doing so. In the feudal society from which capitalism developed, all members of society, in theory, had privileges and obligations which could have been subsumed under the term *property*. In the contemporary Soviet Union, practically all productive assets are under state ownership and control, but individuals have certain rights (in theory) which are safeguarded by the state. In both these noncapitalist societies, individuals have "bundles of rights" or "powers." They have a degree of security in streams of income which are their due as cooperative members of society.

Capitalism and Property

What, then, is distinctive about property in a capitalist society? The author believes the distinctive feature of property in a capitalist society is its assignment as a means to increase output rather than just to distribute it. The assignment of income claims in such corporate societies as medieval Europe and Soviet Russia originated from an attempt to safeguard the security of the individual from other individuals and to distribute income according to the preferences of the rulers of those societies. The assignment of claims to the income flows from assets in a capitalist society finds its primary rationale in providing incentives to individual members of society to increase the economic output available to society.

That the assignment of property claims should increase only the income of the individual who utilizes them is not enough. The members of a society have an interest in granting property rights to an individual member of society only when they enjoy an increase in their own welfare from the recognition of the guarantees given to one of their members.

The principle that society should recognize the claims of individuals when this would benefit society as a whole first gained recognition in the English common law courts at the beginning of the seventeenth century.[1] It was invoked to sanction the substitution of freehold land tenure for the complex system of privileges and obligations which preceded it. It was used to end the public enforcement of monopolies which had the sole purpose of enriching the monopolist at the expense of the public.

This is not to suggest that the principle that property should be guaranteed to an individual only when it would benefit the commonweal has been or is practiced without exception in capitalist societies. This writer only wishes to present this as the underlying logic of a capitalist system of economic organization. In the subsequent chapters the author hopes to show how it led to the evolution of our institutional arrangements.

The Economic Functions
of Property

The vesting of property rights in individuals for the exclusive control and use of land, labor, and capital accomplishes three functions necessary for increasing total economic output: First, it provides incentives for the creation and improvement of assets. Second, it provides incentives for efficient control of existing assets. Third, it rations the use of scarce assets to ensure that they will be used for those purposes which society values most highly. Note that the existence of markets for the valuation of resources is presupposed by the third function and part of the operation of the first two because economic activity is organized on the principle of exchange and the division of labor in a society with any degree of economic development. Property is basic to freedom of exchange, as one must have property rights in assets before one is legally free to exchange them.

The utility to society of granting an individual property in any net

---

[1]See John R. Commons, *Legal Foundations of Capitalism* (New York: The Macmillan Co., 1924), chap. vi and vii. For a contrary view which emphasizes the creation of modern property as a means for the expropriation of the proletariat, see Maurice Dobb, *Studies in the Development of Capitalism* (London: Routledge and Kegan Paul Ltd., 1946), especially chap. I–IV.

increase in the productive capacity of the economy for which he is responsible is *not* intuitively obvious. Suppose that in the absence of individual claims to property in the means of production—labor, capital, and land—all production and consumption were organized around common possession and socially assigned claims to consumption of net social output. Assume, further, that an individual offered to forfeit his right to his communal share of consumption in return for property *only* in his own labor. If the individual's withdrawal of his labor from social production decreased social output by more than the share of consumption which the individual formerly received, society, *ex individual*, would be *worse off* through granting private property to the individual. Society, *ex individual*, would be worse off either because prior to the recognition of individual claims the net contribution of the individual to social output was greater than his consumption or because his withdrawal led to a disproportionate fall in social productivity. In either of these cases, society, *ex individual*, would regard the creation of private property for the individual in his own labor as inimical to its interests.

The Social Gains from Private Property: Locke's example. The one case in which society would have an economic interest in guaranteeing to the individual private property claims in assets is when the society, *ex individual*, would have a greater quantity of economic goods per member than they did while organized communally because the granting of property to the individual had resulted in an increase in output which accrued partly to society.

This matter was explored by Locke and has already been mentioned in Chapter III, in the section entitled The Social Origin of Property: A New Interpretation of Locke. Locke's example of the social utility of private property rests on the hidden assumption that before private property was granted to an individual, society, *ex individual*, was poorer than after the guarantee of property had induced asset creation. In terms of Locke's example, the assumption is that output available to the society, *ex individual*, from ninety acres of unimproved land would be greater than the output available to society including the individual from one hundred acres of unimproved land. This really requires the additional assumption that before the alienation of the ten unimproved acres, the individual in question consumed more than the produce of those ten acres. Or, it involves the individual trading part of the increase in output with other members of society to leave them "better off" from the results of the alienation of part of common possession. This passage is of crucial importance because Locke was trying to demonstrate a point. Locke was aware of the necessity for demonstrating that some gains from property creation would accrue to the members of society apart from the recipient of property claims. Merely demonstrating that social output would increase without inquiring into the distribution of the increased output was insufficient.

Social Gains From Property: A formal demonstration of the general case. A more formal way to demonstrate the social utility of property also allows the identification of the limits to individual and social gains and involves three assumptions: (a) that property rights granted to the individual do not exceed the increment to social output for which he is responsible, (b) that the increment to output is exchanged by the individual with the rest of society, and (c) that the individual has less than complete monopoly power in bargaining over the exchange ratio of the good which he produces in exchange for other goods.

The demonstration is illustrated in Fig. 5–1 by the use of an Edgeworth Box diagram. (The reader unfamiliar with the use of this technique is referred to the Appendix.) In the initial situation, social output and consumption of goods 1 and 2 is indicated by the dimensions of the "box" $ABCD$. Society is in equilibrium at point C consuming quantity AB of good 1 and AD of good 2. At point C, society has reached its highest attainable preference function given a specific supply of resources and state of technology.

Assume that an offer to an individual of rights to possess and exchange any increase in output results in an increase in available resources or an improvement in technology which increases the production of good 1 to B and expands the Box to $AB'C'D$. Society is still consuming at C, and the individual responsible for the increase in good 1 has property in the assets he created to produce $BB' = CC'$ of good 1.

Let the individual have a set of preference functions with their origin at C'. By exchanging a quantity of good 1 for good 2, he can reach a higher preference function. A result of this exchange will be that society is *also* in a more preferred condition. The only circumstance which could prevent society from reaching a higher preference function as a result of the increase in productive capacity and the ensuing exchange would be when the individual could act as a perfect monopolist and force society to move to some point along the original social preference function passing through C. In this limiting case, society would be no "worse off" than before the creation of property. In the diagram any point, X, is assumed to be the final distribution of goods for society and the individual. Point X allows both the individual and society to move to a preferred position. Points Y and Z illustrate the individual and society, respectively, receiving all the gains from exchange in the movement from point C. At point Y, the individual maximizes his gains as a monopolist, but society is on the same preference function as it was before creation of property.

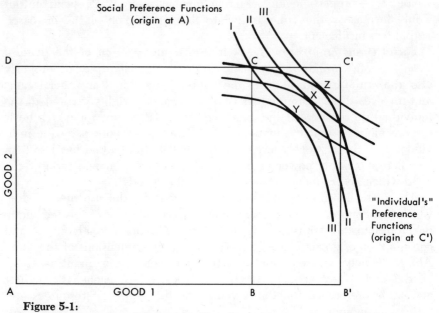

Figure 5-1:
A formal demonstration of the social utility of property.

The utility to society of offering private property to secure increases in total output is, thus, demonstrated in general conditions. The rationale for property need not depend on the *morality* of giving a man property in his incremental contribution to social output. It may rest merely on the assumption that in the absence of the incentive created by a social guarantee, increases in social output would not be forthcoming.

Property and Efficient Use of Resources. The economic arguments for private property based on the desirability of efficient control and allocation of scarce resources assume that in the absence of individual control of scarce resources they would be inefficiently used, that is, it would be possible to increase social production and consumption. The argument for a man having private property in his own labor, in land, and in capital instruments is that if he does not "own" them he will not have any incentive to use them efficiently. The argument is a variant of the one elaborated above for the social utility of property for the creation of new assets.

An interesting note here is that in purely economic terms an argument against chattel slavery can be made on the grounds that when a man lacks property in his own labor and the right to bargain about the disposition of it, he has no self-interest in increasing his output. If he does not increase his output, the gains which other members of society can realize in trading goods and services with him is limited. The owner of a slave has an economic interest in maintaining the slave as he is a valuable asset. This sets a limit to the standard of living to which the slave can be reduced. The slave, however, has no incentive to increase his output as any increase in output belongs to his owner. The physical ability of the slave to withhold his labor makes the realization of increased output difficult for the owner unless he is willing to bargain with the slave over the division of increases in output. The social assignment of property to all men in their own labor need not depend on moral considerations or "natural rights."

The same economic argument applies to land and capital which are utilized by a person who has no property in the assets or their net production. Every individual has bargaining power against society in his ability to limit social output by withholding his intelligently applied labor or by consuming capital. While force or threat may have some efficacy in securing the cooperation of men in production, the incentives offered by property are assumed in a capitalist system to be a superior method of obtaining results. Thus, a wise landowner will be led to give a long-term lease with guarantees of remuneration for tenant improvements because it is a superior method of land utilization. A large corporation may find it advantageous to institute a profit-sharing system for executives. Both arrangements allow individuals with no property ownership in capital assets to secure property rights in the increased productivity of those assets for which they are responsible.

The arguments for private property based on the desirability of securing efficient utilization and allocation of assets like that based on the desirability of creating them relies on the incentive producing the desired response from individual members of the society. One significant difference exists, however. The person who has property in assets need not necessarily have created them himself to possess an incentive to use them efficiently. A *particular distribution* of private property can be defended on grounds of social utility only when it has been created by the men who presently hold claim to the assets. A particular distribution of property cannot be justified *on economic grounds* if the argument merely posits the necessity for the incentive of property to ensure efficient utilization and allocation of extant assets.

The social utilitarian argument for the maintenance of a *given* distribution of property claims is based on the desirability of avoiding the civil strife and disruption which would ensue if existing property claims were suddenly to be disregarded. The argument to maintain a *given* distribution of property is the argument against revolution, and this argument is persuasive only for those who would have more to lose by revolution than to gain by it.

Property and Resource Allocation. The primary economic rationale for private property is the social desirability of increasing the stock of productive assets and their productivity. Given the basic economic problem of limited resources and unlimited demands, property performs a secondary function in allocating scarce resources between competing demands. In a system based on private property, the owners of specific assets ensure they will be used in the way society values most highly by selling them to the highest bidder. Social productivity is increased by rationing the use of scarce assets so that they will be used only when they are the least costly alternative in a production process. We should emphasize, however, that private property is merely an administrative device with reference to resource allocation. In the absence of private ownership of productive assets and a market to insure that price performs an allocative function, a society could allocate resources with optimal efficiency with linear programming techniques.

The holder of property rights in scarce assets ensures optimal allocation of those assets by obtaining the maximum price for their use. In the absence of the rationing mechanism imposed by property, or some surrogate, scarce resources would be used in an inefficient way; that is, net social output could be increased by an allocation of the scarce resources to those willing to pay the highest prices for their use.

This point can be illustrated by reference to the results of the nonexistence of property for so-called "open-access resources." Petroleum and natural gas have sometimes been open-access resources in the past because no property rights were attached to the underground reserves—only to drilling rights on the land surface which was above the reserves. Unless the person who discovered oil had drilling rights on *all* the land over a particular pool of petroleum, it would be economically rational to pump it all out as fast as possible in order to prevent some other person from doing so. This would have two socially undesirable effects. First, it would prevent the recovery of the petroleum at a rate which would maximize the present value of a discounted stream of returns. High production in the present would tend to depress the price of oil while exhaustion in the future would cause future prices to be higher. The lower price in the present would encourage wasteful use of the resource which would be unavailable in the future. Second, maximum recovery in the present would result in higher recovery costs since sinking more wells would increase capital and labor costs (and the dissipation of gas pressure would make pumping more costly).

The absence of property rights in oil pools also tends to discourage exploration for new reserves since an oil company has an incentive to allow others to bear the cost of exploration if they can rush in after discovery and drill wells into the pool. The exploring company can protect itself only by acquiring drilling rights over all the land which they expect to overlay an oil pool.

The lack of congruence between property rights on land surface and oil pools has led to a variety of cooperative agreements and governmental controls to limit and allocate production. These, however, are an imperfect surrogate for a set of property rights which would give exclusive access to a scarce resource.

Fisheries are another "open-access" resource where the absence of exclusive property rights results in inefficiency. The problem with regard to the fisheries is complicated by the existence of an unusual biological yield function but the problem of rational use of the resource is basically similar to the use of land for the growing of forests or grazing. Today, economic rationality would prevent a resource policy which allowed forests to be cut down or land to be exploited without maximizing economic yield over time. The lack of an individual incentive to conserve the use of the resource to give the maximum economic yield over time would result in overcutting or overgrazing. The individual would have an incentive to take all he could before the next man as in the example of petroleum, with the added complication that land and forests when properly utilized are renewable resources. The rational use of grazing or forest land necessitates balancing off present and future costs and prices to get the maximum return over time.

This is partially perceived with regard to fisheries when there is "open access" to the resource since the oceans, unlike land, have not traditionally been alienable into private or state ownership. Biological yield, however, is confused with economic yield, and the usual control measure adopted is to try to control the number of fish taken by limiting the efficiency of the gear, the time that can be fished, the number of fish which can be taken by one person, and so forth. This results always in the inefficient use of capital and labor in fishing (the purpose of the regulation which seeks to limit yield to conserve the stock of fish by promoting inefficiency). The result is higher cost of catching fish through the net loss of productive efficiency. The rational policy would be to limit the human and capital resources involved in fishing. The desired amount of fish could be caught with far less labor and capital and the factors released could then be diverted to other productive uses.

A surplus would accrue to the owner of a fishery, as it accrues to the owner of a forest, if the price of fish exceeds their cost of production by the most efficient means. If the cost of production is driven up to limit the number of fish being caught for conservation purposes, this means that social output falls short of its attainable maximum as resources which would have been used elsewhere are drawn into fishing. Only treating the resource as if it were private property will assure that this does not happen although the accompanying result would be the creation of an economic surplus. In the fishery, incidentally, this could be confiscated by making access to the fishery open to license holders with licenses limited to the number which would produce maximum economic efficiency and sold to the highest bidders. The holder of the license, theoretically, would be willing to pay a price for the license which reflected the capitalized value of the stream of surplus profits—returns above the normal rate of return on capital—to which it entitled him.

The allocative function of private property may result in the private receipt of an income far in excess of the amount which the individual receiving it would be willing to accept for performing the administrative and allocative function of the rentier. There is no economic rationale for society to allow the continued private receipt of this type of income. It would be exceedingly difficult to find any economically rational grounds for the continued policy in capitalist societies of allowing the very considerable economic rents arising from the scarcity of natural resources and land-site values to accrue to private individuals.

The social guarantee of private property to the individual has its logic in the provision of incentives to individuals to create, efficiently utilize, and optimally allocate productive resources. Property rights are a *quid pro quo* which society offers the individual in return for socially beneficial behavior. How extensive does the *quid pro quo* need to be in order to elicit the performance of the desired functions? The recognition of property as a variable bundle of rights provided as an incentive to encourage certain economic functions implies that the bundle of rights might be excessively or insufficiently extensive to perform its desired economic functions for a society at a particular stage of its economic and social development. Fitting the form of property to the socially defined function requires changes in response to technology as well as social purpose. This will be discussed in some historical detail in the next chapter.

Property and
Political Power

A discussion of the economic functions of property which ignores its other functions is too simplistic. Political power defines the distribution of property rights in accordance with political and cultural as well as economic considerations. The specification of property rights must ensure not only the existence of an adequate economic base for a society; it must provide the means for defense against external aggression and internal civil disorder. It must provide for the establishment and maintenance of a social, cultural, and religious life for a society which will give it the social self-consciousness necessary to social survival. Finally, it must accord with a society's conception about equity.

The provision of civil defense, order, culture, and provision for economic growth in a society depends on social allocation of the difference between gross social economic output and the incentives which society must give individual members of the society to ensure their participation in social production. *Theoretically*, society could adjust property rights so that each individual received an incentive just equal to the amount which would induce him to behave in the desired way in creating assets and in utilizing and allocating them optimally. The surplus—the difference between an individual's contribution to gross social output and the amount necessary to offer as an incentive to realize it—would be available for distribution to collective capital formation, security, culture, or distribution to achieve political ends.

As discussed in the section of the preceding chapter on Surplus Value and the Operation of Markets, a distinction related to the one made above has long been made in economic theory in terms of a return to a factor of production in excess of its "cost of production" or long-run supply price. The surplus accruing to the owner of the factor of production represented by the difference between the "cost" of the factor and its price has variously been designated as a "surplus value" (Marx), "rent" (Ricardo), "quasi-rent" (Marshall), or "economic surplus" (Boulding). *Theoretically*, this difference between the payment made to the person controlling the factor necessary to obtain the use of the factor and the price actually paid, could be confiscated by society without diminution in social output.

The social allocation of property rights in a capitalist system, as in other systems, determines the interpersonal distribution of the "surplus" and by that means the uses, for example, capital formation in physical assets and/or education, military expenditures, celebrations and circuses, scientific enquiry, or "culture," to which the surplus will be devoted. The maintenance of political power through distributing property claims to the "surplus" to certain segments of society to assure their support of an existing regime is implicit in the allocation process. It poses an additional constraint on the distribution of property rights in the "surplus" to that posed by the necessity and desirability of maintaining and increasing gross social output. Men are bound to a particular regime by self-interest and will not support a system which allocates less to them than they feel they could obtain from an alternative. This is the effective social and political (as opposed to economic) constraint on the distribution of claims to property which confronts the rulers of all societies including capitalist ones.

In the succeeding two chapters, the reader will be subjected to some condensed and selected historical evidence to support the contentions of this chapter: First, that the evolution of capitalism was accompanied by a recognition of the social utility of granting property guarantees to secure asset creation. And, secondly, that capitalism has led in the United States (and other Western countries) to political recognition of the necessity for adopting property claims to accord with technological change and the demands of less privileged groups for institutional changes which would allow them to secure a larger part of an increasing per capita output. The argument will emphasize the importance of changing technology, changing social objectives, and the limiting factor imposed by the need to provide political stability on the scope and distribution of property.

6

Property, Power, and Technology in Pre-Capitalist Societies

Property is a ubiquitous institution in civilized societies. Some social specification must be made of the form which relationships between men will take. The actual form which property rights do take and the social rationale invoked to justify their distribution, however, varies widely among societies.

This chapter traces the evolution of property relationships in the Western world from force, to divine right, to social contract. It would be comfortable to think that there was a gradual and steady progression from ancient societies to our own in the rationality of social arrangements. Unfortunately, such a sanguine view of social evolution would be difficult to maintain in view of men's repeated attempts to return to earlier forms of defining and defending property rights. For example, the justifications of slavery and colonial exploitation used in classical antiquity have been used to justify rule by force and violence in the recent past by such Western societies as Britain, France, and the United States. The theory of communist organization has emphasized a utopian return to the common possession of assets and distribution according to need, which was characteristic of primitive societies. In contemporary America, many adherents would be found for the view that property rights find their origin in either force or some ill-defined natural laws or divine revelation.

The definition, distribution, and justification of property rights in a society depends on the hierarchy of social objectives and values which a society holds and the character of the technology available for the realization of social objectives. Because values, objectives, and technology have changed over time, the character of property has changed and will continue to do so. A consideration of classical antiquity and medieval Europe and the breakdown of these social systems may help make clear the peculiar features of our own system of institutional relationships.

Classical Antiquity

The Greek and Roman civilizations of classical antiquity are often considered to be the origin of modern Western social and political institutions. Classicists point to the beginnings of political democracy and republican government in the citizens' councils of Athens. Roman law is studied as a major source of the distinctions and terminology of our own legal system.

While the forms and terminologies of social institutions of these classical cultures bear certain similarities to our own, some fundamental differences exist. This is particularly true with respect to property. As we have argued thus far, in capitalist ideology the claims to property are apportioned as an incentive to create and effectively utilize resources for the production of goods and services. In the societies of classical antiquity, claims to assets were divided as the spoils of plunder. They were rewards for military services rendered in the conquest and subjugation of other peoples. They were based explicitly on physical force.

The Grecian cities had their origins as cooperative organizations for the systematic plunder of other societies. The possessions of the warrior citizens were alienated from the possession of other peoples and increased by the labor of the conquered peoples of whom they made slaves. The proportion of the population of the cities who gained the privileges of citizenship depended on the military requirements of the cities. The privileges of citizenship were primarily the rights to share in the spoils of battle and be protected against the threats to person and property from inside and outside the society. Only the citizen had the right of access to the courts in case of a threatened trespass on his person or property by another citizen. Merchants and craftsmen were not likely to be citizens unless they were also warriors. Commercial and manufacturing functions would be performed by slaves in the households of the warrior class. Citizenship and property were a restricted privilege.

The Roman Empire was similarly founded as a military organization designed for the systematic exploitation of conquered peoples for the benefit of the Roman citizenry. For the purpose, the Romans evolved superior administrative machinery to the Greeks. They not only raided; they occupied and farmed the captured land with captured people to provide tax revenue for the support of the imperial establishment. Great estates, *latifundia*, were granted to the knights of the Roman Empire in return for the undertaking on the part of the latter to render specified amounts in taxes and a certain number of recruits for the Roman legions. Slave-labor shipyards turned out slave-manned galleys to carry the produce of the provinces to the Tiber and were administered by a system of contracts let to individual Roman citizens who were privileged to tender.

The Basis of Property in Classical Antiquity. The Roman citizen possessed property in the sense that he had access to the courts for the protection of his possessions. The most important producers' goods, slaves and land, were held at the pleasure of the state in return for military or political services. Conquered land and peoples were alienated from being *res nullius*, "nonproperty," in the Roman law into the property of individual Roman citizens. The state created the productive assets of the society by military conquest and distributed them to the members of the civil society as a *quid pro quo* for military and political services.

The Greek or Roman citizen realized that his assets were seized from barbarians by the state and that his retention of them necessitated his discharge of his military and political responsibilities. In particular, he realized the ever-present possibility of revolt by slaves or subject peoples could only be prevented by the state. The state not only sanctioned property claims to assets. It actually provided the assets.

The functions of private property in classical antiquity were not the same as in contemporary society. There was no question of offering property rights to new slaves or land as an incentive for conquest on a private basis as this would challenge the power of the state. Only the state could "create" new assets. The use of state-created resources was delegated to private control to secure the maximum economic surplus from their use for the state and to bind the loyalty of citizens to the state by self-interest.

The important difference between the ancient and modern conceptions of the function of private property arose from the conception of the state. The ancients saw political organization as a means of military exploitation of subject peoples. The state was a money-making organization for those who controlled it. Property rights in assets were a reward for participation in the organized plunder of men who were *not* citizens of the Greek city or the Roman Empire. The glory that was Greece and the magnificence that was Rome were based on the organized rapacity of an oligarchy in the exploitation of their respective empires.

The Weakness of Force. The fundamental weakness of the Greek and Roman Empires was the low level of agricultural technology on which food production was based. There had been little advance in per worker output of food over the more primitive cultures who fed themselves by food gathering and the tending of flocks. Primitive cultivation of cereals took place, but yield per person was low in the absence of a technology to harness animal power to plowing the earth. As long as cultivation depended largely on human energy, very little surplus of energy was produced over that consumed in the maintenance of a labor force to carry on production.

The very small surplus per worker which could be extracted from agriculture set a limit to the proportion of the population which could be employed in nonagricultural activities. The absolute size of the surplus available to the ruling oligarchy depended on the extent of the subject population. The Greeks were much less efficient than the Romans in the extraction of goods from conquered peoples. They plundered what movable wealth they could find but did not attempt to occupy conquered regions. They would use booty to trade with other cultures and captured slaves for agricultural and handicraft activities in their cities and surrounding countryside. They did not, however, attempt to impose a continuing levy on the areas they conquered. This inevitably limited their "take" and the extent of their empire was geographically limited by the range of their primitive galleys and sailing ships.

The superiority of Roman organization over the Greek was its ability to establish and maintain occupation of subject lands with the Roman legions. Revenue to support the legions and the imperial administration was derived from the imposition of taxes. The *latifundia*, agricultural plantations administered by citizens and worked by slaves, were conceived as a method of increasing output in order to increase the amount which could be extracted in taxes. The managers of the *latifundia* had incentives to improve net output from having their remittance obligations fixed. They had limited rights to the sale or exchange of the land and slaves which comprised their principle assets. These were the possessions of the Empire and their management by Roman citizens was the means by which a surplus was extracted for the purposes of the Empire.

The source of the streams of income from physical assets in classical antiquity, that is, land and slaves, was not what we would regard as the economic processes of investment and efficient utilization. The productivity of the assets did not arise from their creation by the citizen who was given property rights in return. It arose from the military conquests of the state which took the assets from other peoples. The state was not just the source of property relations; it was the source of the physical assets to which property was attached through confiscation from subject peoples. The income from assets was not realized by a set of voluntary arrangements. It was created by involuntary arrangements between master and slave, conqueror and conquered. Citizens made voluntary arrangements for the division of the revenues created by the societies' military ventures. The social rationale of these property arrangements, however, did not rest on property being granted as an incentive for economic production. The arrangements arose from the need to distribute spoils among a warrior class whose self-interest lay in cooperative exploitation of those outside the class.

The Roman Empire disintegrated for a number of reasons. If one considers the economic reasons for disintegration, one finds that apparently imperial control of the provinces on which the Empire was based could not be maintained because the costs of coercion and administration exceeded the gains which could be realized. The maintenance of the legions and the remission of taxes to Rome, given the low level of agricultural and transport technology, was beyond the capabilities of the system. Force proved to be an unviable method of economic organization in the long run because of the inability of the ruling class to make the returns from coercion exceed its cost.

The Middle Ages

The disintegration of the Roman Empire in Western Europe was followed by a heterogeneous millenium (500 A.D.–1500 A.D.) in which the distinctive features of property were determined by the social ideals of Christianity, the peculiar requirements of military technology, and the character of agricultural production.

Faith as the Basis of Society. The legitimacy of political authority in medieval society was not based on force but on faith. The individual member of society had an obligation to accept the ordering of society made by his rulers because of his obligation as a Christian to obey the orders of temporal rulers whom God had placed over him. Medieval rulers governed not by military force but by the grace of God.

All members of society had privileges and obligations appropriate to their divinely ordained status. As members of a corporate body, the church visible and invisible, they had functions to perform like the parts of a human body. They no more had "rights" against one another than the parts of a human body could have "rights" against the other parts of the body. The bargaining between individual members of society over privileges was deemed inappropriate because it would interfere with divine prerogative and undermine the concept of Christian charity for the welfare of one's fellow man.

The rulers of society had divinely ordained duties to care for the welfare of the subjects over which they were given power. This responsibility was analogous to the responsibility of the father for his child. The failure of the ruler to care for his subjects was not a legitimate reason for revolt by his subjects any more than the tyranny of a father could be said to eliminate his children's duty to obey him. The source of the king's power was not his physical power over his subjects or their contract with him to protect their interests but the divinely ordained Constitution of society, itself. Therefore, there could be no question of revolution or of demands for action by the governed. If the king were tyrannical, his subjects could pray for his soul, but for them to take positive action to overthrow his authority would constitute a rejection of the very basis of society-faith in its divine establishment.

Given this ideological framework, the claims of individuals to the use and enjoyment of the fruits of their own labor and their possession of physical assets was extremely tenuous. Individuals lacked procedural safeguards against the demands of their rulers. Further, they lacked the opportunity to have arrangements entered into with other members of society sanctioned and enforced unless it happened to suit the interests of those who enforced the agreements.

Property and Military Technology. A secondary determinant of property relationships in medieval Europe was military technology. The foot soldier of the Roman legion was succeeded by the armored knight on horseback. The invention and diffusion of the stirrup made the trained medieval knight on horseback the modern equivalent of the armored tank. Wielding sword, lance, or mace against men on foot, he had a great advantage in battle and was geographically mobile.

The armies of the kingdoms of the Middle Ages on whom conquest and defense rested were composed primarily of a class of highly trained and expensively equipped, mounted knights. To maintain these armies and provide for the civil administration of the kingdom, medieval rulers settled feudal estates with knights who were to support themselves with the incomes which they could realize from their estates. The granting of the use of a feudal estate by the king entailed the rendering of military services by the knight and his provision on request of a specified number of men and horses.

Thus, an essential feature of property in the Middle Ages was that it was held, as in classical antiquity, by a restricted class of citizens of the state in return for their military services. Unlike classical antiquity, the economic base of the class with political rights was not conquest and the exploitation of conquered peoples as slaves. The economic base was composed of men who had a different status but who were considered to be a part of the same society as their superiors. The serf had no legal rights to do as he wished with his labor and land, but he had privileges as well as obligations. He was a member of society, and moral rules as well as pragmatic considerations limited the extent to which he could be exploited by his feudal master.

Property and Agricultural Technology. A third determinant of property relationships in medieval Europe was the rudimentary level of agricultural technology. Feudal lord and serf, alike, lacked exclusive rights to use land on an individual basis because it could not have been worked effectively in that manner. On the other hand, the chattel slavery of classical antiquity had been abandoned as feudal lords learned that they could get more income with less coercion by settling their serfs with specified obligations in produce and labor rather than trying to cultivate land by slave gangs.

On the medieval manor, land was worked collectively and individually. Plowing required the serfs to pool their own physical effort or their oxen to pull the communal plow. On the other hand, harvesting could be accomplished individually. As a consequence, fields with individual strips scattered about in them became characteristic of medieval agriculture. Each serf had a claim to the produce of certain strips. The strips were allocated in proportion to individual contributions to the plow team. The serf had to plow, plant, and harvest "his" strip in accordance with the decisions reached collectively by the manorial residents. Grazing on the fields after harvest and on the grazing lands of the manor was also proportioned by custom—often in accordance to the possession of draft animals and the strips of land in the common fields.

The Disintegration of
Feudal Corporatism

One of the difficulties in talking about property in the Middle Ages is that the corporate conception of society in which each individual had an assigned function began to disintegrate even before it had come to fruition from forces generated by the system, itself.

Political Ambiguities of Feudalism. The development of the feudal system tended to undermine political absolutism. The political and legal legacy of the Roman Empire emphasized the source of political power as the command of the ruler and the source of economic assets, land and labor, as the action of the state. On the other hand, the reality of the feudal system was frequently different. The power of the king frequently resulted from independent local leaders allying themselves to the monarch out of mutual advantage. And serfs frequently placed themselves voluntarily under the protection of a lord and gave limited and well-defined services in return. Consequently, there existed side by side in the political ideology of medieval Europe conflicting ideas about the legitimacy of power.

Between the king and his vassals there was the relationship simultaneously of subject and sovereign and feudal superior and inferior, each having contractual obligations entered into out of mutual advantage. On the manor itself, the practical problems of organizing agricultural production tended to break down the conception of social arrangements based on *voluntas domini*, the Roman theory of law originating in the command of the superior. The serfs held a more pragmatic view of the origins of privilege and obligation. Their emphasis on the origins of social relationships in implicit social contracts, the *consuetudo manorii*, grew out of the logic of feudalism but was potentially subversive of the system because it tended to undermine the relationship of superior with inferior. Out of this conception of feudalism the common law and the political theories of social contract were to spring.

Rather than spread our view widely over the whole of Europe, let us discuss the breakdown of medieval conceptions of property and political authority in one country—England. This is particularly relevant to an understanding of contemporary American conceptions of property since they developed from the British practices which replaced feudalism and were carried over to America in the seventeenth and eighteenth centuries.

The establishment of a classical feudal pattern in England was made possible by the Norman conquest in 1066. The superiority of the mounted knight to the indigenous unmounted Saxon forces was forcibly demonstrated on the field at Hastings. The Norman knights were settled on feudal estates in England with privileges which stemmed solely from their military functions. All the land of the kingdom belonged to the King by conquest and was settled on his knights both as a reward for service rendered and as a means of rendering future services. Even so, political absolutism began to break down after little more than a century.

The first rejection of the absolute power of the sovereign came in the Magna Carta of 1215. This document is usually hailed as an early proclamation of human rights against the encroachment of an arbitrary government. In fact, it was a feudal settlement forced on King John by his nobles and backed up by their force of arms that he should not deprive them of any of their traditional privileges without a trial in which the outcome should be judged by a jury of their peers. The conception of the King as an absolute sovereign against whom no claim could be maintained was being superceded by action on the part of certain members of the state to guarantee that the King could not deprive them of their privileges in the possession of assets. The Magna Carta established a contract between the sovereign and his subjects to safeguard the privileges of the latter by requiring any actions against them by the King or their peers to be judged by a jury of their peers. This was a limitation of sovereignty.

The rejection of the absolute power of the King needs to be understood in terms of the contradiction between the King's role as ruler by the grace of God and his role as feudal superior to the barons in which he was a leader among military equals, *primus inter pares*. The barons did not wish to reject the King as sovereign, but they wished to enforce the obligations and privileges which existed between feudal superior and inferior. The barons were willing to accede to absolute authority by the King in his political functions but not to his power to abrogate their feudal privileges.

The barons' power, however, was being undermined by changes in military technology. The military superiority of the armed knight was decreased by the development of gunpowder and the cross-bow. This meant that a special, trained class of military men was no longer so crucial to the successful prosecution of warfare. It became possible to raise and equip armies of men with the power of the purse. This played into the hands of kings who wanted to centralize administration and consolidate political power in their kingdoms. In this process they found allies in the merchant classes of the cities who had an economic interest in peace and economic integration of territory into markets in which they could trade with minimum interference on their own activities and maximum interference on the activities of competitors from without.

The power of the feudal oligarchs was greatly diminished vis-a-vis the Crown by the struggles of the fourteenth and fifteenth centuries during which the Crown deprived the barons of their bands of armed retainers. By the sixteenth century the Crown had further diminished the power of the feudal lords by establishing royal courts to interfere with their relations to their peasants and, in particular, to give the latter some security in their tenure of land. The Crown had an economic interest in taking over the functions of the manorial courts in both the collection of legal fees and the establishment of a secure and prosperous yeomanry. The royal courts contributed to the breakdown of absolutism by establishing long leases on lands at fair rents. This was a step toward making land an economic asset in which men could have limited property rights independent of political power vis-a-vis a superior.

The final rejection of the feudal conception of property in land being based on military rather than economic considerations came in 1660 at the end of the Civil War. An act was passed by Parliament ending the feudal tenure of all estates granted by the Crown. The Crown could no longer collect feudal dues or services from the holders of estates and was given, in lieu, the privilege of laying excise taxes on alcoholic beverages. This act made all the land in England legally absolute property since its holders could use or sell it as they chose without royal interference. The King's function as owner (*dominium*) of all the land of the realm was separated from his function as ruler (*imperium*) of all the people. This was a decisive break with the theory of property which had existed since the Roman Empire. It reflected the fundamental changes in power relationships which had been brought about by technological changes in agriculture to which we must now turn.

The Agricultural Revolution and Land Tenure. Parallel to the assertions of political privilege by the members of society which revolutionized the ideological conceptions of society with regard to the nature of individual rights was an agricultural revolution which changed economic organization. One may correctly speak of it as a "revolution" in the sense that the basic attitude toward the use of land changed. The change in the nature of land utilization, further, was to transform the social relationships and lead to modern conceptions of individual property in assets and freedom in their use.

The most essential feature of the agricultural revolution which started in the late Middle Ages was the application of nonhuman power to cultivation. Such simple inventions as the horseshoe and horse collar enabled the horse to be used as a power-engine in the pulling of a plow heavy enough to break up the rich soils of the plains and valleys. The horse had several advantages over the oxen which he increasingly replaced. First, he could pull the same load at twice the speed. Secondly, he consumed oats rather than grass, and sufficient oats to feed a horse could be grown on less ground than the pasture needed to keep an ox. Most important, the use of the horse made possible a large net increase in the per-worker output of food.

The effective harnessing of horsepower to agricultural cultivation made possible an increase in the amount of land which an agricultural laborer could cultivate and also greatly increased his net output of cereals. This meant that the average output per worker in agriculture could, through the use of capital in the form of draft animals, be raised significantly above the level of biological subsistence. This created a potential surplus over the real costs of production which the individual who controlled land and capital could obtain from it. For the first time in history, agricultural land could produce an economic surplus without the "exploitation" of a labor force tied to the land by force of arms or ideologically reinforced tradition.

The same harnessing of horsepower to transportation which had occurred in agriculture reduced the cost of transporting agricultural produce, and towns grew and expanded as they were able to obtain food on favorable terms. A division of labor took place between town and manor which led to a tremendous increase in urbanization and the permeation of an exchange economy based on money to the remotest parts of the kingdom. The expanding demands for food by the towns led to further improvements in cultivation as the lords began to look to their manors as a source of income for a standard of life far superior to that which they had enjoyed earlier.

On the manor, itself, the changes in technology meant changes in the organization of production. As a peasant accumulated capital in the form of draft animals and agricultural implements, he would attempt to get individual possession of a plot of ground which he could work as he pleased with his own capital. Any labor other than his own used in the cultivation would be paid for by a specified payment rather than a return from the harvest or the exchange of his own labor services or capital services directly. He could thus claim exclusive possession of a surplus over his costs of maintaining his animals and his wage payments to other men. His possibility of alienating increases in productivity to his own use rather than having to share them with others led to a breakdown in the cooperative system of production.

From the standpoint of productivity, the system of common cultivation was inferior to a system of individual control. There was a diminished incentive for the individual to work harder or undertake capital improvements if those who contributed nothing would share in the increased output to the diminution of his share. It was also more difficult to get agreement on the improvement of an open field by drainage if the capital cost would have to be apportioned to the claims of all those with rights to strips of land in the open field.

The common possession and use of land dated to a time when the technology of plowing greatly limited the amount of land that any one peasant could cultivate. Plowing was only possible at first with the pooling of labor and later with the pooling of animals. When one man became able to cultivate efficiently a larger plot of land with his own animals, the continuance of a form of common land use was a hindrance to increased productivity which could only be overcome by the creation of individual property in the use of specified tracts of land. This change in agricultural technology led to the "enclosure" of feudal estates. By enclosure all the common lands of the estate would be divided up in proportion to the shares which each peasant traditionally had in the use of land. Instead of the old system of common use of open fields and the commons, the individual peasants would be settled with plots of lands which they could cultivate as they wished and were able. In the process of consolidation, many lost their traditional rights and many sold out their traditional privileges to those with more substantial holdings.

Property, Social Control, and
Possessive Individualism

Several points need to be emphasized about the new status of property in land after the ending of feudal tenure in England in 1660. First, the possession and use of the land still was guaranteed only by access to the courts and the coercive power of the state to restrain action against the person holding property in land. All that had been changed in this respect was the growth of the power of property owners vis-a-vis the state. The *dominium* of the state over all land in the kingdom was denied —only the regulation (*imperium*) was acknowledged. The *dominium* of the private owners of land was asserted to be absolute (not originating in the political power of the state) and was protected by the procedural requirement that any action to deprive an owner of property of his *dominium* could only be accomplished by the judgment of a court of his political equals.

The regulation of the use and enjoyment of property by taxation was recognized to be a necessary function of the state, but it was also realized that *imperium* could be used to deprive the owner of all that was valuable in *dominium*. Consequently, the power of the state to tax was limited by the necessity of obtaining Parliamentary consent to the imposition of any taxes. Thus, the power of the state to regulate without the consent of the owners of property was denied, and the theory that private citizens had absolute power over their property was kept intact by the practice of regarding taxes on property or regulation of its use as arising from the voluntary agreement of the taxpayers to burden themselves for the commonwealth.

If the matter is considered closely, one will see that the security of men in their possession was still absolutely dependent on the power of the state. All that had happened was that sovereignty had been shifted from an absolute ruler to an oligarchy of men with a considerable stake in the security of their possessions. They secured their interests by providing that any legal action against them by the state to confiscate or regulate their absolute *dominium* over their property would only be allowable when sanctioned by the group collectively.

The second point concerning changing conception of property stemming from changes in agricultural technology is more important than the ideological and procedural changes in the relationship of the individual to the state. The technological advances taking place in agriculture were changing the way in which men thought of their relationship to physical things and to other men. The economic position of a feudal lord living on a manor which produced only enough for a bare subsistence for both lord and peasant was based entirely on his power over men. If he worked them as chattel slaves on his own land, he had to compel them physically to produce a surplus over their own energy requirements. When technology permitted substitution of animal for human power and greatly increased output per man, the ownership of land and beasts enabled one man, be he feudal lord or progressive peasant, to secure the services of other men—not by physical compulsion but by a bargain over the distribution of gains from increased productivity. The economic position of a man ceased to be a function of physical coercive powers and came to depend on his judicious use of his capital in the form of animals, agricultural implements, and improvements to the land, and his bargaining power with other men. Men began to think of their economic position as being the result of their own productive powers rather than political position.

This contributed to the downgrading of the role of the state from being the creator of assets by conquest and subjugation of people to a conception of the state as the protector of assets created by men's economic production and voluntary cooperation. The conception of the state changed from being an organization for war and conquest to an organization for the protection of property created by the peaceful and cooperative effort of the members of a civil society. The value of the property one had in the control of land came to be looked on as a creation by the owner rather than by the coercive power of the state.

Religious Objections to Individualism. The substitution of modern forms of landholding for the medieval forms brought a storm of social protest—not only for the way in which it was done, which led to the dispossession of many poor peasants, but for the idea which lay behind it—namely that man should have individual rights to produce and consume as he wished, without regard for the interests of his fellow men. The idealized theory of feudalism emphasized the corporate character of society in which all had a right to share in accordance with their station in life. The modern notion of landholding, by reducing men's relationships with another to the purely economic nexus of an exchange economy, was thought to destroy the essential characteristic of a Christian society, which was the responsibility of one man for his fellow men.

R. H. Tawney wrote that what shocked the religious writers in the age when the medieval conception of society was breaking down was not only the way in which it was done:

> . . . but its repudiation of the principles by which alone, as it seemed, human society is distinguished from a pack of wolves. . . . They sprang to the attack . . . of a creed which was that the individual was absolute

master of his own, and, within the limits set by positive law, may exploit it with a single eye to his pecuniary advantage, unrestrained by any obligation to postpone his own profit to the well-being of his neighbours. . . . It was, in short, the theory of property which was later to be accepted by all civilized communities.[1]

The medieval theory of land utilization had been based on the feudal lord being a trustee for society who rendered both military and political services for the commonweal in return for an income from the estate which he managed. Mistreatment of his tenants would have been a lapse from his duties as much as the failure to render military service to the King, who granted him the land. The peasant was secure in his privileges but must not seek to extend them at the expense of the other peasants on the estate. What distressed the medieval social critic about the modern notion that land could be held as private property with its owner subject to no obligations other than respect of the private property of others was its affirmation of individualism—the fundamental presupposition of our own society that the individual man is responsible only for his own welfare. The medieval theory denied that an individual man should be able to bargain freely about the use of his labor and his possessions.

The Economic Necessity of Individualism for Development. The morality of individualism is not to be judged here. The point must be made, however, that the new conception of property was absolutely necessary to the rational use of land which became a scarce resource as soon as the changes in agricultural technology allowed men to exploit land to produce an economic surplus. As long as the person who had the use of land was unable to calculate the net return to investment of his resources in increasing its productivity, he had very limited incentives to rationalize his administration of his resources. If the lord of the manor was socially obliged to continue to employ and support labor which produced less than its marginal contribution to output, he had no economic incentive to undertake change which would increase per capita output by replacing labor with capital. As long as the user of land was not legally entitled to the use of economic surplus created by his rationalization of production, rationalization would not take place.

The replacement of the medieval notion of the trusteeship of assets with the modern notion of property allowed the person in control of assets to limit his liabilities to claims on the income produced by those assets to those claims which were voluntarily incurred. As long as the person in control of assets was unable to do this, he had a limited and incalculable incentive to try to increase the value of the assets which he

---

[1]R. H. Tawney, *Religion and the Rise of Capitalism* (New York: The New American Library, 1960), p. 151.

controlled. Further, the renunciation of feudal obligation, insofar as it meant that assets were held at the pleasure of the government and subject to repossession at any time, meant the elimination of the political risk which otherwise had to be taken into account in calculating the rate of return of investment.[2]

The end of feudal land possession meant that the most important economic asset in society could no longer be arbitrarily taken by the state and redistributed in accordance with political considerations. Further, it meant that the owner of land was free to use the increased income produced by the asset without recognizing any social claims to the increased income other than those which were voluntarily incurred as part of the process of increasing the income. The power of the individual vis-a-vis society was established by allowing the individual to organize production as he was able, subject only to the constraint that he must obtain the consent of others by means other than politically enforced coercion.

Both the Roman conception of law and property based on command and the medieval belief in existing social relationships being based on divine ordinance foundered on the rocks of economic rationality and the need for a society to proportion incentives to secure the output desired to create a civilization. The replacement of chattel slavery by feudalism was a limited recognition of the need for incentives and security. The breakdown of feudalism occurred as men realized that the security of individual claims to physical assets and to property in one's own labor was economically rational as soon as technological change permitted property to be used as a means of increasing output rather than merely distributing it.

Bibliographic Note:

In the discussion of classical and medieval economic and social institutions in this chapter the author felt that the practice of documenting every statement from specialized scholarly works was not desirable. In the place of footnotes, a list of important sources for the material discussed in this chapter is appended below:

Bloch, Marc, "European Feudalism," *Theories of Society*, Talcott Parsons ed., (New York: The Free Press, 1961).

——, *Feudal Society* (London: Routledge & Kegan Paul Ltd., 1961), chap. xviii–xx, xxxiii.

Heaton, Herbert, *Economic History of Europe* (New York: Harper & Row, Publ., 1936).

[2]An interesting modern treatment of the relationship between political risk and investment behavior will be found in Dan Usher, "Political Risk," *Economic Development and Cultural Change*, Vol. XIII, no. 4 (May 1965).

Michell, H., *The Economics of Ancient Greece*, 2nd ed. (Cambridge: W. Heffer and Sons, 1958). See especially pp. 148–68.

Postan, M. M., ed., *Cambridge Economic History*, 2nd ed. (Cambridge: Cambridge University Press, 1966), Vol. I.

Pound, Roscoe, "Property," in Introduction to the Philosophy of Law (New Haven: Yale University Press, 1954).

Restovtzeff, M., *The Social and Economic History of the Roman Empire*, 2nd ed. (Oxford: Oxford University Press, 1957), Vol. I.

Tawney, R. H., *Religion and the Rise of Capitalism* (New York: The New American Library, 1960).

Ullman, Walter, *The Individual and Society in the Middle Ages* (Baltimore: Johns Hopkins University Press, 1966).

——, *Principles of Government and Politics in the Middle Ages* (London: Methuen & Co., 1961).

Weber, Max, *General Economic History*, translated by F. H. Knight (New York: Greenberg, 1927).

White, Lynn, Jr., *Medieval Technology and Social Change* (Oxford: Oxford University Press, 1962).

7

Market Access, Ideology, and Economic Power:

the birth of capitalism

Property defines the relationships between men. However, in the preceding chapter, our attention has been given almost exclusively to consideration of classical and medieval practices in the use of land and agricultural labor. We must now turn our attention to commerce which was reluctantly tolerated but relegated to inferior status by civilizations prior to our own.

Commerce in Classical Antiquity

Manufacture and trade were carried on in classical antiquity largely by slaves acting on behalf of their masters. Roman senators, for example, were specifically excluded from commerce. One interpretation which could be placed on nonparticipation of the privileged classes in trade is that it would have involved them in bargaining with social inferiors. This would have derogated from their status. Another is that the skills involved were not those of military leadership but of administration and negotiation which were more likely to be found among the merchants captured in conquest than in their captors.

Peaceful trade and commerce were not considered to be the economic basis of classical civilization by its members. Wealth was amassed by military conquest. Slaves and booty, of course, had to be traded and productively employed, but these matters were considered to be of secondary importance to the capture of wealth. The later Roman emperors considered the merchant classes to be parasitic on the state and increasingly attempted to derive revenue from taxation and forced levies on the merchants. These became so onerous that merchants attempted to escape from their traditional occupations. This led to the forced inheritance of occupation by sons from their fathers. The ruin of the Roman Empire may be partially attributed to the decline of commerce, which accompanied the increasing exactions levied on the merchant classes, which weakened the economic base of the civilization. The Roman Empire did not consider the claims of merchants worthy of protection.

Medieval Commercial
Organization

The organization of trade in medieval society led to a type of political organization in the towns which had many parallels with the feudal system in agriculture. The physical existence and military protection of the group of merchants and artisans who comprised a medieval town originated from a charter of incorporation granted by the ruler of the land area in which they were located. The city charter gave the same sort of political jurisdiction to the city corporation over the inhabitants of the city as the feudal lord had over the tenants of his estate. As the feudal lord received his grant of power from the King in return for the rendering of military service to the monarch, the city corporation paid for its political power by purchasing the charter from the monarch and retained it by periodic money payments.

Significant differences also existed in internal organization between medieval manor and town. The political power of the city government over its residents was corporate rather than individual. The directors of the town corporation were leading merchants. The economic life of the town was controlled by the town council through its chartering of guilds of merchants and craftsmen who were given exclusive privileges in the prosecution of certain branches of trade. The medieval guild evolved from the Roman merchant or craft guild and had a similar function— the provision of revenue to support the structure of civil and military administration. The power of the guilds over certain trades was established by the enforcement of the town's courts which were in turn backed up by the royal courts. An inhabitant of the town who sought to do anything contrary to the control of the guild would find their discipline backed up by the town and by royal power.

Monopoly as the Basis of Medieval Economic Organization. The most important economic asset possessed by the town was its grant of power to carry on trade. The most important asset possessed by the guild was its power to carry on a particular trade. The individual member of the guild was a possessor, in common with other guild members, of this asset. The town charter and guild charter were, in fact, charters for the limited monopolization of trade. Monopoly was considered to be an economic necessity for the maintenance of a social order in which certain men had an income from the sale of goods to allow them to perform important political and social functions.

The king needed revenue from the town to support the military and civil expenses of the kingdom. This could be obtained by granting the power to a town to monopolize the trade of a particular area. The town could pay its tribute to the King from part of the monopoly returns it exacted from customers with no alternative source of supply. The revenue for town administration and defense as well as the payments to the grantor of the charter were collected from the individual guilds which held the monopolies of individual trades.

The guild masters were entitled to a standard of life befitting their station as the performers of a political function. The source of their income was the politically enforced monopoly of their trade. Thus, as a parallel with the feudal lord, the income of the guild master was a return for his rendering of political as well as economic functions and depended upon political power. The income from one's position as a guild member could not be capitalized and sold as private property any more than could the capitalized value of net returns from the possession of a feudal estate. This was because of the inextricable involvement of political with economic functions. Also, in theory, there was no net income as obligations were supposed to be commensurate with privileges.

The Breakdown of
Guild Monopoly

As is discussed more thoroughly in Chapter XI, the maintenance of guild monopoly required elaborate restrictions to prevent competition among guild members and to limit entry into the membership of the guilds. The temptations which existed for individual guild members to increase their incomes at the expense of their journeymen and apprentices and to the detriment of other members of the guilds were very great. Thorough-going, politically enforced control was necessary to the maintenance of the system, and this became especially true as soon as either expanding demand, or cost-reducing innovations in production presented opportunities for increased profits.

As soon as technological change began to widen markets by lowering transport costs and reducing the costs of production, competition between towns or between the merchants of a given town tended to break down the control of output and price which was the essence of guild monopoly. Technological changes in transportation and production were accompanied by changes in social theory and political organization.

Ideological Change and the Creation of Private Property in Commercial Assets. A basic ideological change had to take place in the organization of production in manufacturing, as it had in agriculture. A shift occurred from the older idea that income from production was a function of political power and status to the modern conception that it is a reward for activity which leads to a net increase in economic output. The laws and practices had to change so that control of a manufacturing enterprise was not a *privilege* enforced by political power but a *right* which could be taken up by anyone with the capabilities of doing so. Then the value of assets in stock and trade ceased to be an asset to a man *because* he possessed political privilege in market access. The value of assets came to have its source in superior economic performance. It was protected by law from fraud or physical dispossession but was henceforth to have its source in competitive superiority in free markets rather than in the politically granted privilege of monopoly.

Institutional Changes and
Commercial Property

Two specific legal changes at the end of the Middle Ages in Britain paved the way for the modern notions of property and conduct of economic activity. The first was the passage of an act which made minerals the property of the person who mined them rather than the property of the Crown. This meant that landowners gained an incentive to prospect for and mine coal and iron. It opened the way for the exploitation of the earth's resources by private enterprise and was the completion of the reform which had taken place in the possession and use of land for agricultural purposes free from political claims. It signalled the change in the conception of property from being based on political occupation to the conception of property claims as an economic inducement to secure increases in output.

Legalization of Interest. The second change was both very simple and very profound for its effects on the development of capitalism—it was the legalization of the taking of interest and the guarantee of negotiability of debt instruments. In a primitive society, *property* is the right to possess a physical thing and enjoy the fruits of possession and use without the interference of other men. In an advanced society where the management of productive activity is indirect and differentiated, the real claim of property is the right to a stream of income from one's assets when their control is sold to another for that income. The value of the property becomes the discounted present value of a stream of returns. The guarantee of private contracts by society creates property in the promises contained in the contracts. The contracts will have value only if the performance of the private contracts can be socially enforced.

As has been indicated in the previous chapter, the creation of private property in land came about because the lords and peasants who controlled the use of land in England demanded the social enforcement of the voluntary arrangements which had been evolved in regard to the stream of income from land. This came about over the religious objections of an old order. The legalization of interest taking and the negotiability of private contracts came about as merchants demanded a social enforcement of the arrangements they had made among themselves. This was especially important after the royal courts refused to implement the decisions of guild courts which had previously enforced contracts among merchants.

As long as the taking of interest on loans was considered immoral by society, the unenforceability of loan contracts by civil courts made them a very insecure claim. Of course, merchants who dealt in promissory notes, bills of exchange, and other financial instruments knew the necessities of taking interest. Any member of the financial community who used appeals to civil or ecclesiastical authority to avoid making good on his debts would have had no future as a merchant. The guarantee of the members of the financial community was their own good name and property in financial instruments was probably as secure in international high finance as it is today.

Loans to small merchants, peasants, and craftsmen were a different matter. Here, an understandable animus existed against the usurer. It is difficult to know how much the Church's prohibition on the taking of interest for the use of capital affected the availability of loans in the Middle Ages. Evasion of the usury laws would seem to be general if one surveyed all the devices which were actually used to disguise the payment of interest!

The medieval prohibition against taking interest grew out of the Aristotelian doctrine that money was "barren"—that it was incapable of producing anything and that consequently to demand interest for its use was immoral since men would only consent to pay interest under duress. In the context of the times, the prohibition on the taking of interest had some rationale. In the first place, the only governmental demands for capital were for waging war. The Church could not very well sanction loans at interest to finance aggressive wars for plunder. For defensive wars, the levying of forced loans or taxes from the population being protected seemed more moral than allowing moneylenders to extort interest for the finances to defend the commonweal.

The technology of the Middle Ages did not offer much scope for investment in fixed capital. There were no railroads or municipal utility systems to be financed. Feudal land tenure systems provided little stimulus for fixed investments in agriculture. There was no manufacturing in the contemporary meaning of the term—only handicraft production. The capital requirements of the Middle Ages were for circulating capital—credit to finance raw materials in the processes of handicraft production and working capital to finance commodity trade. The amounts which could be managed by one man were usually limited, and part of the medieval philosophy was to discourage growth in the size of an individual firm. A provision that no man could trade except on his own capital was one way of restricting entry into trade in a particular article.

The medieval prohibition on usury was directed toward loans on which payment was certain and at a fixed interest. It was not illegal and immoral (the two were identical in the Middle Ages) to venture capital in a silent partnership for there the gain was contingent on the success of the venture. It was not illegal to buy the right to a stream of rents from land for a capital payment, for the return obviously springs from the fruits of the soil. It was permissible to ask for *interesse* as damages if the principal of a loan was not repaid at the specified time or if not having the use of one's capital caused an actual loss to the lender or a gain foregone.

Still, usury was considered to be a sin. The Church proceeded against usurers with the threat of excommunication. For example, the Council of Vienne (1312) decreed that any communities which sanctioned usury or compelled debtors to pay usurious contracts would have their rulers excommunicated unless the practices were discontinued within three months. Any persons who maintained that usury was not a sin were to be punished as heretics. The city of Florence was the leading financial center of Europe in the fourteenth century, but even there prohibitions on usury were enforced rigorously.[1]

In England the Protestant Reformation in the sixteenth century, with the accompanying suppression of ecclesiastical courts and break with the traditions of the Middle Ages, gave civil sanction to the practice of interest taking. An Act of Parliament in 1552 which had declared interest taking "a vyce moste odyous and detestable, as in dyvers places of the hollie Scripture it is evydent to be seen" was repealed in 1571. It was replaced by an Act which allowed a maximum of 10 per cent interest.[2]

The very act of legalizing interest had the effect of lowering the rate of interest on loans by decreasing the uncertainty regarding their repayment. The enforcement of debt instruments by civil courts created property in debt contracts for the creditor and gave an added inducement to

---

[1]R. H. Tawney, *Religion and the Rise of Capitalism* (New York: The New American Library, 1960), p. 151.
[2]*Ibid.*, pp. 184–85.

the expansion of credit, which was of highest importance to a commercial society.

Negotiability of Credit Instruments. The next step in the development of modern concepts of property in debt contracts came from increasing their liquidity by making them negotiable. After debt contracts had been made property by being made enforceable in a court of law, they were made negotiable property by the legal practice of allowing their assignment to other parties.

Originally, the logic of the debt contract had been patterned on the rent contract between landlord and tenant. The contract for the use of land was not transferable by the tenant to another tenant without the landlord's consent. This restriction had its origin in the feudal notion of land being held by the consent of the feudal superior and being granted as a privilege to another as a personal relationship. Since the essence of the feudal rent theory was that it was an agreement between persons about mutual obligations, the agreement could not be transferred without the consent of both parties. Thus, a debt contract, being likewise a personal relationship, could not be transferred by the creditor to another creditor. Under the old common law developed during the feudal period, if a promissory note was transferred by a creditor, it was no longer enforceable. The agreement of the debtor could, of course, be obtained, but his ability to deny his consent or to ask a price for it impaired the negotiability of the contract.

The practice grew up in trade of assigning promissory notes and bills of exchange—in fact these served as money for the merchant and financial communities. In London, the goldsmiths began the practice of accepting deposits of gold and issuing deposit slips for the commodity stored with them. These commodity slips were transferred from party to party on the understanding that the goldsmiths would honor their bearer. The legality of the transferred contracts, however, was still suspect.

The feature of contract negotiability which disturbed the common law lawyers was that the original creditor might transfer a stronger contract to a third party than he originally had possessed. During the seventeenth century, the practice of British courts slowly changed to allow the creation of perfect negotiability in contracts. In 1704, however, the refusal of a High Court Judge to enforce the promissory notes of a London goldsmith who sought to evade payment led to an act of Parliament in 1705 which established the transferability of negotiable instruments as enforceable at law.[3]

This was, indeed, a revolutionary development. It gave the bearer of a promissory note the right to proceed against its maker and gave the latter none of the usual defenses of fraud or duress in the making of the

[3]John R. Commons, *Legal Foundations of Capitalism* (New York: The Macmillan Co., 1924), pp. 251–52.

contract. If the maker claimed a defect in the contract, he had to pay the bearer and then proceed against the original creditor. The transferor thus gave to the transferee a perfection of contract which he, himself, lacked. This change in social practice greatly increased the scope of property, for now financial instruments could be treated as assets as sure and dependable as physical capital. It also enabled an individual merchant to increase his operations greatly as he could sell credit instruments acquired in the course of his business at low discounts and greatly increase his turnover of capital.

Merchants realized the great advantages accruing from the change in the negotiability of debt contracts. In 1688, Sir Joshua Child had advocated changes in the laws and practices concerning commercial paper. Speaking of the great prosperity of Holland in the seventeenth century, he said:

> . . . the law that is in use among them for transference of bills of debt from one man to another [is of] extraordinary advantage to them in their commerce; by means whereof they can turn their stocks twice or thrice in trade, for once that we can in England; for that, having sold our foreign goods here, we cannot buy again to advantage, till we are possessed of our money; which it may be we shall be six, nine, or twelve months in recovering: and if what we sell be considerable, it is a good man's work all the year to be following vintners and shopkeepers for money. Whereas, were the law of transferring bills in practice with us, we could presently after the sale of our goods dispose of our bills, and close up our accounts.[4]

Legal Reforms and Economic Development. Increasing the security of credit instruments by making them enforceable and transferable was of greatest importance in the history of commercial development. The practices grew up in the everyday transactions of merchants and were later enforced as the law of the land. This permitted the rise of financial institutions to deal in credit instruments, and this in turn increased the efficiency with which the economy allocated capital. The fall in the rate of interest to borrowers stimulated greater investment. The growth and regularization of trade was a necessary condition for the creation of property in credit instruments; a change in legal practice was the sufficient condition.

Negotiability of credit instruments greatly increased the marginal efficiency of capital by increasing its rate of turnover. If a merchant could turn over his capital ten times per year instead of twice by discounting the promissory notes he received in payment instead of holding them until due, a gross margin of 5 per cent on each turn would increase his annual gross return on capital from 10 per cent to something slightly

---

[4]Sir Joshua Child, *A New Discourse of Trade* (London, 1688). Quoted in Commons, *Legal Foundations of Capitalism, op. cit.,* p. 253.

less than 50 per cent. The benefit to society was that the great increase in turnover of working capital would allow for smaller margins and reduction of capital costs.

The greater liquidity of capital resultant from legal changes attracted capital which had formerly been put into land—the only previously secure form of investment. It made possible the rise of banking; bank deposits take the form of a promissory note by the bank and checks drawn against the bank serve the function of money. The Bank of England which was chartered by the government in 1694 was given the right to circulate bank notes—promissory notes drawn on itself—and the right to discount bills. The effect of this was to create a central bank with the power to regulate the supply of money. This was possible only because of institutional changes which perfected credit instruments as a form of property.

Property in such intangible assets as money and credit instruments is a social guarantee to the holder of generalized purchasing power when he grants the use of that purchasing power to the makers of the credit instruments. The makers of the credit instruments can pay interest from the creation of the additional goods whose production is made possible by the abstention from current consumption of the holders of the financial instruments. The creation of property in financial instruments, therefore, has the same rationale as the creation of property in physical things. It stimulates the creation of productive capital.

An important change in social philosophy can be noted in the creation of property in debt contracts which made interest and negotiability enforceable at law. Society stopped making moral judgments about arrangements worked out voluntarily between the parties to a contract except to prevent fraud or duress. The assumption was thereafter made that the parties to any contract were legal equals capable of protecting their own interests. This was the counterpart of the change which had taken place in regard to the use of land.

The Capitalist Revolution

The process of private property creation in land, business assets, and debt contracts which has been discussed in this chapter and the preceding one reflects a basic change in the relation of man to the state and of man to his fellow men. The medieval and classical conception of society had been of relationships being imposed from above. The economic interests of the members of a society were closely regulated in the supposed interests of society as a whole, but political power was systematically used to redistribute income to the ruling classes.

The new conception of society which was replacing the old was an individualistic one in which the individual man called upon the government only to protect him from violence and to compel performance of contractual arrangements worked out by bargaining with his fellow men. The creation of private property in land involved the state giving sanction to a set of new arrangements for the control of agricultural production worked out in the interplay of self-interest of lord, king, and peasant. The breakdown of the guild system was accomplished by individual action of guild members in turning their privileges into property. The customs of businessmen in the loaning of money and the making of contracts were ratified by the state to increase the security of the private property created by contract. In all the cases the individual citizen was taking the active role and asking only for social ratification of the results of bargaining worked out between individuals.

By the end of the seventeenth century, conditions for the emergence of the modern conception of private property were present in Britain. A civil war had been fought to establish a new conception of society based on a compact between men of property to protect the assets which they had created by their own efforts. The classical and medieval ideas of a society based on status and preserved by political power and physical coercion had given way to a modern conception of society as a voluntary organization of individual men to protect their property and their right to acquire it by peaceful, productive means. The new conception had not triumphed by the peaceable acceptance of the old order to doctrines of individual rights and natural liberties. The rights were won by force of arms in a struggle which began with the Magna Carta and ended with the Glorious Revolution of 1688. In the next century the Americans were to find that the enjoyment of the rights and liberties of free men depended upon their being won by force of arms. The Americans, however, had an immense advantage in inheriting a conception of society which was individualistic. We were, as Carl Sandburg has written, "born free."

Bibliographic Note:

In addition to the books referred to in the bibliographic note for the previous chapter, this chapter draws on material from the following works:

Commons, John R., *The Legal Foundations of Capitalism* (New York: The Macmillan Co., 1924).

Heckscher, Eli, *Mercantilism* (London: George Allen and Unwin Ltd., 1935), two volumes.

Samhaber, Ernst, *Merchants Make History* (New York: The John Day Co., Inc., 1963).

Pirenne, Henri, *Economic and Social History of Europe* (London: Kegan, Paul, Trench, Trubner, and Co., 1936).

8

Property, the Individual and the State:

an essay on American theory and practice

A great many questions concerning the character of property were left unsettled by the English "Glorious Revolution" of 1688 and by the American Revolution of 1776. Both were designated as "bourgeois revolutions" by Marx. By this he meant that they represented the seizing of power by the rising and aggressive commercial interests from the older feudal order but that they maintained a class system—now based on property rather than status, but still characterized by exploitation.

Locke and the American Constitutional Settlement

The intellectual apologia of both revolutions was John Locke's political theory. A fundamental ambiguity exists in Locke's theory of civil government which has left the relationship of the state to the economic interests of its members a matter of controversy from the time when the feudal conception of society was abandoned to our own day. As was mentioned in Chapter 3, Locke attempted to justify both an existing distribution of economic assets as well as freedom with a doctrine of natural rights. He made the state the agent of men to protect their property in life, liberty, and estate. The ambiguity in his social-contract theory of government revolves around the nature of the property which the state is created to protect. Is this "property" primarily the economic assets of the members of the state? Or is it equally the "life and liberty" of the members of the state? Locke could be interpreted either way.[1]

101

The basis of participation in political power and the legitimate exercise of political power depend upon the resolution of these questions. They were not resolved in England in 1688, and they were not resolved in the American Constitutional Convention of 1787.

These two general questions, unresolved in the American Constitution, were of greatest significance for the development of the American institutional framework. The first, the qualifications for full membership in the Commonwealth—the franchise—was left to the States. The second, which became increasingly important when the first question was settled, was not settled by the American Civil War and has persisted to our own day—the legitimacy of political control of property.

Compromise at the American Constitutional Convention: Franchise.
Most of the support for the transformation of the weak league of former colonies united under the Articles of Confederation into a stronger Federal Union came from men with substantial economic interests.[2] By Federal Union, they hoped to secure a check on the power of State legislatures to confiscate part of their incomes by taxation, regulation, or other means. They saw the need for additional protection against external aggression and internal revolution. And they had an immediate interest in the creation of a continental market free from internal barriers to trade, the repayment of the debts incurred by the Continental Congress, and the securing of the Trans-Appalachian West.

The men who framed the Constitution took as a matter of course that the Federal Union was a compact among men of substantial economic interests to protect and advance those interests. They were inclined to emphasize the protection of property in its usage as a reference to economic assets rather than the broader Lockean definition of property in "life, liberty, and estate." They succeeded in carrying the day so completely at the Constitutional Convention that the immediate addition of the first ten amendments to the Constitution, the Bill of Rights, was promised them in order to secure the ratification by legislatures of the States who feared that the Federal Government might become as despotic as the English monarchy it had replaced.

The failure of the Constitutional Convention to agree on the qualifications for the full partners to the social compact—the electorate—coupled with conception of the Federal Union as a compact among States, rather

[1]Many critical works have been written on Locke's political theory. A brilliant and original recent work which critically explores the ambiguity mentioned above is C. B. MacPherson, *The Theory of Possessive Individualism* (Oxford: Oxford University Press, 1962). An excellent critical review of the book was written by Jacob Viner, "Possessive Individualism as Original Sin," *Canadian Journal of Economics and Political Science*, Vol. XXIX, no. 4 (Nov. 1963), pp. 548–66.

[2]See Charles A. Beard, *An Economic Interpretation of the Constitution*, new ed. (New York: The Macmillan Company, 1956).

than among people, left to the individual States the determination of the qualifications of the franchise. The only stipulation made by the Constitution was that the election of representatives to the Federal House of Representatives should be by the same franchise as the election of the most numerous house of the State legislature.

The founding fathers did not foresee the rapid broadening of the franchise by the individual States which took place after 1815. The sentiment for universal white male suffrage grew very rapidly in the newly settled States on the Western frontier and communicated itself to the more traditional States of the Eastern seaboard. The process of defending wealth qualifications for suffrage was complicated by the difficulty encountered in securing agreement as to where the line of exclusion should be drawn. The cause of the egalitarians was aided by the difficulty their opponents had in fixing precise qualifications. It was also abetted by the principle of the Revolution itself, no taxation without representation.

Behind the opposition of the wealthier classes to the broadening of the franchise was the fear that legislative power would be used by popularly elected governments to redistribute income and wealth. The belief in the illegitimacy of this use of political power grew out of the interpretation of Locke which made the establishment of civil government to protect wealth by social contract the basis of political power. Men without property could not be depended upon to respect and defend it. This view can be illustrated with an extract from a speech made in the New York Constitutional Convention in 1821 against the proposal of universal male suffrage which was approved by the Convention:[3]

> The notion that every man that works a day on the road, or serves an idle hour in the militia, is entitled as of right to an equal participation in the whole power of government is most unreasonable and has no foundation in justice. . . . Society is an association for the protection of property as well as of life, and the individual who contributes only one cent to the common stock ought not to have the same power and influence in directing the property concerns of the partnership, as he who contributes thousands. He will not have the same inducements to care, diligence, and fidelity. His inducements and temptations would be to divide the whole capital upon the principles of an agrarian law.

Not until the last quarter of the nineteenth century did the fears of the wealthy about the powers of popularly elected legislatures begin to be realized. When legislation was passed affecting their economic power,

[3] *Reports of the Proceedings and Debates of the Convention of 1821 Assembled for the Purpose of Amending the Constitution of the State of New York* (Albany, N.Y., 1821). Quoted in Hofstadter, *Great Issues in American History* (New York: Vintage Books, 1958), Vol. I, p. 256.

the wealthy began to search in the Constitution for the limitation of the power of the state over property. We will return to consider this matter in some detail after we have dealt with two other matters which were not settled by the Constitution and which have wider implications than is sometimes realized concerning the question about the relationship between the state and individuals. Those matters were Negro slavery and the chartering of corporations.

Chattel Slavery

The abolition of the institution of chattel slavery was probably favored by a majority of the American population at the time of the Declaration of Independence in 1776. A clause calling for the interdiction of the slave trade was included in the original version but later excised in order to secure the signatures of the representatives of Georgia and South Carolina. Public hostility to slavery was even greater at the Constitutional Convention but once again, a compromise was reached to secure the adherence of the Southern States to the Federal Union by clauses which prevented the Federal government from interfering with the importation of slaves until 1808 and which made the institution of slavery an option of the individual State which had to be respected by other states.[4]

This compromise was only secured from the representatives of the Northern States because the belief was widespread that the institution of slavery was dying a natural death. Slavery had become increasingly unprofitable in the last half of the eighteenth century in Maryland and Virginia because of falling tobacco prices and rising food prices which caused a fall in revenues and a rise in costs for the plantations. A similar situation prevailed in the culture of rice and indigo in South Carolina and Georgia after the Revolution. George Washington and Thomas Jefferson, both slaveholders, believed that the solution to the problem would come about as plantation owners voluntarily manumitted their slaves or allowed them to buy their freedom.

These expectations were shattered by the advent of the industrial revolution in the cotton textile industry in England and New England and by the invention of the cotton gin. Cotton was ideally suited to slave culture and became immensely important and profitable after the turn of the nineteenth century, thereby giving the institution of chattel slavery a new lease on life. Cotton culture was pushed across the Appalachians into the States of the "New South." Florida was purchased from Spain, the Louisiana territory was purchased from France, and Texas was annexed from Mexico in a great orgy of Western expansion. The Atlantic seaboard Southern States which were unsuited to profitable pro-

[4]*U.S. Constitution*, Article 1, sec. 9:1, Article IV, sec. 1 and 2.

duction of cotton became producers of slaves for export to the virgin cotton lands of the West.

The continued profitability of slavery depended upon relentless expansion to new lands where high yields could be secured. It also depended upon expansion to make the expanding demand for slaves push up their prices and, hence, the capital values of the planters who raised and utilized them.

In the North public sentiment for abolition was increasing. Abolitionism originated partly in humanitarian sentiment and a belief that a democracy could not be firmly built with the continuance of slavery. A more immediate reason for opposition to the expansion of slavery arose from the expansion to the West where the interests of small farmers and the great slave owners were in conflict in competition for Western lands.

The conflict arising from Westward expansion was compromised for a period by allowing slavery in some Western territories, prohibiting it in others, and balancing the admission of slave States and free States to maintain an equality of representation in the Senate. Compromise became increasingly difficult as the two sides became more extreme in their demands. In 1857, the decision of the Supreme Court in *Dred Scott* v. *Sandford* declared that Congressional interference with the practice of slavery conflicted with the Fifth Amendment to the Constitution by depriving some citizens of their property (in slaves) without due process of law. The North, which by this time had become far more populous, was unwilling to see the power of the majority of the electorate frustrated by a judicial restriction of its power to control the institution of slavery.

Slavery, Property, and the Constitution. The American Civil War has been and can be viewed from a variety of vantage points. Its implications for the development of the concept of property and the relationship of the state to property has been insufficiently understood. The immediate cause of the war was the secession of the Southern States, justified by their claim that their constitutional rights to protection of their property were about to be violated. The Southerners passionately believed that their property rights in slaves could not be abridged constitutionally by the Federal Congress. Lincoln, who was very conciliatory to begin with, stated that the important question at issue was whether a majority would rule. The majority of the country was no longer willing to acquiesce in the extension of slavery to new territories and were committed to its gradual and compensated abolition in those States where it did exist.

Lincoln stated that the question at issue in the Civil War was the preservation of the Union. If a dissident minority could secede from a nation when they found their interests prejudiced by the actions of a majority, then factionalism would lead to anarchy. Civil government might be based on a social contract, but Lincoln repudiated the Lockean notion that a government which did not safeguard the property of some of its members absolved them of its support.[5]

The Repugnance of Slavery to Capitalist Ethics. The institution of chattel slavery was profoundly antithetical to the character of a society founded on the individualist postulates of capitalism. This was recognized by many of its proponents who attacked the freedom of Northern industrial workers as illusory and defended slavery on the grounds of care and solicitude of slave owners for their chattels. The continuance of slavery finally foundered on the unwillingness of the Northern states to enforce it.

As was pointed out in the preceding chapter, the basic principle which triumphed in the seventeenth century with regard to the creation of property in contractual arrangements was the social guarantee of contracts which were voluntarily made by the parties. The relationship between the slave and his master was not created by a voluntary contract. It could not be maintained except by force. The Northern States, by harboring fugitive slaves, destroyed the security of investment in slaves by offering them sanctuary. This was expressly forbidden in the Constitution and expressly broken by legislative enactments in most Northern States which prevented the return of captured slaves.

This unwillingness of the Northern States to enforce the institution of slavery destroyed the property rights of the Southerners in their slaves. The Republican Party condoned and was committed to this, and after their election of a Republican president in 1860 the South saw secession as a desperate gamble to force legitimation of an institution which was increasingly repugnant to the North.

It is questionable whether the slaves would have been emancipated without compensation to their owners if the South had not seceded. Lincoln finally signed the Emancipation Proclamation only after tremendous pressure from the extremists in his own party, and then it was applicable only to the slaves held by those who were in rebellion against the Union. It was justified on the grounds of military necessity, and slaves were urged to join the Union forces.

What really ended slavery, as an economically viable institution, was the unwillingness of an ever-increasing number of people to support and honor the property claims of slave owners. In legalistically appealing to the Constitution, the Southerners were ignoring the only real basis of a property claim—public acceptance of the claims of the property owner.

[5]"First Inaugural Address," March 4, 1861. R. P. Basler, ed., *The Collected Works of Abraham Lincoln*, Vol. IV (New Brunswick, N.J.: Rutgers University Press, 1953), pp. 264–71.

The majority of the people in the country, in addition to feeling that they gained no benefit from the continued support of slavery, felt a positive repugnance toward it which no amount of Southern apologia or legal argument could dispel. In succeeding years, a similar fate was to meet the arguments advanced by employers who sought public enforcement of their claims *not* to bargain with labor unions over the wages and conditions of employment on the grounds that decisions concerning these matters were the prerogatives of management.

Corporations: Social Assent to

Private Contracts

The creation and regulation of corporations, like slavery, was discussed at length in the Constitutional Convention. The compromise reached by the delegates on corporations, unlike slavery, was to be completely silent on the issue. This left their creation and control largely to the individual states.

The Old Concept of Corporation: Antagonism to Privileged Monopoly. In considering the antipathies of some of the founding fathers to corporations, we must realize that in the eighteenth century a grant of incorporation was viewed as a grant of privilege. Such a grant was not primarily a device for granting limited liability to the owners of a joint stock company as it is today.

As was mentioned in Chapter 7, corporate charters were granted in the Middle Ages to groups of merchants to control the trade of a particular area. Corporate charters were a cession of sovereignty to a particular group of persons who acquired the power to discipline their own members in the prosecution of a trade and to exclude others from the trade. These corporate monopolies became increasingly unacceptable for the control of internal trade in England by the sixteenth century. When they were granted to raise revenues by the Stuart monarchs in the early seventeenth century, they were a contributory factor to the English Civil War. In the eighteenth century, the activities of such chartered monopolies as the East India Company and the Hudson's Bay Company brought the regulatory activities of the British Crown into conflict with the North American colonies and precipitated the Revolution.

The privilege of limited liability for the stockholders of a corporation was rarely a feature of eighteenth century corporations. In fact, it was explicitly prohibited by the English Bubble Act of 1721 which was extended to the American colonies in 1741. The English Bubble Act was passed as a result of the financial panic which followed the speculative excesses accompanying the sale of the stock of the South Sea Company

—an English chartered corporation with wide commercial and financial privileges and limited liability for the owners of common stock. The extension of the act to the North American colonies in 1741 came about as a result of the failure of the Massachusetts Land Bank along with the ruin of a number of its creditors.[6]

Limited liability of the shareholders of a corporation was a privilege which could only be granted by the state. It transgressed public notions about the sanctity of contract by allowing the shareholders of a corporation to escape the payment of the debts of the corporation in the event that the debts of the corporation exceeded the corporate assets.

When the Federal Congress chartered the First Bank of the United States, the action was opposed by Thomas Jefferson on the grounds that it was unconstitutional and, more importantly, that it was a grant of privilege by the government to a group of political supporters of a monopoly, which would allow them to enrich themselves at the expense of the public. Alexander Hamilton, the first secretary of the Treasury and the sponsor of the chartering of the Bank, countered that the chartering of corporations was not expressly prohibited and that a Bank with special powers was necessary to the regulation of the currency. Another reason for the Bank, however, was the binding of wealthy interests to the fortune of the new government and the Federalist Party. Hamilton saw an historical parallel between the First Bank of the United States and the creation of the Bank of England by the English Parliament in 1694, which bound the powerful financial interests of the City of London to the British constitutional settlement.

When Jefferson became President in 1800, the Republicans did not rescind the charter of the First Bank of the United States, as Jefferson deemed it wise for his party to honor the contractual obligations of the Congress which preceded them. It was allowed to expire without renewal. The Second Bank of the United States, again chartered amidst controversy in 1816, was allowed to expire during Andrew Jackson's administration. Like Jefferson, Jackson believed that the grant of privilege by the Congress to a group of private individuals was unconstitutional and contrary to the spirit of American democracy. This was the last instance in which the Federal government granted a corporate charter to a group of private individuals.

Corporate Charters: Private Performance of Public Functions. The development of the corporate form of business organization must be surveyed in terms of the practices of the individual States in chartering corporations. The end of British rule in 1776 released the States from the

[6]Oscar and Mary Handlin, "Origins of the American Business Corporation," *Journal of Economic History*, Vol. V, no. 1 (May 1945).

restrictions imposed by the extension of the Bubble Act to the colonies, and nothing in the Constitution restricted the States' power to grant corporate charters. For the first half of the nineteenth century, however, as in colonial times, the corporate form for manufacturing enterprises was seldom used, and limited liability was not considered to be an inherent characteristic of corporations.

Before the middle of the nineteenth century corporate charters were granted mainly to bodies which performed some public function. Towns were granted corporate charters to conduct the services deemed proper for local governments. Charters were frequently granted to groups of individuals for the building of bridges, canals, turnpikes, water systems, and other types of organizations where a grant of monopoly in the provision of services and powers of eminent domain were necessary to the successful prosecution of the project. Where these charters were granted, a frequent practice was to limit the returns to the shareholders and either to provide for free provision of services after certain revenues had been attained or to call for the return of excess revenues to a public treasury.

Banks and insurance companies, which were deemed necessary to the conduct of agriculture, commerce, and manufacturing, were frequently granted corporate charters. Here, the purpose of the charters was the guarantee of the fiduciary function of these organizations from mismanagement. This was accomplished by limiting the liability of the shareholders to certain exigencies and certain multiples of their original investment and by making the directors liable without limit for certain types of mismanagement of corporate assets.[7]

Limited Liability as the Essence of the Corporation. Limited liability of the stockholders of corporations started to be the most important feature of corporations only toward the middle of the nineteenth century when charters began to be granted for more risky types of enterprises. This was of great importance as soon as large sums of capital were required for industrial enterprises.

The granting of limited liability to corporate shareholders was the completion of the revolution in property which started in the seventeenth century and was halted by the Bubble Act legislation in 1721. Just as the legalization of usury made debt contracts secure and safeguarded the capital of creditors, and the guarantee of negotiability of credit instruments protected the capital of the person to whom debt contracts were assigned, the granting of limited liability to the corporate shareholder safeguarded his capital by limiting the claims which creditors of the corporation could make against him to the limit of his original purchase

---

[7]Joseph S. Davis, *Essays in the Earlier History of American Corporations*, Vol. II (Cambridge: Harvard University Press, 1917).

of shares. All of these changes greatly increased the security of capital and, consequently, the ease with which it could be secured by those entrepreneurs who needed it to carry on business. Diminishing the risk of the creditor lowered the cost of capital to the entrepreneur.

Just as the sanctioning of interest taking and the guarantee of negotiability of credit instruments had required some changes in the law and in public concepts of the privileges and responsibilities of parties to contract, the creation of the powers of the modern corporation required changes in the public's beliefs about the relationship of the state to the contractual arrangements of individuals. The conceptual change which had to occur was in viewing the grant of incorporation as a contract between individuals rather than as a contract between individuals and the state which granted certain individuals special privileges. The limitation of liability by contract had to be recognized as a right of an individual. The protection of the creditors of the corporation and of individual stockholders of a corporation from the directors had to be recognized as a right which could be established by contract with other individuals. Just as it had to be presumed in the enforcement of interest-bearing debt contracts that the debtor had entered into the contract freely in return for valuable consideration, it had to be presumed that the stockholders and creditors of a corporation with limited liability were entering into contractual relationships with it out of their own free will and with a calculated regard to their own advantage. The public interest in the guarantee of the contractual obligations lay in the beneficial effect that the enforcement of obligations would have on the civil peace and material prosperity of the community.

Corporate Rights "To Be" and "To Do." At the same time that the new concept of the corporation as a device for the legitimate limitation of liability of shareholders had to be accepted, the older concept of the corporation as the recipient of a grant of special powers to control a particular area of trade and commerce had to be rejected. The Dartmouth College case is often cited as an important precedent for the relationship between the state and its corporate creation. In this case, the Supreme Court of the United States ruled that the legislature of the State of New Hampshire could not rescind the corporate charter granted to the college because the state could not impair the sanctity of contracts. The charter of the college, however, did not give the college any privileges in the control of trade or education within the boundaries of the state. It merely gave it the right to exist as an institution offering education on such terms as it saw fit and could negotiate with its student clientele.[8]

[8]*Dartmouth College* v. *Woodward* 4, Wheat, 518.

A far more important development for the definition of the relationship between corporations and the state came in the destruction of the older notion that the state created a privileged monopoly for the holders of the grant of incorporation. In the *Charles River Bridge* v. *Warren Bridge* case which came before the United States Supreme Court in 1839, Chief Justice Taney ruled that the original charter of the Charles River Bridge corporation could not be construed as granting a permanent monopoly in the provision of a crossing over the Charles River in Boston.[9] The company had argued that this had been implied in the original contract of incorporation granted by the Commonwealth of Massachusetts. Taney pointed out that it could never be in the public interest to grant a permanent monopoly to a private group. This doctrine pointed up a change in the public attitude toward corporations. They were to be regarded as creations to provide for private performance of valuable commercial functions for the public, but grants of private monopoly not subject to public control could no longer be tolerated. The creation of valuable property by the grant of privileged monopoly was intolerable for a government pledged to "promote the happiness and prosperity of the community by which it is established."

General Incorporation Laws. The legislative change which accompanied the conceptual change in the public view about the propriety and functions of corporations was the enactment of general incorporation laws in the various states. This allowed corporations to register their constitution and by-laws with the state in which they sought incorporation and to receive a corporate charter on the payment of a small registration fee. This replaced the earlier practice of legislative enactment of specific incorporations for specified purposes. The first state to incorporate business corporations under general laws was New York in 1811, but other states were slow in following this lead. The truth was, of course, that the corporate form was still largely unnecessary in most forms of business because the capital requirements could be obtained on personal terms or through partnerships (sometimes with limited liability).

By the middle of the century, some states were making constitutional provision for the enactment of incorporation of businesses under general laws. Louisiana was the first in 1845 and was followed by New York in 1847 and Illinois in 1848. Two states which later became the headquarters of many large corporations because of their extremely lenient general registration requirements, New Jersey and Delaware, enacted their laws for the registration of corporations in 1875 and 1897 respectively.[10]

[9]*Charles River Bridge* v. *Warren Bridge*, 11 Peters, 420.
[10]G. Heberton Evans, Jr., *Business Incorporations in the United States, 1800–1943* (New York: National Bureau of Economic Research, 1948).

General incorporation laws accomplished the necessary conceptual separation in the corporation's right "to be" and its right "to do." These had not been properly distinguished in the older conceptual framework. General incorporation laws allowed any group of individuals to contract together to specify the reciprocal rights and privileges of the members of the corporation. They did not confer on them special privileges to carry on particular trade other than those rights to market access which belonged to all members of society as part of their economic freedom.

The Significance of General Incorporation: Completion of the Capitalist Revolution. The significance of general incorporation for the individualist conception of society was profound, and its effect for economic development was enormous. The assertion, by the state, of its willingness to enforce the voluntary contractual agreements of individuals without inquiring into their equity was an application of the principle that the individual was a better judge and protector of his interests than the state. It was the completion of the social revolution which replaced feudalism with capitalist individualism.

Limited liability for the shareholders of the joint stock corporation made possible the rise of the modern industrial private enterprise. The substitution of modern freehold concepts of land use for the feudal conceptions of privilege and obligation of the landlord to the community allowed the improving landlord to limit his liabilities and gave him an inducement to invest capital. Similarly, the limitation of the liabilities of the stockholder in an industrial enterprise greatly increased the attractiveness of investment. It made possible the establishment of markets for industrial shares which gave them a liquidity and further enhanced the attractiveness of investment. And finally, freeing the ownership of shares from the liabilities of management and claims on the investors' assets made possible investment by the small saver and corporations in which management was effectively divorced from ownership.

We should note that the role of the state in granting limited liability as a matter of right to corporations established security for the voluntarily contracted arrangements of individuals. This created security in the arrangements which made them property. This was the same type of social ratification as the recognition of the arrangements creating freehold property in land. It was an entirely different undertaking than the state creation of property in chattel slavery, which depended upon the enforcement of involuntary servitude rather than voluntary contract.

The overthrow of the feudal conception of social relationships in eighteenth century England by the establishment of freehold ownership in land was accompanied by revolution and a storm of social protest because this undermined the economic and political superiority of an older order and, in the process, created a great deal of hardship for individuals who had had privileges and protection from society under the older conceptions of privilege and obligation. In the breakup of feudalism, many individuals did not get freehold ownership of land in return for the surrender of their feudal privileges. The strong, ruthless, and aggressive elements of the new individualist order asserted the importance of individual freedom and ignored the practical impediments to the effective use of freedom by individuals who had no economic assets and no tradition of freedom.

In the United States the abolition of slavery was, likewise, possible only with a bloody Civil War. This Civil War undermined the economic and political basis of an old order and the legal freedom of the emancipated Negro slave was rendered of little practical effect because of his lack of land, economic assets, and tradition of freedom in the employment of his own labor. And in the United States, the ruthless and aggressive elements of a new capitalist order paid little heed to the welfare of those whom they had emancipated. Like their seventeenth century English predecessors they turned their attentions to the exploitation of new possibilities for private gain.

The parallels between the overthrow of feudalism and slavery, the Civil War in England in the seventeenth century and the United States in the nineteenth century, are made here in order to contrast them with the peaceful evolution which accompanied the change in social attitude toward corporations. Feudalism and slavery depended upon social support of the coercion necessary to maintain the claims of the property claimants in the two systems. Recognition of the voluntary contractual agreements of members of a corporation to limit their liability required no coercive action by the state—merely the recognition and enforcement of voluntary contracts. In the United States, the initial hostility to corporations was based largely on an older conception of their status as legal persons granted privileges to do certain things—in particular to exclude others from competition in a particular field of business. This type of corporate power had very little influence in the United States owing to the revulsion against it which accompanied the American Revolution. Social recognition of corporate contracts, which merely guaranteed the right of the members of the corporation *to be* a limited liability company, was quickly forthcoming because of the absence of coercion entailed and because of a realization of the benefits which would accrue to society as well as to the contracting parties to corporate contracts. Social acceptance of corporate contracts which permitted groups of individuals to maintain privileged monopolies to the detriment of the public were rejected both because they required coercion and because they made society poorer for the benefit of the corporate monopolists. In the latter half of the nineteenth century, the acquisition by some corporations of monopolistic power without the aid of privileged access to markets created by political exclusion of competition created a new set of problems, which will be considered in Chapter 12.

Property and the State

For two reasons the relationship of the power of the state to the economic assets of the individual became a pressing question after the American Civil War. First, the increasing interdependence of the men who participated in the economy made their power to withhold the use of their property except on their own terms affect the exchange value of the property of others. Second, the progressive enlargement of the franchise led to demands on State Legislatures and the Federal Congress to control the private use of economic power.

Between the Civil War and the end of the nineteenth century, the most ardent advocates of the use of legislative power to protect their interests were the farmers—especially the farmers of the West and the South who were engaged in the production of such staples as cotton, wheat, and cattle for Eastern and European markets. They thought that they were being "squeezed" by the monopolistic power of the railroads who carried their crops to market, the banks who financed them, and the manufacturers who supplied them with machinery and consumers' goods. Their remedies for the alleged economic coercion by their monopolistic suppliers were regulation of the railways, increased coinage of silver to expand the money supply, and anti-trust legislation to stop monopoly in the manufacture and distribution of goods.[11]

Alleged Constitutional Safeguards on Political Control of Property. Finding themselves threatened with legislation in many States, the economic interest groups who were regulated sought protection in the courts. They alleged the unconstitutionality of State legislation controlling commerce on the grounds that it interfered with interstate commerce or that it was a confiscation of property. The States had been precluded from regulation of interstate commerce by the Constitution and the recently passed Fourteenth Amendment (1869) forbade any State to "deprive any person of life, liberty, or property without due process of law." While this had originally been passed to safeguard the civil rights of Negroes from Southern legislators, it was soon being interpreted to protect the economic interests of businessmen and corporations.

In understanding the intellectual climate of the last quarter of the nineteenth century, we must emphasize that the belief was widespread

[11]For a discussion of the legitimacy of farmers' complaints about the cost-price squeeze, see John Bowman, "An Economic Analysis of Mid-Western Farm Land Values and Farm Land Income 1860–1900," *Yale Economic Essays*, Vol. V, no. 2.

that the Constitution did protect the natural rights of the citizens of the republic from regulation by the legislature. For example, when slavery was abolished in 1865, it was done by Constitutional Amendment because the decision of the Supreme Court in 1857 in the Dred Scott case limiting the power of the Federal Congress over slave property was still accepted by a large, influential, and articulate segment of the population. As a consequence when individual States attempted to regulate the use of property in commerce, the Fourteenth Amendment, which extended the prohibition of the Fifth Amendment on deprivation of property without due process to the States, was invoked by those affected who sought to have legislation struck down on the grounds that regulation constituted a confiscation of property.

What was at issue in the controversy over the regulation of property, as with slavery and corporate charters, was the relationship of the state to individuals. There was an important difference, however. The sanction of corporations by general registration merely recognized the freely contracted arrangements of individuals. The state involved itself in no sanction or support of physical or economic coercion. The breakdown of slavery, as suggested above, came about because a majority of the members of the nation were no longer willing to support the physical coercion on which slavery depended. The regulation of private business, sought by legislative majorities, was intended to control the use of economic power of firms with real or alleged monopoly power to coerce *economically* other members of society by their monopoly positions.

Constitutional Control of Economic Power: Munn v. Illinois.

The extension of political control over economic activity during the last hundred years has resulted from the increasing acceptance of the legitimacy and necessity of state control of private economic power. Much of the control, however, has come about without adequate understanding of the changes which were taking place. Much of the misunderstanding was fostered by the courts because of their practice of basing decisions on precedents even in new situations where the precedents did not fit because of basic changes in the economic situations regulated. On the other hand, the opposition to legislative control of economic power has often rested on views about the protection of property and freedom which failed to recognize that the protection of the freedom and property of some from state control might leave the freedom and property of others effectively open to coercion by them. The author's assertions may be supported and further explained by reference to the landmark case concerning the constitutionality of state control of private property, *Munn* v. *The People of the State of Illinois.*[12]

In response to political pressure from the Grange, a farmers' organiza-

[12]*Munn* v. *Illinois,* 94 U. S. 139.

tion, the legislature of the State of Illinois passed a law in 1873 requiring the registration of grain elevators and setting maximum charges for the services rendered by them to farmers in the storage and handling of grain. This regulation of their prices was demanded because of a widespread belief that the elevator operators were acting collusively to maintain higher prices for their services than would obtain under competition between them.

The elevator operators contested the constitutionality of the legislation in the Illinois and United States Supreme Courts. They pleaded that the legislation constituted regulation of interstate commerce by a single State. They also alleged that the legislation confiscated part of the market value of their assets through a diminution of their earning power, which they contended violated the Fourteenth Amendment prohibiting a State from depriving owners of their property without due process.

In the United States Supreme Court in 1877, Chief Justice Waite, speaking for the majority, ruled that the Illinois legislation was constitutional. Realizing that the case in question would establish an important precedent, Waite attempted to place his decision in a broad perspective. He went back to the Magna Carta to take note of the existence in the tradition of the common law of the principle of limitations being placed on the power of the State to deal arbitrarily with its members. Nevertheless, he noted that the State of Illinois had not deprived the elevator owners of their property; the legislature had merely regulated its *use*, and this was a necessary and proper (although not necessarily wise) action. The power of the state to regulate commerce had never been at dispute in the common law. He quoted the former Chief Justice, Roger Taney, to the effect that the regulation of the transactions of the members of a state was the essence of sovereignty.

Dealing directly with the applicability of the Fourteenth Amendment, Waite noted that the absence of any definition of "deprive" in the Constitution necessitated an inference as to its meaning from prevailing notions about the confiscation of property by regulation. Up to the time of the passage of the Fourteenth Amendment, it was not supposed that statutes regulating the use or price of private property constituted deprivation. The Fourteenth Amendment had as its purpose only the guarantee to the citizens of all States the enjoyment of their civil liberties and equal protection under the law. It did not introduce any new liberties.

The Constitution, said Waite, protects the rights of citizens under common law. An important principle of the common law was that when private property "was affected with a public interest, it ceases to be *juris privati* only." This was a quote from the seventeenth century English Lord Chief Justice Matthew Hale. This principle, said Waite, lay behind a long tradition of regulation of the charges of common carriers.

Even though no exact precedent could be found for the regulation of grain elevators, clearly they came under the same principle as common carriers and, hence, could be regulated as they were patently "affected with the public interest."

Waite rejected the argument that the owner of property was constitutionally entitled to a reasonable compensation for its use and that this could only be established judicially. "In countries where the common law prevails, it has been customary from time immemorial for the legislature to declare what shall be a reasonable compensation under such circumstances, or perhaps more properly speaking, to fix a maximum beyond which any charge made would be unreasonable." The core of Waite's decision was the argument that the Fourteenth Amendment had not affected the traditional powers of the legislature and that the traditional powers of the legislature included the regulation of property used for business purposes.

The minority position, presented by Justice Stephen J. Field, has long been famous in American judicial history because it later became the basis for judicial determination of the reasonableness of prices and rates of return on capital of public utilities. More important for our purposes, however, was the manner in which it pointed up the inapplicability of the precedents cited for legislative regulation of private property and the need for recognizing a new situation to which the Constitution needed adaptation.

"Affected with the public interest," Field pointed out, was a term with a specialized meaning and limited application. Common carriers and other types of business "affected with the public interest" were subject to regulation because their very existence depended upon an implicit or explicit grant of public power or sovereignty. Common carriers used the roads or navigable waters which belonged to the public and subjected themselves to regulation as a *quid pro quo* for using them. Thus, a railroad might be regulated under this category because its existence depended upon a public grant of monopoly in a limited geographic area, the granting of the power of eminent domain in construction, and state help in financing.

Field pointed out that the extension of the police power of the state to regulate the use of any property which was devoted to a use in which the public had an interest would subject all business to public regulation since the public had an interest in the prices charged by any business. The elevator operators did not operate with any privileges granted by the public, and if they could be regulated on the precedent claimed, then no protection was offered in the Constitution for any private property used in business against the majority of a legislature.

In his decision, Waite had maintained that the State Legislature had the right to regulate property as long as it did not confiscate it. It was this point to which Field directed his attack. He argued that the inclusion of property along with life and liberty in the Fifth and Fourteenth Amendments to the Constitution merited its protection in the broadest sense. All that was valuable in property sprang from its use, and if the State Legislature could deprive the property owner of his income from property by the regulation of the prices which he could charge, then they could effectively deprive him of all that was valuable in property.

Field argued for a liberal interpretation of the Constitutional protection afforded to property. Just as the Constitutional prohibition on the deprivation of life without due process of law was construed to prevent the government from mutilating the body by amputating limbs and organs, just as the prohibition on deprivation of liberty was construed to guarantee a person more than freedom from physical coercion and confinement, the prohibition on deprivation of property should guarantee the individual property owner against more than confiscation of his possession and title. The legislature *should* be considered as constitutionally prohibited from the regulation of business which deprived the owners of part of the exchange value of their property.

While Justice Field properly pointed out that the economic value of assets in a society organized on the basis of exchange depends on the power to sell the use of those assets, the acceptance of his argument that the Constitution should be construed to protect from regulation an existing exchange value of assets would involve the state in the sanctioning of coercion. What Waite and his colleagues in the majority had accepted and tried to justify on the basis of erroneous precedents was that the state could not protect property claims which involved economic coercion if a majority of the population refused to accede to the coercion. The elevator operators were able to coerce the farmers economically when they conspired together to fix charges because they had a monopoly in the provision of a service necessary to the marketing of grain. The Illinois legislature had attempted to control that coercive power by its regulation.

Field's argument about the sanctity of the exchange value of property from control by the state was parallel to the argument used by Chief Justice Taney in the Dred Scott decision. It disallowed the refusal of a majority of the population as represented in a legislature to continue the sanction of economic arrangements between individuals which involved coercion. The difference between slavery and monopoly is that in slavery the state is enforcing physical coercion while in monopoly it is sanctioning economic coercion. Both arguments limiting the legislative power rest on the supposition that the Constitution protects an existing system of economic arrangements by imposing constraints on legislative control of arrangements. True, in the case of slavery the state had to enforce actively the property slave owners possessed in their chattels by appropriate legislation and police action, while no legislation or positive action by the state was necessary in the case of private monopoly. Still, economic necessity deprived the farmers of part of their income as surely as the Black Codes deprived slaves of freedom.

The Implications of Munn v. Illinois for the Concept of Property. The majority decision in the Munn case was an important milestone in the development of the concept of property. It established the legitimacy of legislative control of the economic power of private property. This was to increase as the United States changed from a nation of small merchants and farmers to an industrialized state of large corporations and labor unions.

We should emphasize that the legislative circumscription of the powers of individuals to use their assets as they pleased accords with the theory of property developed in Chapter V of this volume. The rights accorded to an individual in the use of his assets by the state is proportioned by the state as an inducement to secure the performance of valuable functions by the individual. Protecting a monopolistic position allows the retention by an individual of a larger income from his assets than would be necessary to ensure their employment in uses beneficial to society.

The minority decision, as mentioned, was also very important in that the regulation of prices and rates of return on capital of public utilities by the courts rather than the legislature was established soon after the Munn case by a decision of the Supreme Court in 1890.[13] This decision accepted that public-utility type companies were publicly created and enforced monopolies which were legitimately regulated by the state. The decision also recognized, however, that the private owners of these public utilities needed a guarantee of a "fair" return on their capital. If the control of prices by the state denied them a rate of return equal to what they could realize in other investments, it was confiscating part of their property. We should note, once again, that the "property" which the state had to protect was "fair" return on assets. The state "had" to assure the protection of property in a fair return because in the absence of a guarantee, the capital would not be forthcoming to finance the development and operation of public-utility type concerns by private investors. The guarantee of the sanctity of private property of investors in publicly regulated utilities sprang from no "natural right" to a fair return but from public recognition of the necessity of inducements to secure a given response by individuals. Protestations about "natural" or "Constitutional" rights of individuals to the exchange value of their property

---

[13]*Chicago, Milwaukee, and St. Paul Railway Co.* v. *Minnesota* 134 U. S. 418 (1890).

by Stephen Field and successive generations of Americans were really superfluous and conceal the real source and protection of the rights of individuals—the self-interest of society in granting them rights to elicit certain desirable actions.

The regulation of the economic power of monopolies by the state when those monopolies were not created by the state was not satisfactorily resolved by the Munn case. The elevators represented a marginal case. Their owners were able to maintain a collusive monopoly primarily because the railroads, which did have state-created monopolies in various geographic locations, were able to limit the building of competing elevators in conjunction with the owners of existing elevators. Had the legislators and the courts wanted to control the power of monopoly in the provision of elevator services by using the precedents of the common law, they might have attempted to use the old common law doctrines of conspiracy in restraint of trade. Under the conspiracy doctrines, either individuals or the state could have brought action against the elevator operators. Proof of conspiracy in restraint of trade would have made them liable for damages. This course of action was to be taken in the Sherman Anti-Trust Law of 1890 and will be discussed more fully in Chapter 13.

The precedents governing the regulation of common carriers were not applicable in *Munn* v. *Illinois*. Nor were other precedents immediately relevant because the existence of monopoly without a grant of state power to enforce it was a new development in political economy, brought about by a change in the character of economic production. In the past, monopoly had only been possible with a specific grant by the state to the chartered monopolist of privileged access to particular markets. The state's power to create monopoly entailed its power to regulate the use of monopoly power. Now, a new set of circumstances was arising in which industrial firms could gain monopoly powers, not through privileged access to markets, but through technological superiority, access to resources, economies of scale, and other advantages which individual firms could use to give them indisputable control of markets. The new barriers to entry were not created by the state but by the individual firms, themselves.

Justice Field made an extremely valuable contribution to our understanding of the concept of property when he called attention to the need to prevent social confiscation of the exchange value of property by legislation. What he failed to deal with, however, was *what* exchange value society needed to protect. The protection of the exchange value of an asset resulting from the monopoly position of the owner of the asset could not be maintained against a legislative majority.

The exchange value of an asset which *ought* to be protected from confiscation by regulation is the value which would be realized in competitive markets. This principle was adopted in the Minnesota Rate Case of 1890 as the principle governing political control of public utilities. There are practical problems in identifying a "fair," or competitive, rate of return and specifying accounting and valuation practices to secure it. Nevertheless, the establishment of this principle was of fundamental importance in resolving the relationship of society to the economic assets of the individual member.

Economic and Political Power:
the Triumph of the Contractual
Origin of Property

At the outset of this chapter we suggested that the fundamental dualism in Locke's theory of civil government between the protection of property and the protection of life and liberty had not been satisfactorily resolved by the American Constitution of 1787. This writer believes that the decision of the majority in *Munn* v. *Illinois* and succeeding cases which affirmed the Constitutional right of popularly elected legislatures to control the use of economic power settled this dualism by restricting the protection of property to the claims of individual property owners which did not rely on the coercion of other members of society.

Social limitation of private monopoly power involving the confiscation of the exchange value of assets owing to monopoly is not a deprivation of property. It is not because the state could not undertake to give the guarantees of property to economic arrangements which allowed the monopolists economically to coerce the rest of society. Conversely, guarantees of property to the owners of economic assets of the exchange value of those assets in competitive markets was proper since it involved no coercion of other members of society and gave the necessary security to voluntary arrangements in which society had an interest.

The decision that the American Commonwealth should protect the life, liberty, and property of all its members was made, consciously or unconsciously, when the wealth qualifications for franchise were dropped. Once this had been done, the eventual use of political power by the majority to protect itself from the coercive power of a minority wielded with the assistance of the state was inevitable. Political control of the use of economic power has come about as a result of the efforts of the members of the state to protect themselves by the use of political power. Legislative control of the power of private businesses with monopoly power could not be prevented by appeals to the Constitution any more than could the abolition of slavery.

9

Economic Freedom:

the logic of exchange and the nature of social control

Private property is one cornerstone of a capitalist system; free exchange of goods and services is the other. Just as property establishes security for the individual in the possession and use of his legitimately acquired assets, free markets allow him to bargain about the exchange of these assets on mutually advantageous terms with other members of society. Property rights give a person freedom *from* unlawful coercion by other individuals or the state; rights of market access give a person freedom *to* pursue his self-interest subject only to securing assent from the members of society affected by his actions.

The argument of this chapter is that the restraints placed on the exchange transactions of individual members of a society depend upon the technological characteristics of production and the structure of political power in the society. Thus, the argument is parallel to the one elaborated in Chapter 5 for the delineation of the scope of property. Freedom of exchange is not regarded as an "inalienable" or "natural" right of man (whatever those terms mean). Economic freedom, like property, is a socially created and defined set of rights granted to individual members of a society from a calculation that this will serve social interests.

Economic Freedom and Other Freedoms

Freedom to participate in markets without restriction is sometimes posited as a freedom which *ought* to be regarded as fundamental as freedom of speech, worship, and conscience.[1] A basic difference exists between economic freedom and these civil liberties, however. The practice of free speech or worship according to the dictates of conscience does not interfere with the freedom of others to exercise their freedom. If one man has freedom of speech, another's freedom of speech is not curtailed in theory or practice. One man's form of worship does not interfere with another's.

Economic freedom is different because every exchange transaction has two sides. Both parties may gain from an exchange—if they did not perceive a gain from exchange they would not participate voluntarily. However, some of the gains from trade are divided, and under some circumstances one party may take all, or the lion's share, of the gains from exchange to the dissatisfaction of the other party. If, for example, one party to a transaction can make a "take-it-or-leave-it" offer while the other party has only that option, the superior bargaining position of one party leaves little effective freedom to the other. Sanctioning the freedom of one party to make a "take-it-or-leave-it" offer on his own terms when the other party has no alternative effectively confirms differences in the existing balance of power between the parties. If freedom is the power to do certain things, sanctioning the superior bargaining position of one party effectively allocates freedom to him and makes the freedom of the other theoretical rather than actual. Social limitation of the bargaining power of one party limits his freedom of action in order to increase that of the other party.

We should note that even civil liberties are subject to control where the action of one person may affect the interests of another. Freedom of speech does not include license to libel another. Political freedom in the United States does not include the power to advocate forcible overthrow of the existing Constitutional arrangements. Freedom of worship according to the dictates of conscience does not allow behavior or practices which the community finds prejudicial to public order.

The Social Utility of
Voluntary Exchange

Freedom of exchange is a *means*. Market freedom allows an individual to increase the value of his assets by exchanging their use with others in return for valuable consideration. The community has an interest in sanctioning division of labor and exchange because it increases wealth. It has an interest in regulating the conditions of exchange because this affects the distribution of income. The distribution of bargaining power

[1]See, for example, M. Friedman, *Capitalism and Freedom* (Chicago: University of Chicago Press, 1962), chap. 1 and 2, and F. A. von Hayek, *The Road to Serfdom* (Chicago: University of Chicago Press, 1944), chap. 7.

along with the assignment of property claims determines the allocation of "surplus" between uses and persons. A society effectively limits the freedom of its members in exchanges between themselves by making certain exchange transactions illegal or unenforceable.

As was demonstrated in Chapter 5, the social utility of establishing the property claims of individuals depended on those individuals exchanging their property with society under conditions in which they are not able to annex all the gains from trade. In Chapter 8, the dependence of the value of assets on the conditions of market access was discussed with relation to property in the economic power of monopoly. The conditions under which one can exchange an asset sets the limits to the value of property which can be realized in exchange. Social limitations on the exchange transactions of the property owner are part of the dimensions of property defined by society.

The Limits of Free Exchange. For purposes of argument, it might be useful to follow the convention of Chapter 5 in dealing with the rights granted by society to the individual. Recall that the argument elaborated there posited that society had an interest in granting property in assets to the individual who created them as an incentive for their creation. Society would benefit, in the general case, from property creation since the individual would exchange the increment in output with society for other goods, which would allow society to move to a higher preference function.

The interest of society in exchange with the individual would be to maximize its gains from trade by preventing the individual from exchanging his goods for society's for any more than the minimum which would induce him to create property and exchange it. The individual's interest, on the other hand, would be to exchange his goods for the highest obtainable price. A diagrammatic statement of the situation can be seen in Fig. 9–1, which restates Fig. 5–1.

The "Individual" has a property claim to CC' of good 2 which he has produced in response to the incentive offered by society of exclusive claim to the use or exchange of CC'. The "Individual" will not voluntarily consent to an exchange of good 1 for good 2 at any ratio which would leave him at a point between his preference function I (which passes through C) and the origin of his set of preference functions, C'. He will not voluntarily consent because any exchange which left him with a holding of goods 1 and 2 which was between his preference function I and his origin at C' would be, by definition, a nonpreferred position to C.

Society, on the other hand, would be unwilling to agree to any exchange of good 2 for good 1 which left it with a distribution of the

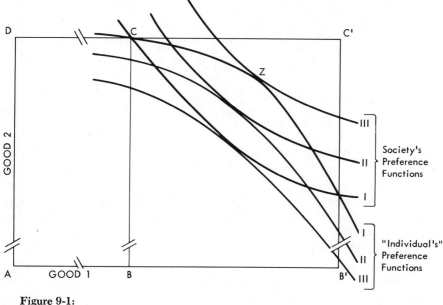

Figure 9-1:
The limits of voluntary exchange.

two goods represented by a point between its preference function *I* and the origin of its preference functions at *A*. Any such point would represent a distribution of goods nonpreferred to *C*.

A definition of property which included the right to exclusive possession and use would guarantee the individual *CC′* of good *1* and any combination of goods *1* and *2* which lay on the preference function *I* passing through *C*. Since Society would never have any self-interest in offering the exchange of good *2* for good *1* which would result in a combination of goods which lay on a point between its preference function *I* and the origin at *A*, this must be regarded as the upper limit of any freedom of exchange granted by society to the individual. The effective limits to freedom of exchange between the individual and society, then, are the preference functions passing through *C* which form the ellipse in which the final exchange position will be located.[2]

The argument for allowing an individual to exchange his goods with society is that society will be "better off" by the exchange. The "proof" is obvious; society will only consent to exchange which leaves it in a more preferred position after the exchange than before. This, however, is not an argument to allow the individual freedom to bargain over the

---

[2]The best-general introduction to the economic and philosophical problems involved in an analysis of the social utility of exchange is I.M.D. Little, *A Critique of Welfare Economics* (Oxford: Oxford University Press, 1950).

ratio of exchange. The interest of society, as against the individual, would be to gain the most preferable position possible consonant with securing the individual's assent to the transaction. This would be point Z in the diagram.

Restrictions on Voluntary Exchange
Social Control of Markets

The bargaining strength of the individual depends upon the alternatives open to society. This is the major reason for the importance to society of avoiding monopoly and fostering competitive supply of goods and services. If there are many suppliers, their competition in offering exchange transactions with society will force them to offer the most favorable exchange ratio consonant with their own self-interest. (The interested reader is invited to consult a standard book in economic theory for an exposition of the characteristics of the optimum welfare position reached in conditions of perfect competition in goods and factor markets.)

The exposition of the argument in the preceding section has been made in terms of society and an individual. The logic of the argument is not changed if a second individual replaces society as one of the parties to the exchange. Now, we may think of society as a third party setting the rules and conditions under which bargaining and exchange will take place. Any restrictions placed on the bargaining procedures which can be used by the individuals, or restrictions on the ratio at which goods could be exchanged, will involve society in altering the outcome which would have taken place in the absence of socially imposed rules or restrictions on market freedom—the freedom to bargain over any point within the ellipse. Any action taken by society to alter the ratio of exchange between individuals will alter the distribution of the gains from exchange.

While every individual would have an interest in being a monopolist in order to secure the maximum gain from the exchange of his good with the other members of society, society has an interest in having a maximum of competition, and institutional arrangements will be made to increase the knowledge and options available to the buyers of goods and services.

A second reason why societies will try to maintain open access to markets is that the political creation or sanction of monopoly positions will lead to internal faction and the attempt by groups to use the power of the state to increase their income and wealth by controlling market structure and power in their interests. This could lead to political instability as the group lacking access or protection of their interests would seek to take over political control. The control of markets is, of course, an objective of political power, but while all members of a society have an interest in maintaining perfect competition and open access of markets, only specific individuals and groups have an interest in the maintenance of market conditions favorable to themselves. The more representative of the interests of society as a whole the government is, the less likely it will be to structure market power in favor of specific interest groups.

Conspiracy. In order to prevent the private control of markets, conspiracy must be prevented. This can be accomplished by refusing to enforce collusive agreements or, even more effectively, by making collusive agreements an illegal act punishable by suitable penalties. Because the presence of monopoly profits will always make it advantageous for individuals outside the collusive agreements to compete in supplying goods, and because each individual conspirator will have an interest in breaking the conspiratorial agreement as long as his partners still keep it, private control of markets will be difficult unless given social enforcement. The freedom of individuals to make contracts will, therefore, not usually include the freedom to make conspiratorial contracts to restrain the sale of goods or services. Labor unions present an important and complex exception discussed below.[3]

Public Goods. The freedom of individuals to exchange goods and services free of social control will be modified to a greater or lesser extent to finance what are sometimes called "public goods." The most important public goods are defense against external aggression and the maintenance of internal law and order. Since an individual would enjoy the benefits of these public goods whether he paid for them or not, they will have to be financed by some method other than voluntary purchase. Education, literature, and art also have some of the characteristics of public goods which, therefore, require some sort of political action to supply them on a principle other than individual purchase and sale.[4] In some societies, "public goods" are financed essentially by sanctioning private collection of economic "surplus," which is then devoted to the provision of these public goods. In other societies, these public goods are financed by a tax levied on either goods or the income accruing to owners of the factors of production.[5]

[3]See Chapters 13 and 14.

[4]An excellent survey of the issues and literature in the theory of public goods will be found in Mancur Olsen, Jr., *The Logic of Collective Action: Public Goods and the Theory of Groups* (Cambridge: Harvard University Press, 1965).

[5]See Chapter 6.

Technical Monopolies. Another reason for limitation of access to markets may be the desirability of monopoly on technical grounds. In some cases, to permit free entry might result in higher costs for a society when duplication of facilities would prevent the utilization of available scale economies. When a monopoly is publicly established and enforced, however, control becomes necessary to prevent private gains resulting from the absence of competition.[6]

The Social Interest in Competition. Under most circumstances, a society has an interest in assuring that open access to markets produces competition to prevent particular individuals from gaining a strong bargaining position vis-a-vis society as a whole. Well-organized markets in which both buyers and sellers possess information about the "state of the market" will contribute to good performance. Social enforcement of contracts and, in particular, the prevention of fraud whereby one party to the contract fails to render what he purports to give in exchange are a means of improving knowledge about the market. Under this heading, occupational licensing to assure the public that providers of services can perform a given standard of service is practiced. Goods have to be properly labeled as to content and, in some cases where private groups are unable to establish suitable standards, public authorities specify and enforce those standards. Limitations on the freedom of individuals to buy and sell goods on other terms than those specified by the society are an important contributor to order which, in turn, helps to protect public health, safety, and interests from private action.[7]

Imperfect Markets and Bargaining

The logic of social action in the regulation of exchange activities is to establish alternatives to promote competition where possible and to limit the bargaining power of parties who would otherwise have considerable power because of the existence of few alternative choices. If competition does not exist, a policy of "laissez faire" confirms a given distribution of bargaining power. It allows certain members of society (or the government in a corporate society) to control the use of "economic surplus."

Factor Markets and Goods Markets. Thus far, our discussion of markets and social restrictions on exchange has not differentiated between "goods" markets and "factor" markets. In a society of any degree of

[6]See Abba P. Lerner, *The Economics of Control* (New York: The Macmillan Company, 1957).

[7]Milton Friedman has called attention to the abuses to which social controls have been applied by private interests. Friedman, *op. cit.*

development, individuals do not primarily produce goods with their own labor, land, and capital and exchange them with other individuals for goods. They sell the use of the factors of production, labor, capital, and land in which they have property for money with which to buy goods. The exchange terms on which they can sell their productive services to the organizers of production determine the share of total product going to the owners of the factors of production and the entrepreneurs who organize the production.

In competitive markets, one expects the relative prices of goods to be proportional to their relative "costs of production." In an alternative cost framework this means that the exchange ratio between two goods will reflect how much production of one good would have to be foregone to release the productive resources necessary to produce the other.

The payments going to the owners of productive factors in a developed society do *not* reflect their cost of production. Land, labor, and capital are not commodities which are produced in response to changes in the returns to the owners. The returns to the owners may exert some influence in the long run over the supply of the productive factors made available. Higher wages may marginally increase the amount of labor which the individuals in a society are willing to sell. We no longer believe that it will cause families to have more children. An increase in the rate of return on capital may lead to more saving. It might also lead to less. The land available for various uses can be marginally increased. Nevertheless, we tend to think of the supply of the factors of production as being rather unresponsive to changes in the prices offered for their services *in the society as a whole*. The supply of factors to any particular firm in the economy, of course, will be highly responsive to price.

The upper limit to the payment offered by an entrepreneur to an owner of factor services will be his estimate of the net output he could produce by employing the factor. In the terminology of neo-classical economic theory, a profit-maximizing entrepreneur would continue to employ factor services up to the point that the value of the marginal product of the last unit of factor input was equal to its cost to him.

The lower limit to the payment which the entrepreneur can make for factor services is the alternative income which the factor owner would secure in other employment. If the individual entrepreneur is purchasing factor services in perfectly competitive factor markets, the quantity of factor services he employs makes no difference to their price. If the supply of factor services is not infinitely large in proportion to his demand for them, the individual entrepreneur must take into account the effect of his demand for them on their price. The lower limit may rise as the quantity employed increases.

Factor Price Indeterminacy. In the perfectly competitive long-run equilibrium of economic theory, competition between entrepreneurs for factor services will ensure that their employment is extended to the point where the value of the marginal product of each factor is equal to its supply price. Unfortunately, the perfectly competitive long-run equilibrium of theory is seldom, if ever realized. When a firm is purchasing factor services under conditions where the owners of those services have limited alternatives and where the supply price of the factors is a function of the quantity of factor services the firm employs, the firm will maximize its profit by limiting its employment of the factor with the rising supply price. The firm may thus pay the factor owner considerably less than the value of the marginal product of the factor—the upper limit to the payment to the factor owner which the firm would make on a profit-maximizing decision. This holds true regardless of whether the firm is selling its output in perfectly competitive product markets. The situation is summarized in Fig. 9–2.

In Fig. 9–2, the VMP curve (value of marginal product) shows the net contribution to output of the last unit of factor service employed. It is a "demand function" for the factor in that it shows how much an entrepreneur would be willing to pay for that quantity of factor services if forced to do so by competition. The supply function for the factor exhibits rising costs for greater quantities of the factor. (If the factor market in which the firm purchased factor services were perfectly competitive, the supply function would be a horizontal line at the going competitive price. The intersection of the horizontal supply function with the downward sloping VMP function would determine the quantity of the factor employed and the price received.)

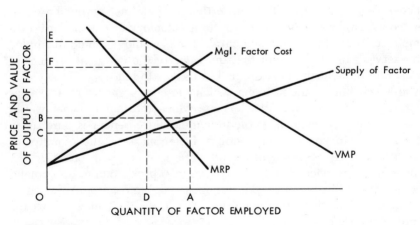

Figure 9-2:
Supply and demand for factor services.

The function labeled "marginal factor cost" shows the addition to the total cost to the firm of employing an additional unit of the factor. It rises more steeply than the supply curve because each additional unit of factor employed raises the cost per unit, and thus the total factor cost. The MRP ("marginal revenue product") function is appropriate for the firm which operates in imperfect product markets. With increases in employment and output, the price for the product which will clear the market falls. Thus, the profit-maximizing firm selling in imperfect product markets must take into account the decrease in the price of its product which occurs as output and employment increases. The MRP function shows the increase in total revenue derived from the employment of an additional unit of the productive factor.

Fig. 9–2 utilizes functions appropriate for short-run equilibrium. The factors of production, other than the one being observed, are assumed to be fixed. The slopes and positions of the diagrams are used for expositional purposes only. The point to be made is that in an imperfect factor market, the profit-maximizing firm will pay the owners of the factor of production less than the value of the marginal product of the factor. If product markets are perfect, the firm in Fig. 9–2 would employ a quantity of the factor, OA, determined by the intersection of the VMP and Marginal Factor Cost functions and would pay a price OB per unit of the factor—the price for which that quantity of the factor could be secured.

If the firm were operating in imperfect product markets, profit maximization would entail the equation of the MRP and Marginal Factor Cost functions which would result in an employment of quantity, OD, of the factor at a price of OC, the price at which that quantity of the factor could be obtained.

The profit-maximizing firm does not coerce the owners of the factors of production in the purchase of their services. It pays the price necessary to secure a given quantity of factor services. (One could even say that it pays more than necessary to those owners of the factor services which would have been willing to take less.) The profit-maximizing firm "exploits" the imperfection of the factor markets which limits the alternatives, and hence, the bargaining power of the owners of the factor services. Given their lack of alternatives, the profit-maximizing firm pays less for a given quantity of factor services than it would have been willing to pay. In terms of Figure 9–2, the firm competing in perfect product markets would have been willing to pay OF for quantity OA of the factor. The price difference, BF, times the quantity, OA, represents a "surplus" which the entrepreneur who purchased productive factors and sold goods was able to appropriate. The firm operating in imperfect product markets is able to appropriate a "surplus" from its customers as well as its suppliers of productive factors.

The Effect of Economic Growth on Markets. In general, the process of economic development might be said to increase the alternatives, and hence, the competition in the markets for goods. Improvements in transportation lower the cost of transportation and thus increase the size of markets and the number of firms competing. Improvements in communication increase the knowledge of market possibilities for both producers and consumers. As incomes increase, consumption of many items becomes postponable, and a variety of wholly different types of goods and services are competing for the consumers' expenditure.

The process of economic growth, however, may very well make factor markets more imperfect through the increased specialization of the factors which increases their productivity.[8] Capital in hand tools may not be nearly as productive in a given process as a machine tool designed for the job, but they may be transferred more easily to a variety of other processes. A highly skilled textile operative may find difficulty in finding an alternative position in which she is as productive if her job is changed by automation.

Specialization of production may make pieces of capital equipment suited to only one type of employment with practically no alternative use. Specialization by human beings may make them highly productive in one line of work but with few alternatives in a specific geographic area. Owners of capital can compensate for the riskiness of specialization by investing their money in fixed interest debts so that the firm bears the risks, or can buy equity shares in firms which depreciate fixed capital rapidly, and/or diversify. Individuals who invest time and money in specializing their labor services may find their alternatives limited and themselves, consequently, in a weak bargaining position in labor markets.

An analysis of the effects of economic growth on the range of indeterminacy of factor prices is outlined in Fig. 9–3.

In Fig. 9–3, Generalized Output is shown on the vertical axis and Specialized Output is on the horizontal axis. In the initial situation, a quantity *AC* of Generalized Output is produced by a society. One individual in the society produces and consumes amount *BC* of the Generalized Output and society, *ex individual*, produces and consumes quantity *AB*.

The individual specializes his factor services (labor, capital, or land) in the production of Specialized Output. In order to do this he must stop producing *BC* of the Generalized Output to produce quantity *AF* of the Specialized Output. After specialization, society, *ex individual*,

---

[8]The importance of specialization in reducing the costs of production is analyzed in an article which takes its title from Adam Smith's famous dictum by George A. Stigler, "The Division of Labor is Limited by the Extent of the Market," *Journal of Political Economy*, Vol. LVIX (June 1951).

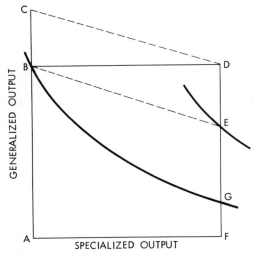

Figure 9-3:
Specialization and factor price indeterminacy.

produces quantity *AB* of Generalized Output and the individual produces *AF* of Specialized Output. For the individual and society, the cost
of producing *AF* of Specialized Output is *BC* of Generalized Output
which is not produced.

The individual produces only the Specialized Output but wishes to
consume only Generalized Output which he secures from society by
exchanging Specialized Output for it. If we follow the convention used
earlier and treat the rectangle, ABDF, as an Edgeworth Box with society
at the lower left hand corner and the individual at the upper right, we
can illustrate the limits of exchange. Society's preference functions originate at *A* and the preference function passing through *B* also passes
through *G*. The individual's preference functions originate at *D* but are
not shown. The individual wishes to consume only Generalized Output,
and his preference functions would be shown as lines parallel to *AF* and
BD.

The lower limit to the amount of Generalized Output which the individual could secure from society in voluntary specialization and exchange
would be quantity *DE* equal to *CB*. The individual would not give up
producing and consuming *BC* to produce *AF* of the Specialized Output
unless he could trade at least to reach as high a consumption level as
before. (In the long run, the price of one good in terms of another cannot fall below the reciprocal of their transformation ratio.)

The upper limit to the quantity of Generalized Output which society
would be willing to trade to the individual for Specialized Output would
be the quantity *DG* which would leave society with quantity *FG* after

exchange. This upper limit is determined by society's preference function which passes through B and G. At G, society would be in an equally preferred position to B, and any lesser quantity of Generalized Output would leave society in a less preferred position.

The quantity of the Generalized Output which the individual will be able to acquire from society in exchange for his production of Specialized Output will be between DE and DG. This is the range of indeterminacy in bargaining. The upper limit is the value of the Specialized Output to society and the lower limit is the alternative cost to the individual.

Economic Growth and Factor Price Indeterminacy. What the author wishes to demonstrate is that an increase in factor productivity will increase the range of indeterminacy. In Fig. 9–4, the Edgeworth Box of Fig. 9–3 is repeated with an increase of Specialized Output to F'. This increase in Specialized Output is a representation of what happens during economic growth. An increased quantity of one good can be produced with the same amount of productive factors. Thus, the alternative cost of producing one good in terms of another is decreased.

In Fig. 9–4, the range of indeterminacy $E'G'$ is greater than the original range EG. It must always be greater because of the convexity of the social preference function passing through B, G, and G'.

The crucial point to be drawn from the analysis is that the gains from specialization and exchange *and* the range of indeterminacy in exchange ratios increases as economic growth takes place. The operation of markets, therefore, becomes of increasing importance as specialization of production and exchange increase the potential gains available to both individuals who specialize and society as a whole.

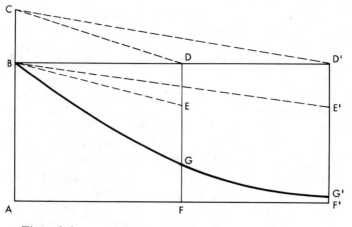

Figure 9-4:
Economic growth and increasing indeterminacy.

Our analysis has been conducted as though our individual exchanged the Specialized Output produced with his factor services directly with society. While this may be the case with small farmers and with purveyors of services such as doctors, lawyers, barbers, and the corner automobile mechanic, in the usual case, individuals in our society sell their factor services to entrepreneurs. The profit-maximizing entrepreneur has an interest in purchasing factor services at the lowest price obtainable and selling the output which he organizes from their use at the highest prices. The upper and lower limits for the owner of factor services are, in the usual case, the upper and lower limits for the entrepreneur to pay the owners of factor services. The entrepreneur could pay the owners of factor services in Fig. 9–3 a quantity of Generalized Output DE and then exchange the Specialized Output AF which he purchased from the owners of the factor services for DG of the Generalized Output. This would net him a surplus equal to EG. This quantity of Generalized Output, EG, could be bargained away from the entrepreneur by the owners of factor services under certain conditions.

Factor Price Indeterminacy and

Labor Unions

The most notable device for bargaining away part of the "surplus" from the entrepreneur (or the public) is a labor union. For a variety of reasons connected with the mobility and homogeneity of capital and the organization of capital markets, there is not such a widespread tendency for capital owners to organize collusively.

A labor union is a conspiracy on the part of its members to act as a monopolist in the sale of a particular type of labor service. To be effective it must have effective control of its members and power to prevent nonmembers from offering labor services to the employer with whom they are bargaining. If a labor union is not a coercive conspiracy, it cannot be effective.

The labor union poses a number of very difficult questions for a society organized along the lines of free bargaining between all parties over the prices of goods and services.[9] In the absence of labor unions, individuals selling their labor services who have limited alternatives may be paid considerably less than the value of their marginal contribution to output. Social restrictions on the organization and power of unions may allow one segment of society (and usually a relatively poor segment) to be exploited (paid less than the value of their marginal product) by entrepreneurs.

[9]See Chapter 14.

On the other hand, an effective labor union will raise the prices of factor services. If it does so to some entrepreneurs who are producing a particular commodity but not to others, it may force them out of business. If it raises labor costs to all entrepreneurs producing the commodity, the society as a whole will pay higher prices for the good, and income will be redistributed toward the members of the union.

Finally, a host of problems are connected with the freedom and security of an individual member of the union. An effective union will limit its membership and, thus, deny access to employment in certain instances to certain men. To be effective in bargaining, a union must be able to control its members, which limits their alternatives. To control effectively employment in a particular industry, a union may even have to be able to prevent an employer from moving the location of operations, substituting machinery, or subcontracting out particular types of work.

Summary

The scope of an individual's economic freedom is determined by his property and the limitations placed by society on the exchange contracts which he makes with other members of society. Limitations on the individual's freedom to exchange are made by society to protect its members from being exploited when the imperfections which exist in markets would otherwise enable individuals to enrich themselves by taking part of the consumers' or producers' surplus from them in voluntary exchange transactions.

The analysis of this chapter has been largely preoccupied with exchange bargaining under conditions of imperfect competition. In the long run, perfectly competitive equilibrium of economic theory, there is *no* bargaining problem, because all goods exchange at prices relative to their cost of production in terms of other goods and the owners of all factors of production receive a price for their use equal to the value of their marginal output. In the long run, perfectly competitive equilibrium of economic theory, there is no need for social interference with the voluntary exchange of goods and services by individuals, for none of them has any power to effect an exchange bargain with another which would deprive him voluntarily of part of his "surplus." The only role for the state *is* to enforce the contracts voluntarily made by individuals.

In the real world of short-run changes, uncertainty, inertia, resources fixed in particular uses, and ignorance about alternatives, there is much scope for bargaining about the prices of goods and the services of productive resources. The analysis of this chapter should lead the observer of social institutions to expect interference with the market freedom of individuals as a rational response to the problems created by imperfect markets. The acceptance of a laissez-faire attitude by the members of a society subject to the use of economic power by others would be an irrational response unless some fatalistic belief existed that there was no point in trying to interfere with the existing order because it was, in some sense, naturally ordained.

The control of markets by a society will reflect the distribution of political power in the society. Attempts to redistribute income by altering the receipt of economic surplus by producers and consumers through restriction on exchange will accord with the consensus of the ruling group concerning social priorities. Limits exist as to the amount of redistribution which can be accomplished with a given distribution of property, but the limits grow progressively larger in the course of economic growth.

10

The Control
of Markets:

*a medieval
comparison*

Economic freedom is not an end in itself. A wide degree of freedom from politically controlled economic activity is a cornerstone of a capitalist society because the members of a capitalist society believe that free markets can be made to produce acceptable results.

To understand the advantages and difficulties of free markets in capitalist societies we must inquire into the practices and problems of societies which have started from a different set of assumptions about the viability and social acceptability of the results of free markets. An historical inquiry into practices prior to the nineteenth century or into the larger part of the contemporary world reveals that the bulk of mankind has relied to a greater extent on political direction and control than voluntary action for the organization of economic activity.

Rather than cast our net too widely, we will confine our examination to the control of economic activity in Europe in the late Middle Ages and to the Soviet Union in recent times. In both societies there has been a complicated interplay between ethical presuppositions about the morality of the income distribution and interpersonal relations that were believed to result from the uncontrolled bargaining of individual members of society and the political and technological problems peculiar to these societies. One of the most interesting conclusions to be drawn from an examination of both societies is that control of economic activity by the state was progressively relaxed because of the demands of economic growth. This is particularly interesting since we will argue in succeeding chapters that the impact of economic growth on American society, which has historically been based on a maximum degree of freedom from political control, has led to greater social intervention in the economy. Convergence in economic philosophy, therefore, might be held to be a result of the demands of technology rather than an outgrowth of ethics.

The Legitimacy of Social Control of Economic Activity in Medieval Europe

The theory of the legitimacy of the control of all assets by the state during the Middle Ages was discussed at some length in Chapter 6. In essence, the theory was that the land and the men who inhabited it had been created by God. Individual men did not have any absolute rights in the use of assets. They were trustees with privileges depending on their station in life. Society was a corporate entity in which each member had a proper function, and attempts by an individual to "bargain" with other individuals or with society collectively would have been viewed as improper as the attempt of a child to bargain with his parents or his brothers. As has been noted, a considerable gulf existed between the statement of the ideas by kings and philosophers and their implementation in the realities of everyday life on the manor and in the town markets.[1]

John Locke's assertions of the human origins of property and government in the seventeenth century reflected the repudiation of the medieval political theory which took place in Western Europe at the end of the Middle Ages. The commercial practices which were formerly based (or rationalized) on them continued to exist on into the nineteenth century, however, as they suited the interests of powerful economic groups who had acquired and extended their wealth under the old system.

When Adam Smith inveighed against the complex web of market controls in his *Wealth of Nations* in 1776, he was criticizing the remains of the medieval system. He was writing on behalf of the rising manufacturing interests who found themselves constrained in obtaining labor and frustrated in exploiting market opportunities. He was also arguing that the regulations originally designed to protect and improve the labor force did the opposite and were used by particular interests to exploit those they claimed to protect.[2] Smith did not condemn all attempts

[1]This point is explored by Walter Ullman, *The Individual and Society in the Middle Ages* (Baltimore: Johns Hopkins University Press, 1966), pp. 53–62.
[2]Adam Smith, *The Wealth of Nations*, E. Canaan, ed. (New York: Modern Library, Inc., 1939), Book I, Chapters 6 and 7.

by the state to control the transactions of individuals, but he argued that the attempts which were being made usually had the wrong effects.

Smith's treatise was an attempt to replace an old conception of a corporate society with a new conception of an individual society in which the voluntary transactions of individuals pursuing their self-interest would produce the good results desired by all moral men. In his attempts to break down the guild restrictions of the period with regard to the employment of workmen, Smith advanced some propositions with regard to the "rights of labor" which were as revolutionary as those advanced by Locke with regard to the "rights of property" a century earlier.[3] The revolutionary character of both thinkers lay in their rejection of the notion of a corporate society in which every man had a status with commensurate privileges and obligations which was inherited and not subject to change by the initiative of the individual.

The basic premise of the medieval conception of society from which its control of markets was derived was that a town (the basic political unit) was a Christian brotherhood. The merchants and craftsmen of the medieval town formed the town corporation which enacted and enforced the laws governing the operation of economic activity as well as the civil, religious, and defense needs of the town. Members of the town corporation were only able to participate in the economic and social life of the town in accordance with their status in the corporation. Their exclusion from the rights and privileges of members would have made it impossible for them to carry on business. They were morally and religiously bound in their dealings with the other members of the town by their common membership in the Church where they took the sacraments together. Trespassing against the moral laws of the Church could lead to their religious excommunication by the denial of the sacraments and the loss of hope in life after death. The coextension of the political, economic, and religious community of the town legitimated its control of economic activity.

Several observations need to be made on the place of the towns in the Middle Ages. The society in which the town merchants operated was profoundly suspicious of their activities. The merchants had, as it were, bought their way out of the feudal system and maintained their immunity from feudal responsibilities by the continual payment of tribute to the feudal lords. They were a constant aggravation to the "Lords, Spiritual and Temporal" for several reasons: First, the towns were a constant magnet for labor, and during times of population scarcity, the mere presence of towns forced concessions upon the part of feudal lords to their serfs. Second, the merchants were a rival political

[3]See Eli Ginzberg, *The House of Adam Smith* (New York: Columbia University Press, 1934), Chapter 3.

and military power to the established order, and at the close of the Middle Ages were strong supporters of the royal power in national unification and subjection of the old feudal aristocracy. Third, their economic activities heralded to a new society based on different conceptions of human relationships, some of which the Church regarded as immoral and exploitative.

It may seem strange to the modern mind that the Church would condemn economic exploitation by merchants while being silent on the relationship of serf and feudal lord. The serfs were bound to the land and required to render certain payments and services to their feudal lord. The Church and society saw in this relationship, however, mutual obligation rather than exploitation, even while acknowledging that the relationship could be abused.

In the last analysis the towns were tolerated because they performed services which were desired by the feudal lords. Not only did they allow the exchange of manorial output for goods which could not be produced, but they also were a source of income, particularly income in a liquid form which could be used to finance dynastic ambitions or merely a higher standard of living for the feudal lords. In the end, the impact of the town broke down the feudal system by pervasively spreading a market economy with production for exchange rather than manorial subsistence. The old relationships of status were replaced by negotiated contractual arrangements, and the need for wider markets led to the creation of national states in place of the small units of sovereign power.

The most striking characteristic of the medieval towns was the extent to which economic and political power was concentrated. The right to control trade was the acknowledged prerogative of the sovereign power enforced by his military power. The merchants of the towns battled and bargained for the grant of this sovereign power and realized that it was a privilege of great value. The charter of incorporation of a town was a cession of privilege from a sovereign power. It was a cession of sovereignty, itself, since the towns were empowered to regulate the lives of the members of the town corporation. They were able to retain power only as long as they posessed sufficient wealth to protect themselves with their own retainers or by buying the protection of feudal lords. Further, the willingness of the sovereign lord who had ceded them sovereignty to let them continue to exercise it depended upon their usefulness to his purposes or their power to resist him.

The Necessity of Social Control of Markets. The security and prosperity of the medieval town depended on the control of markets. If control were lost or weakened, the town was endangered in its very existence. In markets in which the citizens of the town were consumers, elaborate regulations to protect all the citizens by perfecting the market were instituted. When the terms of trade vis-a-vis the customers or suppliers of the town could be improved by collusion, the action was taken because it was in the town's interest. Operating always under the constraint of limited elasticities of both supply and demand, definite advantages could be realized at the expense of the outside world. And why not? It was a disadvantage to the entire town to let merchants drive up prices paid to foreign suppliers and drive down prices paid by foreign consumers through competition. The benefits would accrue entirely to foreigners. As long as the impact of imperfect markets benefitted the town at the expense of foreigners, the political structuring and control of markets was entirely rational and led to no internal conflicts of interest except over the division of the gains from trade by the collusive merchants.

For purposes of exposition one might say that the members of a medieval town thought of the demand for the products produced by their guilds as being fixed in the sense that their limited market had a fixed amount of purchasing power to spend on that article. They thought of the per-unit costs of production as being constant, and the guilds resisted any innovations which might have had the effect of reducing cost by reducing employment because this would have displaced apprentices and journeymen whom they were socially bound to retain in employment.

These expectations are shown in Fig. 10–1 by a demand curve of unitary elasticity and a constant cost supply curve.

Guild policy was aimed at restricting production to OA so that a price of OC could be maintained which would furnish a net return to the guild

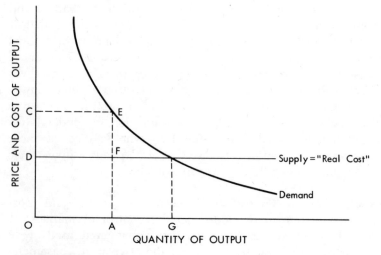

Figure 10-1:
Supply and demand expectations of a medieval town.

of *DCEF*. This could be used for the maintenance of the guild masters and the town establishment which made their monopoly enforceable. The increase of output to *OG* would have eliminated a net return to the guild.

A prime objective of the commercial policy of the towns was to divert trade from other towns and to control as much of the trade of the hinterland of the town as possible. The more trade that passed through the hands of the merchants of the town, the richer the town would be. It was also considered to be necessary to control the transactions of the town's merchants with outsiders, however, to prevent competition between them which might have had the effect of raising the prices of goods purchased from suppliers or driving down the prices of goods sold. Thus, one may say that the policies of the towns were aimed at increasing the volume and improving the terms of trade in the goods in which the merchants of the town specialized. These policies, of course, checked one another since the terms of trade and the volume of trade were inversely related. If suppliers were offered too little or customers asked too much, volume of trade would suffer.

The policies of individual towns were checked by competitive towns, and warfare between towns was often the result of commercial rivalry. The commercial control of areas adjacent to the towns and the forcible exclusion of competitors was the essence of economic power. The city of Cologne, for example, controlled trade on the Rhine by being able to bar other merchants from the trade. Vienna exercised the same power on the Danube. The Hanseatic League was the precursor of modern international cartels. It was an arrangement between dominant merchant groups in a number of cities in northern Europe to collaborate effectively in controlling the trade in certain commodities in the areas bordering the Baltic and North Sea. The struggles of Venice, Genoa, and Florence for control of the Italian trade were incessant. Military and commercial control were coextensive in the Middle Ages.

The level of profits and the wealth and power of the merchant groups in the towns were dependent on their success in blocking other towns and avoiding competition among the merchants of a particular town. Both suppliers and consumers were external to the political community of the town. Their exploitation in trade through the limitation of alternatives could not result in any internal conflict of interest in the community since the community enforcing the trade regulations was separate from those on whom they imposed a burden. The historian Schmöller noted:

> All the resources of municipal diplomacy . . . and in the last resort of violence were employed to gain control over trade routes and to obtain staple rights: to bring it about that as many routes as possible should lead to the town; as few as possible pass by: that through traffic, by caravan or ship, should, if possible, be made to halt there, and goods

en route exposed and offered for sale to the burgesses. The whole . . .
Law . . . was an instrument wherewith to destroy, or, at all events, to
diminish the . . . competitors from outside.[4]

Staple rights is a euphemistic term for the control of trade in a certain
commodity. One of the most famous was the Wool Staple which operated
in Britain in the Middle Ages. In the tenth and eleventh century, Italian
merchants received grants of monopoly in the export of wool from the
Crown in return for loans and payments to finance civil and military
expenditures. In the twelfth and thirteenth centuries these privileges
were progressively taken over by merchants in the various English towns
who were able to form a collusive oligopoly in both the purchase and
sale of the staple. They were able to depress the price at which they
purchased wool in England and to inflate it in Flanders by their policies.
The long-run effects of the policy, interestingly, were to stimulate the
manufacture of cloth in England by giving it decisive cost advantages
over that produced in the low countries. In the short run it was the
foundation of many medieval fortunes.[5]

The towns operated as small islands in the sea of feudalism. Their
charters were purchased from the local feudal lords, and the citizens of
a town were organized, in many respects, as a trading corporation. They
regulated the economic activity which they could control in the interests
of their members. Strangers, nonmembers in the town corporation, were
enjoined from exchange transactions in the towns except under conditions
specified to give the advantages in trade to the town burghers. Traveling
merchants were obliged to lodge with members of the town guild—not
for purposes of encouraging hospitality or social intercourse—but so that
the burgher could see that the alien merchant did not make any deals
on the sly.

In medieval London, foreign merchants were only allowed to live
and trade in an area called "the Steelyard." This was a privilege granted
by the Crown rather than the merchants of the City of London and was
a source of constant irritation to the London merchants who succeeded
in abrogating the privileges of foreigners during the reign of Elizabeth I
as a part of the policies of national unification.

The Medieval Fairs. The only place where foreign merchants were not
placed at a disadvantage with resident merchants in their dealings was
at the fairs which were organized during the Middle Ages for the purpose
of allowing trade between merchants exclusive of town control. The most
famous of the medieval fairs were those of the Champagne region of

[4]Gustave Schmoller, *The Mercantile System* (New York: The Macmillan Co.,
1893), pp. 10–11.
[5]See Eileen Power, "The Wool Trade in the Fifteenth Century" in M. M. Postan
and E. Power, ed., *Studies in English Trade in the Fifteenth Century* (New York:
The Macmillan Co., 1933).

France. These reached their greatest importance in the thirteenth century and lasted in different cities of Champagne for nearly the entire year. The location of the fair was crucial to its success, for it lay between the woolen cloth producing areas of Flanders and the Italian cities which imported many luxury goods from the Orient and the Levant. Economic transactions at these fairs were similar to modern practices except that the merchants would deal in goods which they had brought with them— the practice of selling and buying from samples for future delivery having not yet developed. The fairs had to have their own courts to enforce a code of commercial conduct. Malpractice by a merchant at a fair could result in exclusion not only of the merchant in question but the merchants of his town. Thus, commercial law first began to be enforced on an international scale by the merchants, themselves.

In addition to the exchange of goods, the Champagne fairs were of immense importance to medieval commerce because they became a center of financial transactions. Traveling merchants brought the currency of their own areas with them to the fair, and a lively market in foreign exchange emerged. Even more important, goods began to be purchased by the drawing of bills of exchange to avoid the risks of traveling with large amounts of cash.

The prelates of the Church played a very important part in this development because they had a superior credit rating. If a bill was drawn against a merchant in a distant town, some uncertainty existed regarding its repayment because of the possible unwillingness of his town to force him to pay his debts even in the face of exclusion of all the town's merchants from the fair. The prelates of the Church, on the other hand, could be excommunicated for the nonpayment of debt and consequently played an important part in the development of international trade by giving the certainty to financial instruments so necessary to the successful prosecution of commerce. The fairs of the Middle Ages were made possible by the Church, which was the only nonlocal political unit of the Middle Ages with effective control over its members. The interest of the Church in the financial transactions lay in the transferral of the tithes collected in commodities in its widespread dominions to Rome in the form of negotiable instruments. The medieval fairs are an interesting exception to the prevailing commercial practices of the period.

The Problem of Controlling Output

In addition to exercising a monopoly of trade in a given geographic area and excluding foreign merchants from competition, the medieval town corporation had to prevent its own members from competing with one another. In the absence of regulation, individual merchants would have tried to increase their share of total trade. The attempt to do this would have led to competition and diminished the profits of monopoly which were made possible by the limitation of the supply of goods. The town corporation dealt with this problem by delegating control of particular trades to the guilds which were allowed to enforce price and output restrictions on their members.

Three devices were used to limit the expansion of one member of the guild at the expense of another. One was the requirement that a member of the guild be ready to sell raw materials to the other members of the guild at his cost—a device to prevent monopoly through cornering the supply of raw materials. The second device was a limitation on the number of apprentices which could be employed by a craft-guild member. A third requirement stipulated that a guild master could not "farm out" work outside the guild until he had first offered the work to fellow members of the guild. All of these requirements worked against the interests of guild members individually, and they broke down progressively.

In their origin, the craft guilds were associations of independent producers who banded together to control production and competition. Their regulations were designed to prevent individual members from gaining at the expense of other members of the guild. Partly for this reason regulations governing the employment of apprentices and journeymen were instituted. The stipulation that apprentices and journeymen should be able to become masters in the trade after a given number of years was a limitation on entry into the craft, as was the limitation of the number of apprentices and journeymen which could be employed by any master.

Prices were regulated by the guild in keeping with the medieval notion of "the just price"—cost of production plus a margin which would allow the maintenance of a "customary" standard of living. Quality was closely controlled by the guild—both to prevent the sale of merchandise which would reflect adversely on the reputation of the guild and to prevent surreptitious competition by quality variation.

The Control of Labor. The apprentices obviously constituted a cheap labor supply for the master craftsmen. On the other hand, the masters were responsible for both the welfare and education of their apprentices. The logic of the system was that apprenticeship was an investment which would pay off for the individual when he became a privileged master craftsman. The system, of course, was open to great abuse, and over time apprenticeship progressively degenerated into a device to insure a cheap supply of labor. The guilds became controlled by the masters who fixed wages and prices to suit their own interests.

In the later Middle Ages, journeymen formed together in guilds to bargain for their interests against the masters in an early forerunner of the modern labor union. These journeymen guilds were declared illegal by the town governments, which were controlled by the employers and their allies. However, the guilds continued to exist nominally as religious societies with the real purpose of acting as journeymen's unions.

The original philosophy of regulation of labor in the medieval guild system was well suited to the technological constraints which operated in the society. Markets were limited by the low level of income of the mass of the agricultural population and the high cost of transportation. There were no economies of scale in handicraft production which would have made a different system more efficient. Thus, demand was limited and inelastic. The welfare of the towns depended upon the limitation of competition, and the regulation of employment in the guilds was a necessary part of the political economy of the medieval town. The original intention was not to exploit the worker in the relationship between master, apprentice, and journeyman. The intention was to maximize the gains from trade to the town by limiting supply to the consumers outside the town walls.

Just as medieval society controlled the markets for commodities, they suppressed the development of a free labor market. The feudal serfs were not "free" to sell their labor services. Neither were the members of the medieval guilds free to buy and sell labor services. The apprenticeship system on which guild control of competition was based had as its primary purpose the limitation of output by the control of the number of workmen in a particular trade. By limitation on production the guilds could price their goods to yield a return which enabled the guild masters to maintain a certain standard of living in the community. If individual guild masters had not been limited as to the number of apprentices and journeymen they could employ, the profits of particular trades would have been lowered by increased outputs driving down prices.

The Logic of Preventing Bargaining. Not only was the apprenticeship system and prohibition of journeymen's guilds necessary to the control of production—it was also necessary to prevent labor from bargaining away part of the monopoly profits from the guild masters. The preservation of the idea of a corporate society in which men were compensated to enable them to maintain a certain status in the community rather than by a wage bargain pressed on both sides was equally part of the philosophy of the guild system. The idea that an employer should be able to hire as he pleased was as foreign to the conception of mutual dependence as the idea that a worker should be free to bargain individually or collectively over his wages.

Men were not free in medieval society to leave one job or locale for another without securing the permission of civil authorities. In sixteenth century England, rapid economic and social changes led to a great deal of disruption and displacement of labor. The Elizabethan "sturdy beggar" became an object of some social concern, and national policy was turned to the problem of controlling employment. The Statute of Artificers and Apprentices passed in 1563 codified a good deal of the old guild and feudal customs and regulations pertaining to the laboring population. The basis of the law was the statement of the universal obligation of men to be gainfully employed with the social obligation laid upon local governmental administration to see that they were.

All men not apprenticed were obliged to work in agriculture, and even those who were apprenticed were required to do agricultural labor at harvest time. Wages were to be fixed by the local Justices of the Peace in accordance with the cost of living. Employed persons were forbidden to leave the parish in which they were employed unless they could produce evidence from their employer that they had been released from their work.

Protection of the
Town Consumer

The regulation of commercial activity in the Middle Ages had both an internal and external dimension. The policies of the town's merchants in their dealings did not apply in their transactions with those inside the town community. Medieval regulations were designed to prevent the taking of advantage by one party to a transaction where both parties were a member of the same community. This was in contrast to relations with outsiders where taking advantage was not only permitted but encouraged and enforced because the interest of the entire town population lay in diverting as much trade as possible to the merchants of the town and securing the most favorable terms of trade.

The rather narrow view of dealings in trade with those outside the town contrasts markedly with the regulations on trade within the towns. In the first place, in dealing with the necessities—particularly food and fuel and clothing—there were elaborate provisions, practices, and customs to protect the townspeople. In part, these practices were necessary to survival. The towns could not afford to have a precarious supply of necessities which would make it vulnerable to political or military pressure.

Another primary purpose of the regulations was to improve the terms of trade on which the townspeople could obtain supplies from the surrounding countryside and to prevent any monopolistic or unfair practices which would have increased the cost of necessities. With a fairly inelastic demand for food and fuel, and a limited local area of supply, very small changes in supply could exert marked influence on prices. There were real opportunities to the town's suppliers to "hold them up to ransom," and it was of great importance to the towns to prevent this from happening.

The first step taken by the town authorities was the regularization of trade in commodities. Sales could only be made at specific times and specific places. This was an attempt to "deepen the market" and increase the number of alternatives open to buyers at any given time. Frequently, regulations were established to give the townspeople the first chance to buy. At the Smithfield Market outside London, the members of the London butchers guild were allowed to begin purchases at 8 A.M. and others were not allowed to make purchases until 10 A.M.[6]

The medieval prohibition on "forestalling," on going outside the town markets to buy up supplies before they were offered, was designed to prevent anyone from cornering the market in a particular commodity in order to raise prices to the townspeople. In Paris, as in other cities, local ordinances prevented anyone from going outside the city to meet a convoy coming with supplies to the market.

On the other hand, the towns sometimes collectively forestalled competition for supplies by making an offer before the goods were brought to the market. In Bristol, when a ship came to port, the merchants of the town would sometimes collude to decide what prices to offer for the cargo. At Liverpool, the mayor had the right to make the first offer for the purchase of imports before they were offered for sale in the town markets.[7]

The prohibition against "engrossing" was a device adopted by merchants to prevent any of their number from cornering the supply and becoming a wholesaler. This prohibition was usually applied to foodstuffs and fuel where the trade was carried on by petty retail merchants. It did not usually apply to the trade in the various staples or foreign goods where monopoly was desired to increase the revenues of the town at the expense of foreigners.

In a market, it is in the interest of the consumers to have accurate information as to the availability of goods and their quality. The prohibition against "regrating" was designed to prevent the increase in prices by spreading false rumors of scarcity.

Widespread attempts were made to standardize quality and prevent

[6]A. Pearce, *History of the Butchers' Company*, p. 43. Quoted in Maurice Dobb, *Studies in the Development of Capitalism* (London: Routledge & Kegan Paul Ltd., 1946), p. 94.

[7]E. Lipson, *Economic History of England*, Vol. I (London: A.&C. Black, Ltd., 1915), p. 245.

the sale of adulterated goods. The courts in medieval England fined bakers who sold inferior or short-weight loaves, butchers who sold rotten meat, and brewers who sold weak ale. The City of Paris forbade the adulteration of beer, the misrepresentation of wine, or the coloring of butter. In London, offending merchants were dragged through the streets with the substandard articles hung around their necks.[8]

The Just Price. In their trade with one another, the members of the community were under a moral obligation to sell goods at the "just price." The notion of a "just price" was understood in terms of a price which represented cost of production plus "normal" margin to sustain a customary standard of living for a merchant or craftsman. There was, however, no objection to increases in price which were caused by *natural* scarcity. Objection was made primarily to the use of monopoly power to raise prices over the "just price" which would have prevailed in perfectly competitive markets. The Church objected to exploitation in exchange transactions, coercion of the weak by the strong. Exploitation, for the medieval Churchmen, meant charging more than "the just price" by taking advantage of the market or structuring the market to make it possible.

St. Thomas Aquinas emphasized that the essence of a "just price" was that both parties to an exchange should benefit equally. Behind the subjective notion of "equal benefit" was the idea that taking advantage of the need of one's fellow man was immoral when the seller had a monopoly position in the supply of the thing needed by the buyer, which was frequently the case in the Middle Ages. The condemnation of usury sprang from this consideration. If a man had money which he had no "need" of himself, it was immoral for him to take advantage of another's "need" for the money to extract a payment for its use.

The same distinction was made in the regulation of money-lending between *Interesse* and usury. A man might demand and receive *Interesse* if by loaning money to another he lost the opportunity to make a profitable transaction. The word *Interesse* comes from the Latin *intereo* meaning "to be lost" and the payment of *Interesse* was sanctioned by the Church as just on the ground that a lender of money should not be deprived of a possible gain because he had helped a fellow man in need.[9]

The application of the term *usury* in the Middle Ages was not confined to loan transactions. *Usurer* was a term of abuse similar to *monopolist* in our own terminology. Just as we do not mean that the man designated by the term *monopolist* is the sole seller of a particular commodity

[8]H. Heaton, *Economic History of Europe* (New York: Harper & Row, Publ., 1936), pp. 194–95.

[9]Sidney Homer, *A History of Interest Rates* (New Brunswick: Rutgers University Press, 1963), chap. vi.

but rather a man who uses his market power to take advantage of his fellows, the Middle Ages understood *usurer* to refer to any man who took advantage of his fellow men by driving a bargain in which he took advantage of the weakness of the position of the other party to the transaction.[10]

Profits, themselves, were not regarded as evil. It was the way in which they were used which was good or evil. It was laudable to make money if the money were given to the Church or the poor but not if it were spent on self-indulgence.

The Disintegration of Social
Control of Markets

The medieval practices with regard to the control of markets were broken down by the growth of trade, which accompanied improvements in productivity in transportation, agriculture, and industrial production. Political unification of markets in Britain, France, and finally Italy and Germany broke down the localism of economic activity and with it the practical possibilities of collusion and control of markets. Conditions for the breakdown of the political privileges of the guilds came earliest in England for two reasons. First, the country had a centralized administration from 1066 on, and the power of particular towns over particular markets could only be enforced at the expense of other towns protected by the same political authority. At an early date the various English towns began to protest about royal policies which guaranteed other towns the control of trade to their disadvantage. Royal grants of monopoly in trade after the sixteenth century were exclusively for the prosecution of trade overseas. It was such charters for trade which led to the settlement of the North American colonies through such companies of merchants as the Virginia Company, Massachusetts Bay Company, and Hudson's Bay Company. We have already noted that attempts by the Crown to continue the regulation of American markets in the interest of some British mercantile interests was an important contribution to the American Revolution.

The old town guilds were empowered by Parliament to enforce the apprenticeship regulations which they, themselves, enacted. By the sixteenth century, however, the courts were not enforcing the power of the guilds on their members. Entrepreneurs who wished to escape the apprenticeship restrictions and limits on the number of journeymen they wanted to employ merely moved outside the towns. After the beginning of the seventeenth century the common law courts in England began

[10]R. H. Tawney, *Religion and the Rise of Capitalism* (New York: The New American Library, 1962), p. 157.

to refuse to enforce restrictive practices by the guilds. Just as in the case of the feudal landlords where the royal courts had taken the power of the manorial courts over the residents of the manors, the royal courts took over the judicial powers of the guild courts against guild members. This came in response to the conflict of interest between the subjects of the kingdom who objected to being exploited by guild monopolies. Further, the feeling was that the policies of the guilds promoted idleness and kept men from pursuing a trade and was, therefore, against the commonweal. By the eighteenth century the law was largely a dead letter from nonenforcement.

The last vestige of the medieval conception of community responsibility for the labor force was in agriculture where the so-called "Speenhamland system" continued until 1832. Under this system the wages of agricultural laborers were supplemented by their parishes to bring them up to the level considered necessary for subsistence. The system was widely attacked by the manufacturing interests in areas of labor shortages because they maintained that it prevented surplus labor in agriculture from moving into industrial employment.[11]

An Overview of Medieval
Economic Philosophy

A summation of the medieval philosophy of a corporate society in which the economic regulations of members of the society were closely regulated in line with social objectives is not easy. The moral basis of the philosophy was the acceptance of the notion that all men had a certain status in society which was foreordained by Divine Providence. A man's status carried with it certain obligations to one's fellow man. To seek to advance one's own interest at the expense of others was destructive of society.

The prevailing belief was that economic conditions were essentially static so that the only way in which one man could grow richer was through making other men poorer. The guild master who sought to increase employment and production was wicked because he deprived other members of society of gainful employment and prevented them from honoring the universal obligation to work.

In 1723, Mandeville summed up the medieval philosophy of market

[11]For a defense of the rationality of the system, see Marc Blaug, "The Myth of the Old Poor Law and the Making of the New," *Journal of Economic History*, Vol. XXIII (June 1963), pp. 151–84.

The supposed effects of the Speenhamland system are accorded great influence in nineteenth century opposition to social reform by Karl Polanyi in *The Great Transformation* (Boston: Beacon Press, 1957), chap. vii–x.

control in saying: "Private Vices by the dextrous Management of a skill-ful Politician may be turned into Public Benefits." Only a half century later, Adam Smith substituted a faith in the "Invisible Hand" for the "skillful politician" as the means by which private interest was controlled for the social good. The medieval philosophy of market control differed from the optimistic policies of social laissez faire not in a belief that there were natural forces directing economic activity but in the belief that the natural forces might be socially undesirable. The belief in a benevolent physiocracy governing economic activities was not an article of faith until it was propounded as an alternative by Adam Smith.

Bibliographic Note:

The works listed below provide a general treatment of material covered in this chapter.

Clapham, J. H., *A Concise Economic History of Britain from the Earliest Times to 1750* (Cambridge: Cambridge University Press, 1949), chaps. V, VIII, IX.

Lipson, E., *An Introduction to the Economic History of England*, Vol. I (London: A. & C. Black, Ltd., 1915), chaps. VI–X.

11

Soviet Economic Organization[1]

The range of freedom in economic matters open to the citizen of the Soviet Union is very circumscribed. With minor exceptions, collective ownership of the means of production means that the individual cannot bargain with other individuals over the sale of goods or services. In the small private sector which still exists in agriculture and the professions, one person cannot legally hire another to produce goods, nor can one legally purchase goods for resale.

Except for the small private sector, all decisions about prices, output, investment, and the distribution of personal income are made by the state. In the supposedly transitional phase of "dictatorship in the name of the proletariat" which precedes the achievement of the communist utopia, the income left for consumption after the allocation of a large proportion to capital formation, defense, and education is distributed "to each according to his labor."

Freedom to Work

Every member of Russian society has an obligation to work for society as a whole. In addition to the absence of property income which would provide an income in the absence of employment, the Soviet citizen is not legally free to leave employment for a period exceeding one month. The one month provision is a recent relaxation of control. Between 1940 and the repeal of the law in 1956, employees of all state enterprises were forbidden to leave their jobs without permission. Breaking this law (or even tardiness of more than twenty minutes) was a criminal offense which made the offender liable to forced labor. The law was repealed in 1956 because of its unpopularity and the difficulty of its enforcement. Peasants on the collective farms are still not free to leave them except under certain circumstances.

Control of Production

Industrial production in the Soviet Union is directed by the *Gosplan* —the State Planning Commission. The individual industrial plant is supervised in its day-to-day operations by a manager, but he has very little scope for discretionary action. He is obligated to produce in accordance with a plan which specifies his output (usually in terms of physical units), and allocates to his plant given quantities of raw materials, capital equipment, and a "wages fund," which is used to pay the employees of the enterprise in accordance with the wage scales established by the *Gosplan*.

Managers of the state enterprises are encouraged to fulfill (or exceed) the plan by monetary inducements in addition to the consequences for promotion or demotion. They, in turn, can offer bonuses to the plant's labor force for exceeding piece-work norms. Overfulfillment of the planned output by the plant may also result in collective benefits for the plant's labor force in terms of recreation facilities or housing.

Agricultural production is carried on by state farms which are run along the same lines as industrial enterprises and by collective farms which are producers' cooperatives. The latter are required to deliver to the planning authority specified quantities of agricultural output at prices considerably below those prevailing in the "free market" and below those offered by the state for above-plan deliveries. The members of the collective farms receive shares in the net proceeds from the farms' activities, but their main income derives from their sale of produce which they market from their own small plots of land. While these private plots account for only about 3 per cent of agricultural land, they are responsible for about one-third of total agricultural output.[2]

Labor unions exist in the Soviet Union, and membership by employees is almost universal since members receive advantages in the receipt of pensions and disability payments. While the unions are responsible for handling any grievances of individual members with management, little evidence exists that they show any proclivity to represent the interests

[1]This chapter is based largely on Alex Nove, *The Soviet Economy: An Introduction*, rev. ed. (New York: Frederick A. Praeger, Inc., 1966). Unless otherwise noted, statements of fact contained in this chapter are excerpted from this source.

[2]Gregory Grossman, *Economic Systems* (Englewood Cliffs, N.J.: Prentice-Hall, Inc., 1967), p. 80.

of their members. Most important, labor unions cannot bargain over wages or strike. They exist primarily as administrators of certain social welfare benefits and also act as an arm of the state in trying to secure increases in labor productivity.[3]

The Soviet government finances defense, capital investment, and all the other expenditures of the economy largely through revenues generated by its pricing policies. The most important single source of revenue is the "turnover tax" which is levied on a differential basis on all commodities produced by state enterprises. A second important source of revenue is the surplus realized in the compulsory purchases of agricultural commodities from the collective farms at very low prices. Income tax, which is levied at different rates on different occupational groups, is a small source of governmental revenue. This, of course, makes administrative sense. Why should the government, as employer, make a deduction from the incomes of its employees rather than just adjusting their net pay downward?

All exports and imports are handled by specialized corporations acting under directions from *Gosplan*. Those commodities are exported which are not required to fulfill the domestic part of the plan. They are very often exchanged on barter terms with other countries, and the imports received by the Soviet Union sometimes are not in any great need. The government attempts to use foreign trade for political purposes, and in its dealing with satellite countries, the Soviet Union has had considerable complaints of "exploiting" its trading partners by the terms of exchange which are set.[4]

The problems encountered by the Soviet Union in its attempts to operate an economic system in which there is little individual freedom to bargain or respond to shortages and surpluses have not been completely overcome. Any assessment of the material accomplishments of the system, however, must take into account the rapid economic growth which the nation has achieved since 1917 despite many formidable obstacles. In less than half a century, the Soviet Union has changed from a backward agricultural society with extremely low living standards for the mass of the peasantry to a modern, industrialized nation with nearly universal literacy and the potential, if not the realization, for a high mass-consumption society.[5]

[3]Gaston Rimlinger, "The Trade Union in Soviet Social Insurance: Historical Development and Present Functions," *Industrial and Labor Relations Review*, Vol. XIV, no. 3 (April 1961).

[4]For an assessment, see Horst Mendershausen, "The Terms of Soviet-satellite trade: a broadened analysis," *Review of Economics and Statistics*, May 1960, pp. 152–63.

[5]The definitive work on Soviet growth is Abram Bergson, *The Real National Income of the Soviet Union Since 1928* (Cambridge: Harvard University Press, 1961).

Income Distribution and

Incentives

The claim of a communist system is that it can solve the problem of distribution equitably while a capitalist system cannot. We have no way of checking on this claim as there are no published figures on income distribution in the Soviet Union. Considerable disparities in wages exist for different classes of labor, but, of course, the disparities introduced by incomes from capital, which are a major cause of inequality in capitalist countries, do not occur. The concealment of the figures and the frequent diatribes against "petty bourgeois" notions of equal incomes by party ideologues are suggestive evidence of substantial inequality and restiveness about it.[6]

The Soviet economy is most open to criticism in the provision of incentives and the rational allocation of scarce resources. The greatest failure of the economic planners has been in raising agricultural output sufficiently. Some have attributed Khrushchev's demise to the failure of his agricultural policies. The problem, however, has proved highly intractable ever since the Revolution. It was dealt with in the 1920s by the abandonment of agricultural collectivization and the substitution of the New Economic Policy (NEP), under which peasants were allowed to farm land for their own gain and to sell agricultural goods in free markets. This was stopped in 1929 as part of the first Five Year Plan, and the peasants were brutally collectivized by Stalin, partly for political and ideological reasons, and partly in an attempt to increase the amount of food which could be squeezed from the farm at lower prices. The logic of Soviet industrialization has always rested on the necessity of expropriating a surplus from agriculture which could be used for feeding an industrial labor force which was largely used for building capital goods.

The Russian planners have attempted to increase agricultural output by coercion rather than positive incentives. Forced deliveries to the state at low prices are the means of doing this. The state has been successful in expropriating part of the agricultural surplus from the peasants, but the concomitant result has been a stubborn refusal of the peasants to increase their net output very rapidly. The Soviet Union would have a very serious food problem if it were not for their reluctant continuance to permit the peasants their small private plots.[7]

Incentives and Responses. In industrial production, the incentives geared to plan fulfillment in terms of physical units rather than profitability have led to considerable anomalous behavior. Many incidents exist

[6]Nove, *op. cit.*, p. 127.
[7]*Ibid.*, pp. 187–95.

involving shoe factories producing only one (small) size of shoe because their quota was specified merely in terms of quantity, or of nail factories producing only huge nails when output was stated in tons and only small nails when it was stated in number. Emphasis on physical specification has left much to be desired in accommodation of production to users' needs, which is ironic considering Marx's criticism of capitalist production being for exchange rather than use.

Specification of output in value terms has escaped some of the problems of quantity specification but caused others, because the prices are fixed by the planners and may not reflect the relative importance of needs. The specification of output in gross value terms (rather than value added) leads to production of articles incorporating expensive raw materials and components produced by other state enterprises.

Alec Nove quotes an example of the conflicts involved in contradictory output goals for machinery supplying and using firms. An aircraft manufacturing enterprise was able to show considerable increases in productivity by making design changes which would decrease the carrying capacity of the aircraft by two kilograms. The production saving was estimated at 10,000 rubles per aircraft. The loss in carrying capacity to Aeroflot, the state airline, on the other hand was on the order of 400,000 rubles per year.[8]

Incentives and Innovation. Probably the most serious shortcoming of the Soviet incentive system is its effect on innovation. Since goals are established in terms of an existing production process, it is usually more advantageous for an enterprise to increase output with an existing system than to substitute a new and untried one for which new production goals will be established in any event. The "dynamic efficiency" of the Soviet economy does not compare well with the West. The spectacular gains which the Soviet Union has made in increasing per capita output have largely been the result of the very high rate of gross capital formation, and the shift of labor from primary industries (agriculture, forestry, and mining) to secondary industries (manufacturing).[9]

Planning and Resource

Allocation

The coordination of supply and demand accomplished by the price system in capitalist economies is dealt with by planners in the Soviet Union who set output goals for the entire economy and then allocate inputs to all the state enterprises. Soviet planning is done by a system

---

[8]*Ibid.*, pp. 179–80.
[9]Bela Belassa, "The Dynamic Efficiency of the Soviet Economy," *American Economic Review*, May 1964, pp. 490–502.

of "materials balances," in which input requirements of the various sectors and enterprises are set against the planned output. Shortages and surpluses are then adjusted to produce a balance. A great difficulty in the system is lack of a system of relative prices to reflect differential scarcity and the variations in the importance of the demands by state enterprises for inputs. For example, scarce copper might be allocated to one state enterprise which could, with little difficulty, use more plentiful aluminum, while it was denied to another state enterprise which, therefore, had to curtail its output. Partly for doctrinal reasons which specify that commodities should exchange in terms of their (labor) cost of production, and partly because higher prices for scarce goods exercise no rationing or incentive functions in a centrally planned system, the relative prices used by planners for accounting and control purposes do not reflect shortages and requirements very accurately. This leads to requests by plant managers and responses by planners which are frequently responsible for production falling below the attainable levels. This problem is partially being met by the introduction of linear programming and the derivation of "shadow prices," which are, in fact, the "alternative costs" of neo-classical economic theory.

Beginning in 1955 after Stalin's death, an era of critical examination of the organization of Soviet production began and was accompanied by debates among Soviet economists about what could be done to improve the performance of the system. Conspicuous among the "reformers" was Yevsei Liberman who advocated considerable decentralization of decision making to the managers of individual state enterprises and the evelution of performance in terms of "profits" rather than plan-fulfillment. His proposals, which were published in *Pravda,* advocated the partial retention of the "profits" made by individual plants for bonuses and other incentives.[10] He has, of course, been vigorously attacked by the "centralizers"—the planners, who saw in his proposals not only serious problems for their "materials-balance" approach but also a dangerous approach to doctrinal heresy.

All sorts of pragmatic objections can be raised to Liberman's proposals because of the nature of the relative prices which are set by *Gosplan.* A more fundamental change which would have to be made in the Soviet system before Liberman's proposals would be completely logical to adopt would be a system of prices which reflected relative scarcity. This has been advocated in several forms by such econometricians as Novozhilov and Kantorovich, but their proposals have been vigorously attacked by some of the party ideologists who fear that bourgeois economics is being brought in under the disguise of mathematics. On the other hand, as

[10]For a statement intended to explain to Western readers the differences between "profits" in a capitalist and communist system, see Yevsei Liberman, "The Soviet Economic Reform," *Foreign Affairs,* October 1967, pp. 53–63.

eminent an Academician as Strumilov has defended the need for recognizing the fact that scarcity is a problem which cannot be dealt with by assuming that declarations of its temporary character make temporary measures to deal with it unnecessary.[11]

The Reforms of 1965. In September 1965, sweeping reforms were made in the Soviet planning and administrative structure and practices.[12] Managers of state enterprises were given increased discretion in operation. Most important, sales was substituted for gross output as a measure of plan achievement. Some of Liberman's proposals for bonuses based on profits were adopted, and incentives were geared to *increases* in sales, profits, and the profit rate.

One of the most important theoretical changes was the adoption of a charge to state enterprises for the use of capital. Previously, the lack of a charge to state enterprises led to large requests for capital equipment and a great deal of misallocation of scarce capital between competing uses for which no way existed of assessing relative importance.

We do not yet know how the reforms announced in 1965 will affect the practices of Russian economic organization. It does appear that the system is moving toward a greater degree of freedom. The manager of one plant may now sue the manager of another for nonfulfillment of a contract which leads to the loss of bonuses. It is not very far from this to a recognition of the property claims created by contract between individuals and between individuals and the state. While Russian workers do not have freedom to bargain over wages, their freedom to change jobs has given them *de facto* power to bargain because their classification is subject to some discretion by the plant manager and those facing shortages of particular types of skilled workers find that they can attract and retain them only with higher classifications and bonuses. The necessity of providing incentives, on one hand, and the advantages of a more decentralized and realistic system of allocation and control, on the other, are forcing the masters of the communist state to give some freedom and property to their subjects.

Common Characteristics of

Corporate Societies

One is tempted to draw analogies between Soviet and medieval European society even though there are such contrasts in technology and ideology between them. Their common conception of the corporate character of human society and the immoral and destructive character of the

[11]For a discussion of the debate and an attempt to interpret the issues, see Nove, *op. cit.*, pp. 286–303.
[12]*Ibid.*, pp. 331–35. See also, Liberman, *op. cit.*, pp. 55–57.

ethic of self-interest embodied in economic freedom and private property make their responses similar in many respects.

Ideology. First, we should note that both societies are based on the pursuit of a transcendental ideal only imperfectly realized in this world. For medieval society, the idea of a Christian brotherhood united by a common faith and subject to a divinely sanctioned earthly authority justified the submergence of the individual to the interests of the group. The rewards of faith and obedience were to be realized in the next world. The communist dictatorship of the proletariat is enforced in order to bring about a classless society in which there is peace and harmony.

Both societies are subject to great emphasis on ideology. Both emphasize the interpretation of the true doctrine revealed in the "scriptures," and both fear that heresy will be committed in an attempt to accommodate doctrines to the problems of the day or to justify the pursuit of self-interest. The interpretation of the Marxist-Leninist writings and their tortured accommodation to the problems of the day would have done justice to any of the Medieval Schoolmen!

The Obligation to Work. In both societies, the obligation of all men to work for society is affirmed and enforced by law. In both societies, the right of labor to bargain collectively over wages is denied on the moral grounds that this would allow selfish individuals to increase their own income at the expense of society and on the practical grounds that it would allow the mass of the population to bargain away part of the social product which the rulers wished to use for collective expenditure on defense and culture, capital formation, and their own consumption.

Property rights are not acknowledged in either society in land, in physical assets other than personal possessions, and, of course, in a man's own labor. Land can theoretically not be alienated into private use because it is a collective possession for the use of society as its rulers see fit. As the value of productive assets in medieval society depended upon the town's control of markets, the physical plant of Soviet society has been created by the labor of past and present generations of workers and belongs to them collectively. The managers of the plants are merely the agents of society, just as the guild masters were.

The Soviet collective farm bears striking resemblance to the medieval manor. In some respects this can be explained by historical continuity. The disestablishment of feudalism in Russia in 1860 did not really end the system in practice, and at the time of the Russian Revolution, agricultural village organizations, the *mir*, were translated into the collective farm. The peasants are still required to work on the land of the estate, and they are bound to it by law. They deliver a specified quantity of agricultural output to the agricultural ministry rather than the feudal lord and divide up what is left. They have small plots of land which they are allowed to cultivate for their own use.

Market Controls. In their control of prices, the Soviet authorities have their counterpart of the medieval concept of "the just price" in their attempt to make relative prices reflect "socially necessary labor." Their prohibition of free exchange embodies their abhorrence of any one individual exploiting his communist brother by charging him a price in excess of socially necessary labor. Hiring another person to produce goods would have to be exploitatory or otherwise there would be no incentive in doing so. Of course, the state can realize a surplus in production and exchange because this is used for expenditure in the interests of society collectively. The medieval justification of the control of trade to exploit foreigners, of course, had the same rationale and justification.

The Medieval Schoolmen dealt with the taking of interest on money by saying it was permissible if it resulted in a loss for the owner who was unable to take advantage of favorable commercial conditions because he had loaned it to someone else. The *Gosplan* has found it necessary to introduce an interest charge to state enterprises for the use of capital to avoid the losses which would be suffered by some firms from not having capital because other firms are using the scarce article.

In both societies, a surplus to finance collective expenditures is raised through control of the prices of inputs and the sale of outputs rather than taxes. Medieval trade monopolies were designed to maintain the town establishment by controlling competition to prevent suppliers from being paid the value of their marginal product and to prevent customers from obtaining goods at prices which represented their marginal costs. In Russia, the workers and consumers, who are the members of the society enforcing the trade regulation, are systematically "exploited" by the state's monopoly of all economic activity.

If Soviet citizens are gaining more freedom, it is because the rulers of Soviet society are finding that their subjects are no longer satisfied with promises of "pie in the sky" when they know that the system is capable of providing them with more consumption goods. The subjects are bargaining for more and getting it in return for increased output. State control of production is being relaxed in order to stimulate technological innovation. The inability of medieval society to control technological innovation by the guild members led to the breakdown of the guild system. Peasants in both systems purchase property rights in the land they till and pay for them out of the increased output which they then have the incentive to produce.

The Lack of Alternatives for the Soviet Citizen. One major difference between medieval society and modern Russia which may frustrate the growth of individualist institutions is political. Russia is, to a much greater extent, a closed society in which political power is much more closely held. The medieval serf could escape from one manor to another region, and the ambitious guild craftsmen could move outside the town walls and set up a more modern manufactory to compete against the old guild. Russia is a unified state with controlled borders. The Russian citizen has no alternative use for his labor or any savings he might accumulate other than to sell them to the state on the prices which it determines. Russian rulers have to cope with the problems of incentives and the allocation of scarce resources. They do not have to brook competition with private power in their internal organization. The freedom which would be forced on the state by the existence of alternatives is precluded by the limitation of any alternatives. It is the existence of alternatives which enables the individual to escape the yoke of social control. This led, eventually, to the more individualistic society which developed in Europe at the close of the Middle Ages.

Corporate Societies:

Theory and Practice

The last two chapters have not aimed to give a comprehensive exposition of the theory and practice of corporate societies in their control of markets but rather to suggest some of the basic presuppositions which underlie the attempts at social control. The basic presupposition of a corporate society is that the individual should *not* be free to strike exchange bargains with other members of society. A man is *not* held to have the exclusive property in his own labor and not allowed to establish property in streams of income from the control of production. The defenders of a corporate conception of society have always contended that freedom of the individual from social control was a masque for privilege. One could ask, on the other hand, whether the assertion of social control of markets by political authority was not a bare-handed attempt to create privilege for the few in the guise of protection for all.

The defenders of the feudal order claimed moral superiority for an economic system which emphasized mutual obligation rather than the reduction of all human relationships to the cash nexus of an exchange transaction. In theory the patriarchal conception of human society was idyllic, but in practice it was a society in which human relationships were enforced by physical violence. In theory, the Marxian vision of a society in which all men are equals and in which distribution of the riches of cooperative effort are shared according to need sounds superior to a free market society in which men are equals only in their lack of social protection and given free reign to exploit one another in exchange. In practice, however, dictatorship in the name of the proletariat bears a close relationship to the tyranny of the oriental despots who rule in theory by divine right but in practice by physical violence and brutal suppression.

12

The Control

of

Monopoly

The discussion of the changing character of property rights in earlier chapters has attempted to show how the rights and privileges attached by society to the use of assets have changed in response to social needs and values. Even in a society which has extensive "private" property, controls are placed on the use of assets. Private enterprise is not "free" enterprise in the sense that the state will sanction *any* contractual arrangements voluntarily arrived at by individual members of the society.

The preceding two chapters have discussed the controls placed on the operations of markets by two societies which were described as "corporate." In both, markets were carefully controlled by the state on the assumption that uncontrolled private enterprise would produce socially undesirable results. American society, on the other hand, has been premised on the belief that a large degree of individual economic freedom was desirable and that it could be made to produce socially acceptable results. The necessity of political action to make markets work in a socially acceptable manner has meant continued redefinition of the scope of private enterprise to preserve competition and prevent the growth of private power unchecked by competition.

The Roots of
Anti-Monopoly Policies

In Chapter 9, we pointed out that while a society always realized a gain from exchange, its gains were maximized when competition forced the suppliers of goods to sell them at the lowest price acceptable to the supplier. An even stronger objection traditionally raised against monopoly has been the deprivation of employment of men and capital occasioned by monopoly control of markets.[1] The objections of competitors eliminated by a monopolist are much stronger than those of consumers since the losses are so much more important to the individuals concerned. The political pressure of producers rather than that of consumers was important in the passing of the Sherman and Clayton anti-trust legislation in the United States. The pressure of small retailers led to the "fair trade" provisions of the Robinson-Patman Act of 1935. Nevertheless, the existence of monopoly or tendencies toward it have traditionally been represented to the public as a danger to be controlled on the grounds that it was against "the public interest" to have any suppression of competition.

Common Law Conspiracy Doctrines. The historical roots of the American policy on monopolies are to be found in the decisions of the common law courts and in Parliamentary acts in England in the early seventeenth century. It will be helpful to mention these laws and decisions as they help to explain the origins of some of the difficult questions of public policy in contemporary anti-trust legislation.

As discussed in Chapter 10, medieval trade regulations on external trade created, sanctioned, and enforced monopolies to allow the gains from monopoly to be enjoyed by the medieval town at the expense of those outside the town community. National political integration made continued political support of monopoly more difficult because it placed the rulers in the position of allowing one group of their subjects to gain at the expense of another group.

Political unification in England was complete by the end of the sixteenth century, and the attempts by the Stuart monarchy in the early seventeenth century to finance their activities by the sale of monopoly charters in order to avoid calling Parliament came into vigorous opposition from both Parliament and the common law courts.

In the famous Case of Monopolies in 1602, a monopoly in the manufacture of playing cards which had been granted by the monarch was held invalid by the courts on the grounds that it was against the *public* interest. It was held to be against the "Commonwealth" on the grounds that it deprived men of work and led to higher prices and poorer quality goods for the public. In 1624, Parliament passed the Statute of Monopolies which invalidated all grants of monopoly by the Crown except those patents granted for inventions.

In the internal regulation of trade, medieval prohibitions on forestall-

---

[1]In 1602, the English Lord Chief Justice Popham noted that monopoly promoted unemployment and the impoverishment of workers. *Darcy* v. *Allein*, Trin. 44 Eliz. (1602) quoted in Commons, *Legal Foundations of Capitalism, op. cit.*, p. 227.

ing, engrossing, and regrating were designed to improve the operation of markets and protect the town's consumers by preventing monopoly. These were carried forward by the courts in a particular way. Parties who attempted to monopolize trade were not prosecuted for the monopolization itself, but for *conspiracy* against the public interest. It was held that monopoly was impossible to maintain in the absence of a conspiracy or a legally sanctioned monopoly because of the impossibility of controlling competition. Therefore, the courts not only refused to enforce contracts which attempted to control the output and price of articles by producers but made the existence of such contracts evidence of a criminal conspiracy against those excluded from the trade and the public generally. The courts did not examine competitive behavior or market structure in the prosecution of monopoly—only intent which was evidenced by conspiratorial activity.

The Sherman Anti-trust Act. In the United States, Federal legislation to control monopoly was first introduced by the Sherman Anti-trust Act of 1890, which did nothing more than reiterate the common law doctrine on conspiracy and monopoly. The Act affirmed:

> Every contract, combination in the form of trust or otherwise, or conspiracy in restraint of trade or commerce among the several States or with foreign nations is hereby declared to be illegal. . . . Every person who shall monopolize or attempt to monopolize or combine or conspire with any other person or persons to monopolize any part of the trade or commerce among the several States or with foreign nations, shall be deemed guilty of a misdemeanor, and, on conviction thereof, shall be punished by fine not exceeding $50,000, or by imprisonment not exceeding one year, or by both said punishments in the discretion of the court.

The Sherman Act equated monopoly and conspiracy in the manner of the common law. Section 1 of the Act condemns any conspiracy in restraint of trade, and Section 2 includes under the coverage of the Act anyone who monopolizes or attempts to monopolize. In the adjudication of the Act the Supreme Court has, by and large, refused conviction based solely on the evidence of monopoly. This is partially explainable by the difficulties of definition and evidence regarding monopoly, but it also reflects the Court's attempt to enforce the intention of the Congress in passing the Act.[2]

The Sherman Act was passed during a period of marked economic and social change in the United States. The rapid pace of industrialization and technological change coupled with the penetration of competitive forces into formerly local markets brought bankruptcy to many

[2]For an interesting (now somewhat dated) examination of anti-trust policy in the United States, see Edwin S. Mason, "Monopoly in Law and Economics," *Yale Law Review*, Vol. 47, no. 1 (Nov. 1937).

firms. Most of the elimination of smaller firms was a part of the necessary process of economic growth. The inefficient were driven out of business by the lower costs of the efficient firms who had adopted modern technology. However, some firms were driven out of business by price warfare in particular markets, railroad rebates, and exclusive agreements "tying" particular suppliers and customers in order to drive competitors out of business. Thus, much of the agitation for control of "the trusts" came from small businessmen who feared the licit and illicit competition of big firms.

A second source of agitation for the bill came from the public at large which blamed "the trusts" for all economic ills. The farmers in particular thought that suppliers of manufactured goods were conspiring to keep prices up while their own prices were driven down by a conspiracy of railroads, elevator operators, and grain speculators. In retrospect it appears that they based their argument on false evidence, for in ·the period of general price decline between 1875 and 1895 the prices of farm products fell less than the prices of manufactured products. Nevertheless, the farmers undoubtedly had some legitimate grievances.

In any event a great deal of evidence exists from the Congressional debates and other sources that the law which was passed was never intended by its supporters to be effective in checking size *qua*-size. The Act has, in fact, been called "the mother of trusts" because by making agreements between firms over prices and markets illegal, it stimulated overt combination by merger of firms which had formerly cooperated. This was remedied by the "anti-merger" provisions of the 1913 Clayton Act.

The framers of the Sherman Act did not mean the same thing by "monopoly" as do economists. They meant unfair competitive practices rather than control of markets through technical superiority. When one of the sponsors of the Sherman Act, Senator Hoar, was asked whether a firm would be considered a monopoly if it dominated a trade through superior skill, he replied: "The word 'monopoly' is merely a technical term which has a clear and legal significance, and it is this: it is the sole engrossing to a man's self by means which prevent other men from engaging in fair competition with him."[3]

Ambiguities of Anti-trust Legislation. Senator Hoar, notwithstanding, monopoly means different things to different people, and this has bedeviled enforcement of anti-trust legislation. In strict economic terms monopoly means the existence of only one seller in the market. In practical discourse, however, economists frequently speak of the monopoly power of firms who do have competitors, especially if tacit or explicit

[3]*Congressional Record*, 21 (1890) 3152.

cooperation exists between the firms in marketing policies. Various performance tests have been proposed to identify the extent of monopoly power; they include percentage of the market controlled by one or a few firms, the ratio of price minus marginal cost to price, and rate of return on capital. None of these is completely satisfactory in theory, and the measurement problem leaves much to be desired in practice. To the author's knowledge neither of the last two have been used in legal proceedings. The first, share of the market, was used to convict the Aluminum Company of America of monopoly in 1946 and in the Brown Shoe Company case in 1962 but was severely criticized in both cases because of the way in which it was applied. In the Alcoa case the relevant market was taken to be primary ingots of aluminum. The fact that aluminum ingots compete with scrap aluminum and other metals in their various industrial uses was not accepted by the Court as evidence that Alcoa had serious checks on its monopoly power. On the other hand, Alcoa was not broken up, and with a few notable exceptions large American corporations which have grown through efficient management and the reinvestment of profits have not been broken up by the Courts.[4] The Brown Shoe Company case was, in many respects, even more arbitrary and a merger was forbidden by the Court's decision.

The legal concept of monopoly, as Senator Hoar correctly emphasized, does not focus on market power but on restrictive agreements or conspiratorial agreements not to compete. The tradition of the common law against monopolies found its origins in opposition to the grants of exclusive privilege by the sovereign. These were struck down by nonenforcement by the common law courts in the seventeenth century on the grounds that they were against the commonweal. This began the tradition of considering restrictions on trade to see if they were or were not "in the public interest." This culminated in the United States in the "rule of reason" doctrine enunciated in anti-trust cases in the United States from the turn of the century up until the end of the Second World War when it was rejected in the Alcoa case.

No definitional problem exists with conspiracy. The meaning of "conspiracy" is very straightforward. The Justice Department's Anti-Trust Division has little difficulty in obtaining a conviction if the charge can be proved. It is very difficult, however, to obtain evidence which will stand up in court. The parties to a conspiracy, obviously, are not going to incriminate themselves, and it is practically impossible to obtain other witnesses to conspiratorial action which can be elaborately concealed. The convictions of executives and companies in the electrical equipment

[4]For a discussion of the criteria of monopoly used in anti-trust proceedings in recent years, see Edwin S. Mason, "The Current Status of the Monopoly Problem in the United States," *Harvard Law Review*, Vol. LXII, no. 8 (June 1949).

industries in 1962 was a masterpiece of sleuthing unparalleled in the annals of the Anti-Trust Division of the Justice Department.

The principles on which the courts would presently base a decision are difficult to guess, and uncertainty, itself, has imposed a powerful check on the actions of large firms who fear indictment. There are two reasonable grounds on which to base social policies against monopoly and restrictive practices. One is political—the desirability of keeping economic power widely dispersed to prevent the monopoly of political power by large economic interests. The second is the protection of the consumer from exploitation by monopoly power. The argument against "unfair" competition is really a derivative argument from the first two. There is no rationale in preserving a less efficient economic unit for its own sake. It may be done to preserve a wider distribution of economic power for political reasons, or it may be done to prevent a less efficient firm with greater financial resources from driving a more efficient firm out of business by various forms of coercion in order subsequently to monopolize and exploit the consumer.

The economic philosophy which lies behind the Sherman Act, the Clayton Act, and the Robinson-Patman Act is the same. The consumer can only be protected from exploitation by the presence of competition in the markets in which he buys his goods. If competition destroys competitors, the consumer will ultimately be exploited—therefore, competition must be controlled to prevent "unfair" competition from reducing the number of competitors. Monopoly is condemned *per se* because even in the absence of exploitation of the consumer, the monopolist has the *power* to exploit. Collusion is bad *per se* because it can have the intent only of exploiting the public by preventing competition. Evidence of either monopoly or collusion is, therefore, sufficient to prove the offenders guilty of action contrary to public interest.

The Inadequacy of Old Ideas
About Monopoly

The difficulty with the common law notion of conspiracy and monopoly is that the two are not synonymous in our society. A firm or group of firms can monopolize the production and distribution of a particular good without any exclusive grant or restrictive covenant. A firm or group of firms can establish a *de facto* monopoly by achieving a scale of production and distribution which permits lower per unit costs than any competitive firm could hope to match without the same scale of operation. If a firm's long-run average costs of production reaches a minimum only with an output which takes the largest part of the market, no possibility of perfect competition exists. Common law ideas were evolved when scale economies were not present in the handicraft production which characterized most trades prior to the industrial revolution. Then monopolies were only possible by conspiracy. The existence of a monopoly was evidence *per se* of conspiracy. This is no longer true in the modern world.

Monopoly power in most cases in the modern United States does not depend upon conspiratorial collusion—it depends upon patents, technological superiority, economies of scale, and the barriers to entry caused by public acceptance of certain branded products. This is not to deny that the anti-trust laws have been effective in curbing some of the worst types of collusive agreements. Agreements to restrict production and raise prices among individual firms are not enforced by courts as they can be in some European countries. In fact, a company which sought the performance of a restrictive covenant or damages for its nonfulfillment in American courts would not only be denied satisfaction—it would be prosecuted for conspiracy on the evidence of the contract which it sought to have enforced. This has helped to preserve competition by making secret agreements unstable. The Sherman Act went no further than to affirm the common law on this account, however, and no evidence exists of any courts sanctioning conspiratorial contracts prior to 1890.

The economic arguments for social control of monopoly deserve a great deal more scrutiny. Economic theory takes as axiomatic that the "firm" will maximize its present value by price and output policies. In a situation in which the firm has control over a market, the firm will restrict output and price it above marginal cost of production. Thus, the consumer is "exploited" by being forced to pay a higher price than would obtain under perfect competition. The allocation of resources is suboptimal because price—the social valuation of a commodity in consumption—is not equal to marginal cost—the social valuation of scarce resources in use.

The traditional arguments against monopoly depend upon the firm's maximizing policies leading to restriction of output with consequent increase in price, and their lack of stimulus to be efficient and to innovate because of the lack of competitive pressure. Both of these arguments are extremely difficult to evaluate empirically. Several authors have shown that the misallocation of resources which could be inferred from the pricing policies of monopolistic industries in the United States is extremely small—less than a fraction of 1 per cent of Gross National Product.[5]

[5]For a discussion, see G. C. Bjork, "Sin and Size: An empirical estimate of income loss and redistribution by the 500 largest U.S. industrial firms," A. C. Harberger, "Monopoly and Resource Allocation," *American Economic Review*, May 1954; and Harvey Leibenstein, "Allocative Efficiency v. X-Efficiency," *American Economic Review*, June 1966.

The difficulty with this type of evaluation of the extent of monopoly power is that it assumes that monopoly power can be measured by the rate of return on capital. Misallocation of resources is measured by asking how much increase in output in monopolistic industries and how much decrease in output in other industries would be necessary to equalize the rate of return on capital. The possibility of the gains from monopoly being annexed by aggressive bargaining by unions, being shared by management in large salaries, bonuses, stock options, and expense accounts, and being invested in large advertising and sales expenditures to maintain monopoly cannot be taken into account by this method of measurement. Yet, one needs only to look at the disparity in earnings between executives and wage labor in such monopolistic industries as automobiles, electrical equipment, and petroleum and in such competitive industries as agriculture, retail trade, and textiles to realize that part of the gains of monopoly are being realized by the employees of monopolistic industries.

As was pointed out in Chapter 9, with imperfect product markets and imperfect factor markets part of the gains from monopoly could be bargained away from the monopolist. This not only alters the relative prices of goods, but it changes the distribution of income. As discussed in Chapter 10, the medieval towns had to forbid labor unions in order to prevent the journeymen from bargaining away part of the monopoly gains created by the town's regulation of markets. Unions, similarly, are prevented from bargaining about wages in the Soviet Union. This problem will be discussed more fully in the following chapter as the legalization of collusive action by workers in labor unions in the United States poses some extremely thorny problems for public policy.

Monopoly and
Dynamic Efficiency

A second ground on which the assumption that monopoly is against the public interest may be questioned is on the dynamic effect of monopoly on cost and efficiency. The statement cannot be made that over the course of time a perfectly competitive industry would lower the cost of production and price of goods more than a monopolistic industry. The proponents of perfect competition and vigorous anti-trust enforcement point out that the monopoly firm is secure in its hold on the market and does not need to innovate and cut costs as much as does the firm in the perfectly competitive market. On the other hand, the supporters of monopoly argue that the incentive of greater profits is still there and the returns on innovation are potentially much greater since they cannot be dissipated by competition. Further, the monopolistic firm is always open to the challenge of new technology and the loss of its monopoly position. Finally, it has access to capital on cheaper terms from internal sources than would firms who would have to float issues in the market which might make risky innovation easier.

Assessing the claims for monopoly on dynamic grounds is difficult. Aggregate rates of economic growth to the United States over different periods of time in which the economy might have been deemed "more monopolistic" or "more competitive" are impossible. The growth rates of particular industries characterized by different degrees of concentration are inconclusive because of the myriad factors which influence the measured rate of growth in productivity.

A firm with monopoly power does, however, have more incentive to undertake research on process inventions in the field in which the monopoly power is wielded. This is true because of the defensive strategy of not allowing a potential competitor to get a technological edge. Not all knowledge and technical improvement can be effectively patented, and the holder of a monopoly power in a particular market can better assure that the benefits to him of an invention will exceed the costs of invention than can the developer of a new process in a competitive industry. Nevertheless, no conclusive empirical evidence exists to support the superiority of monopolistic firms in invention and innovation. A contrast of the innovative behavior of large and small firms in industries characterized by different degrees of monopoly power by one author led to rather inconclusive results.[6]

Monopoly Structure and

Firm Behavior

A possible explanation of the failure of firms to behave like monopolists, even when they have extensive market power, may be found in their management. The traditional economic model of maximization of present value by the firm assumes that the financial interests of the management of the firm are co-incident with the owners of the firm. Many observers of the modern corporation have pointed out the divorce between ownership and control.[7] Possibly a policy of short-run profit maximization by a corporate executive might maximize the value of the stockholders' equity

[6]Edward Mansfield, "Size of Firm, Market Structure, and Innovation," *Journal of Political Economy*, Vol. 71, No. 6, December 1963, pp. 556–76.

[7]The classic book on the subject is A. A. Berle and G. C. Means, *The Modern Corporation and Private Property* (New York: The Macmillan Company, 1932). A more recent restatement is A. A. Berle, *Power without Property* (New York: Harcourt, Brace & World, Inc., 1959).

but, at the same time, lead to a smaller present value for his expected stream of earnings because the employment market for corporate managers puts a higher premium on rate of growth of sales, technological progressiveness, or other factors than simple return on capital.[8]

Suppose, for purposes of argument, that the present value of the shares of stock in a corporation would be maximized by a policy of output restriction and price control to yield a high rate of profit on stockholders' equity. Suppose, on the other hand, that the salary of the corporate executive who heads up the company or one of its divisions depends upon the market for executives and that in that market, executive compensation is based more on the size of operations or the rate of growth of operations controlled by the executive than on the rate of return on capital he is able to secure for the shareholders of the corporation. Under these circumstances, the corporate executive would be likely to implement price and output policies designed to produce more goods at a lower price than would result in profit maximization.

Of course, there is a restraint to the size maximization policies of the executive. The pursuit of simple size maximization would bankrupt the corporation, but before that happened, stockholders would grow restless with the fall in the value of their shares and might attempt to turn out the management regime. The equities market would not furnish any capital for expansion on favorable terms because of the fall in value of the company's shares, and it could not be internally financed because of the shortage of profits resulting from sales expansion at the expense of profitability. The first effective check on sales maximization will be the necessity of earning what "the market" considers to be an acceptable rate of return on equity shares of the corporation in question. The difference between profit maximization and sales maximization subject to a market-imposed lower limit on profitability is illustrated in Fig. 12–1.

Total revenue, total cost, and total profit are measured on the vertical axis as a function of output. The total cost function shows the presence of substantial fixed costs with variable costs, which increase slowly at first and then begin to increase at an increasing rate as the firm incurs higher sales and distribution costs and even higher production costs as bottlenecks are encountered in production. The total revenue function

---

[8]The "sales-maximization" hypothesis was first advanced by William J. Baumol, *Business Behavior, Value, and Growth* (New York: The Macmillan Company, 1959).

The underlying hypothesis that executive compensation was based on sales rather than profitability (rate of return on capital) was tested with moderate success in A. O. Elbing, J. W. McGuire, and J. S. Y. Chin, "Executive Incomes, Sales, and Profits," *American Economic Review*, Vol. LII, no. 31 (Sept. 1962), pp. 753–61. A more recent elaboration of the argument has been made in A. Downs and R. J. Monsen, Jr., "A Theory of Large Managerial Firms," *Journal of Political Economy*, Vol. LXXIII, no. 3 (June 1965), pp. 221–36.

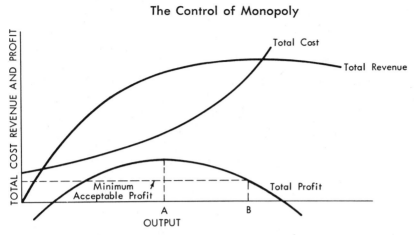

Figure 12-1:
Sales maximization vs. profit maximization.

reflects the combined influence of increasing output and decreasing per unit price as the firm is forced to set lower and lower prices to sell a larger volume of output. The profit function is the difference between the revenue and cost functions.

Sales maximization is obviously unfeasible since it would involve the firm in infinite losses. The classical model of profit maximization would derive an equilibrium output at A where profits are at a maximum. Sales maximization subject to a profitability restraint would result in the expansion of output to B. At output B, the firm would be earning that rate of return on its capital which the market considered "acceptable" for a firm of its risk potential.

This "acceptable rate of return" is, of course, as difficult to identify in practice as are other economic entities. The executive, however, does have a "gut" feeling about what it is. If he falls below it, the market will depreciate the value of the firm's shares. If he earns more, the market value of the stocks will rise.

Management Behavior and Sales Maximization. Now one might ask: "Will not the corporate executive continually err toward profit maximization as this will drive the price of the stocks up and make the shareholders happy? Given the likelihood of stock options, will this not be in his own best interest?" These are both very good short-run arguments. The question is what will happen if profits are driven up in one year or for a couple of years? Then the market value of the stock will appreciate to take account of present and expected profitability, and any decline in profitability or even a slowdown in the rate of growth of profitability will cause the stocks to fall (absolutely or relatively) in market price with resulting capital losses and dissatisfaction. Under these conditions one could argue that security is the best policy for the corporate executive. This is especially so if output restriction and the exercise of monopoly power are likely to expose the firm to public criticism, union demands for a share in the profits, and/or investigation by the anti-trusters.

If the price and output policies of the corporation with monopoly powers tend toward sales maximization subject to a market restraint rather than pure profit maximization, the result will be to move price and output decisions toward the perfectly competitive result since the "acceptable" market rate of return will be the market rate of return on capital of the perfectly competitive model of resource allocation.

The crucial assumption in the analysis is the behavior of the corporate manager. If his income is determined by the alternatives open to him in the market for corporate executives, and if these tend to be correlated with size and growth rate rather than profitability, then economic rationality and maximization of present value will determine the outcome sketched above. We have not even considered alternative goals of security, altruistic public service, or power which would also militate toward the behavior indicated rather than the behavior of the traditional monopolist.

The shareholder in this situation is not coerced by the corporate executive. He is coerced by competitive markets for capital. The corporate executive is really taking into account the cost of capital. He is seeing that the shareholder receives the competitive rate but no more. The stockholder is coerced only in the sense that the capital market is used to force him to accept a normal rate of return rather than the amount which the corporation could afford to pay.

The shareholder can always sell his stocks and invest in another company if he does not like the policies or dividends of the company in which he holds stock. In the last analysis, he can vote out the regime and hire managers who will maximize profits, but to do this he may find that the higher salaries necessary to get executives to do as he wishes will consume the higher dividends he hoped to obtain. In the last analysis, the typical modern shareholder is *not* an entrepreneur entitled to the profits of superior management and wisdom—he is a rentier receiving interest on his capital reflecting the market rate of return plus a risk differential.

A second interpretation of competitive behavior of firms with market power is that they do not use it because they are afraid that if they do they will lose it. This argument means, in fact, that the existence of long-term monopolistic behavior is ruled to be an impossibility because of potential competition. The consumer is always protected from exploitation by *potential* alternatives.

The Control of Monopoly

Monopoly and "Countervailing Power." John Galbraith[9] has advanced an interesting thesis in *American Capitalism* about the control of monopoly power in our society. He postulates that the existence of any power center will call forth a countervailing power. On the one hand, the growth of large corporations brings about the rise of strong labor unions, and, on the other hand, the growth of large customers with monopsonistic power to counter the monopoly power of the producer. He adduces as evidence the large automobile companies with which the steel companies must deal and large retailers such as A & P and Sears Roebuck to counter the power of General Foods and General Electric. This is a very intriguing thesis. Unfortunately, the way in which monopsonistic buyers are compelled to pass on the benefits of their bargainng power to the ultimate consumers is not included in the theory. There are no large consumer cooperatives to force concessions from the monopsonists. The power of the automobile companies and the chain stores is not counterbalanced by their customers but by their competitors.

Unfortunately, some "countervailing power" is checked by the Robinson-Patman Act which provides, on the one hand, for the maintenance of "fair trade" prices and, on the other hand, prevents price discrimination by sellers to large buyers except in those situations where equivalent cost reduction can be demonstrated. This protects, at the same time, the monopolistic manufacturer and the inefficient retailer by protecting unit profit margins. It robs the ultimate customer from the cost reductions which could take place from the expansion of production and economies of scale in distribution. It ultimately protects the return on capital only of the monopolistic manufacturer.

Monopoly Behavior and Economic Rationality. The provisions of the Robinson-Patman Act, like many other attempts at social control of monopoly are based on economic reasoning of limited application. Accepting for the present the axiom of maximization of present value by the firm, under what conditions would a maximizing firm find it rational to drive out competitors by selling at less than cost and sustaining losses? Only in a situation in which the present value of the losses incurred is less than the present value of the monopoly profits which would accrue in the future from driving competitors out of business. Unless a would-be monopolist can control entry to his industry by a political exclusion of competitors, a limit on future profits posed by the threat of entry of competitors always exists. In addition, the present value of future profits is considerably lessened if they are discounted at the 5–15 per cent rates of interest which are used by entre-

[9]John K. Galbraith, *American Capitalism* (New York: Houghton Mifflin Company, 1957).

preneurs in their calculation of investment decisions. Under most conditions, the losses sustained in eliminating a competitor would be a very poor investment for the firm attempting to maximize present value.

The primary type of "unfair competition" singled out in the Clayton and Robinson-Patman Acts was the granting of discounts to large purchasers and of discriminatory prices to drive out competitors in particular geographic areas. Admitting that these practices exist and that they are liable to drive smaller retailers and wholesale merchants out of business, it is difficult to see that they are against the public interest if they result in lower retail prices through the reduction of trade margins. Rational sales policies by manufacturers and large trading organizations would *not* lead them to incur short-term losses in the usual instance for purpose of gaining a monopoly. If scale economies are to be enjoyed in distribution, then it is in the public interest to realize them. Arguments may exist for preserving small merchants by frustrating economies of scale, but they are not economic.

The Contemporary Relevance of
Anti-Trust Policy

The protection of the consumer from exploitation in modern American capitalism rests on the philosophy of promoting competition amongst his suppliers. He is well protected from restrictive agreements and collusive practices by the Sherman Act. On the other hand, the long-run interests of the consumer in a high rate of growth in productivity *may* be better advanced by monopolistic market structures as long as the market power is not exercised for short-run output restriction. This has been implicitly recognized in the enforcement of the Sherman Act by the Supreme Court in the past under the so-called "rule of reason."

The noted American historian, Richard Hofstadter,[10] has called attention to the fact that in the heyday of public sentiment for "trust-busting" little was actually accomplished. In recent years public indifference to monopoly has been accompanied by vigorous activity by the Justice Department and by court decisions which blocked mergers which might "substantially lessen competition" by reducing the number of firms in an industry or by increasing the market share of one of them. Hofstadter concludes that American opposition to "bigness in business" and economic power has largely been motivated by political ideology rather than the economic threats posed by monopoly.

One needs to ask at this juncture of time whether the anti-trust activi-

[10]Richard Hofstadter, "What Happened to the Anti-trust Movement," in *The Business Establishment* (New York: John Wiley & Sons, Inc., 1964), pp. 113–51.

ties of the Justice Department are in the "public interest." They have blocked and discouraged mergers which might have led to increased efficiency. The uncertainty they engender in the plans of the business community and the legal costs of anti-trust prosecution and defense impose an economic cost on the community at large. One could even ask whether they are self-consistent. The proponents of several proposed mergers turned down by the Justice Department have claimed that the mergers would lead to increased competition and improved economic performance in several industries by creating larger and more effective competitors out of a fusion of smaller firms.

The testimony[11] presented by the executives of the electrical equipment manufacturers convicted for price-fixing in 1962 claimed that the absence of collusion over prices would have driven the smaller firms out of business. Thus, the alternatives open for the larger companies were claimed to be price-fixing, which would keep the smaller firms in business, or competition, which would lead to monopoly by Westinghouse and General Electric. In either case, the companies would be prosecuted under the Sherman Act. It is frequently alleged also that General Motors would drop prices and increase production except that this would increase their share of the market and lead to Justice Department prosecution!

The control of monopolies in the United States has been based on the now questionable assumption that monopolies could not exist without either a political exclusion of competition or a conspiracy to prevent it. The iniquity of monopoly has been adjudged on the questionable assumption that the inevitable result of the lack of competition would be higher prices for the consumer. The desire to protect small entrepreneurs from "unfair" competition has rested in large part on a yearning to return to the early nineteenth century Jeffersonian idyll of small merchants and farmers.

It is time to rethink our social control of markets. The old common law ideas about monopoly and conspiracy were evolved for a society with a wholly different technology and set of social ideals. If we are going to prohibit monopoly on the grounds that it is against the "public interest," it might be desirable to place the burden of proof that monopoly, as opposed to conspiracy, is against the public interest with the public prosecutor rather than assuming that market power is bad *per se.*

---

[11]See Clarence Walton and Frederick Cleveland, *Corporations on Trial: The Electric Cases* (Belmont, Calif.: Wadsworth Publishing Company, 1964).

13

Social Regulation of Labor Monopoly

While legislative and judicial practice in the United States has continued to enforce the old common law prohibition of monopoly and conspiracy to monopolize in the sale of goods, it has accepted monopoly and conspiracy in the sale of labor services by labor unions. From the middle of the nineteenth century the courts became progressively more unwilling to treat labor unions as illegal conspiracies. Unions were exempted from anti-trust prosecution by the Clayton Act of 1913, and since the passage of the Wagner Act in 1935, labor unions have been actively encouraged by the Federal government.

Contemporary Labor Legislation

The controlling legislation with regard to labor-management relations in the United States is the "Wagner Act," the National Labor Relations Act of 1935 as amended by the "Taft-Hartley Act," the Labor Management Relations Act of 1947, the "Landrum-Griffin Act," the Labor Management Reporting and Disclosure Act of 1959. The basic philosophy of labor-management relations in the United States is the creation of bargaining units of "equal economic power" to prevent the exploitation of the weakness of the bargaining power of the individual worker by the large employer. This was to be accomplished by the association of individual workers in "unions of their own choosing" for bargaining purposes.

The Need for Labor Unions in an Advanced Society. The economic logic which lies behind the Wagner and Taft-Hartley Acts is the creation of labor monopoly to counteract employer monopsony in particular labor markets. The monopsony problem becomes progressively more serious the more advanced society becomes because of the increased specialization of skills of the worker.[1] In an underdeveloped society the mass labor market is fairly undifferentiated—an unskilled worker in one industry can move to an unskilled job with another industry if he feels that his wages and working conditions are substandard. There is also the option of self-employment in agriculture. The same option is not as open to a skilled worker, however. For example, a skilled meatcutter may be a valuable employee to a packing plant, but his only other alternative may be unskilled work elsewhere. In this situation, the meat-packing industry has the worker in a monopsonistic situation—the meat-packing industry is the only buyer of his skilled services. In this bargaining situation, the industry may exploit the worker in bargaining because of his lack of effective alternatives. The logic of labor legislation is to prevent this happening by confronting the monopsonist with a monopolist.

The problem of monopsony is further complicated by the geographic immobility of the individual worker. This immobility is a result of the specialization which leads to higher productivity. The worker is also likely to be tied to a particular job by having a pension vested in the job and seniority rights which cannot be transferred—even to another plant of his employer or to another plant in the industry. Further, the worker is likely to have a financial stake in a home which he does not want to lose—moving to another house will entail considerable financial expense. Economic growth contributes to labor immobility.

The essence of the modern labor market is very imperfectly competitive for certain types of skilled workers. In one particular job, they can make very high pay. Their alternatives are jobs with considerably lower pay. The union exists to prevent the employer from exploiting the lack of alternatives open to the individual worker by refusing to let the employer make a "take it or leave it" offer to individual workers. The union allows the workers to bargain with the financial and legal expertise which can be purchased only by workers collectively.[2]

The rights of labor unions and their effective power under existing legislation has come to them from rejection of the old common law notions about the evils of conspiracy. The unions have been allowed to organize and exercise power to counter the powerful bargaining position of employers in imperfect labor markets. The absence of labor unions

[1]See the section on "The Effect of Economic Growth on Markets," in Chapter 9.
[2]For an account of unions as purveyors of specialized services to their members, see James A. Kuhn, "Business Unionism in a Laboristic Society," in Ivar Berg, ed., *The Business of America* (New York: Harcourt, Brace & World, Inc., 1968), pp. 284–309.

would leave too much bargaining power to employers. On the other hand, we presently give too little emphasis in the regulation of labor unions to the two problems which the common law prohibitions on conspiracy attempted to control the power of unions to coerce individual members, and the power of unions to raise the prices of the commodities they produce to the public.

The Abandonment of the
Illegal Conspiracy Doctrine
in the United States

Before considering these problems, let us review the way in which we have evolved our present practices. The idea that workers should be free to associate and form unions for the purpose of bargaining with an employer or group of employers in a particular industry is of relatively recent acceptance in the United States. Under the common law, an association of workers which attempted to secure a "union-shop" contract or which bargained collectively by the threat of a strike was liable for prosecution for conspiracy against the public interest. The reasoning involved in this doctrine is exemplified by a decision handed down in Philadelphia in 1806 which is representative of the common law doctrine of conspiracy.[3] The indictment charged a group of cordwainers (shoemakers) with: "contriving, and intending unjustly and oppressively, to increase and augment the prices and rates usually paid and allowed to them [when they did] combine, conspire, confederate, and unlawfully agree together . . . that they . . . [would not work] but at certain prices and rates. . . ." It was also charged that they: "unlawfully did combine, conspire, confederate, and agree together, that they . . . and each and every one of them should and would endeavor to prevent by threats, menaces, and other unlawful means, other artificers from working and laboring in the said art and occupation, but at certain large prices and rates which they [fixed]."

The prosecution in the case agreed that any man had an unquestioned right to ask any price for his labor that he saw fit. Any man could attempt to get his employer to give him $100 for making a pair of boots. That would be a legal right. It was only illegal to combine to raise prices.

In his charge to the jury, the judge said the relevant question was whether the combination of workmen was injurious to the public welfare. He noted that prices were usually regulated by supply and demand. The

[3]Philadelphia Cordwainers' Case, *Commonwealth vs. Pullis,* 1806, Mayor's Court of Philadelphia. Cited in Robert E. Mathews, ed., *Labor Relations and the Law* (Boston: Little, Brown and Co., 1953), pp. 9–10.

combination of workmen would tend to make the price of the article they produced subject to the will of a few interested parties. This would make it difficult for an employer to carry on his business because of the uncertainty of his labor costs. This would be ruinous to the commerce of a city and, therefore, against public welfare. It would remove the incentives for the individual workmen to excel. It would compel all workmen to join the association in order to obtain employment. He asserted the basic common law doctrine of conspiracy "What is lawful for an individual is not lawful for a group of individuals. The law is clear even though the principle on which it is founded is not clear."

Several years later, in a similar suit against some shoemakers in Pittsburgh another judge made the following statement in his charge to the jury:[4]

In the investigation of subjects like that now presented to the court and jury, the mind is easily misled. We naturally look at the contending parties—here we see on the one hand, a number of journeymen, whom we are led to regard as poor men, opposed to their employers, some of whom are represented as wealthy. The human mind spontaneously revolts at the idea of oppression; and the attention of the jury is invariably drawn to this point; as if the true question were, whether the journeymen were the oppressed, and the masters the oppressors—whether the profits of the one class be not too great, and the remuneration of the other inadequate.

But it would be taking a very contracted, and by no means a just view of this case, to consider it as a controversy between the employers and the journeymen. And your time would be very unprofitably employed, in calculating the respective profits of the one or the other. With the regulations of wages, or the profit of the one or the other, you have nothing to do. It has been truly said that every man has a right to affix what price he pleases on his labour. It is not for demanding high prices that these men are indicted, but for employing unlawful means to extort those prices. For using means prejudicial to the community. Confederacies of this kind have a most pernicious effect, as respects the community at large. They restrain trade: they tend to banish many artisans, and to oppress others. It is the interest of the public, and it is the right of every individual, that those who are skilled in any profession, art, or mystery, should be unrestrained in the exercise of it. It is peculiarly the interest of a trading and manufacturing town (such as Pittsburgh) that such freedom should exist. Without it, trade and manufactures cannot flourish; it is, therefore, important to all to cherish such freedom. A by-law restraining trade would be void. A by-law to prohibit journeymen shoemakers from residing in Pittsburgh, unless they should become members of and contribute to, a certain association; or unless they would work at certain prices; or prohibiting a master workman from employing whomsoever he pleased, would be ridiculously tyrannical. It

[4]Pittsburgh Cordwainers' Case, 1815, *4 Commons and Gilmore.* Cited in Mathews, *Ibid.*, p. 11.

would be void. If the municipality cannot thus restrain trade, or interfere with the rights of the citizens, shall such restraint be imposed by
a combination of individuals?—Can that be lawful and right in the one,
which would be tyrannical and void in the other? . . .

As respects individuals, I consider the price which the journeymen may
charge their employers, or the price at which those employers may vend
their boots, of little consequence; if the citizens residing in this part of
the country could not be supplied at a fair price, by mechanics in their
neighborhood, they would obtain the article elsewhere, or it would be
obtained for them. Boot and shoe shops would be opened upon a scale
sufficiently large to supply the consumption. These articles would be
brought from Philadelphia, Baltimore, New York, Boston, and other parts
of the union; or if the manufacturers throughout the United States should
be so blind to their own interest, as to approach extortion, importations
from Europe would cause the price of the article to find its proper level.

We should indeed have abundance of the manufactured article; but we
should cease to be the manufacturers. Is this a slight consideration in a
manufacturing town? And can they be guiltless who enter into combinations which have a manifest tendency to produce such a result?

Conspiracy and "the Public Interest": Assumptions. In the Philadelphia
cordwainers' case the presiding judge made a very telling remark when
he asserted that the law against conspiracy was clear even when the
principle on which it was founded was not. Conspiracy by workmen to
bargain away part of the profits of guild monopolies was prohibited by
law in the feudal towns as it would have dissipated the profits necessary
to the support of the town establishment.[5] Conspiracy by workmen was
discouraged in mercantilist policies on the ground that it would weaken
the competitive position of the town in selling its output. This is alluded
to by the judge in the Pittsburgh case.

In terms of the individualist philosophy of the early nineteenth century, and abstracting from any interpretations of legal judgments in terms
of class interest, the application of the law against conspiracy on the
grounds of "public interest" depended on the assumption that the cordwainers sold their services in competitive labor markets, which prevented
the shoe manufacturers from paying them less than their contribution to
output (the value of their marginal product). If the labor markets were
not completely competitive, unions could increase the bargaining power
of the workmen and, consequently, their wages. The increase in wages
would have come at the expense of the profits of the manufacturer rather
than in the form of higher prices for the public.[6]

The legal prohibition of bargaining to protect profits would not have

[5]See the above section on "The Logic of Preventing Bargaining," in Chapter 10.
[6]See the above section on "Factor Price Indeterminacy and Labor Unions" in
Chapter 9.

directly protected the public interest and would have placed the courts in the position of protecting the economic power of one group at the expense of another. The judge's statement that wages were determined by supply and demand was a misleading notion since it ignored the possibility that when the labor force had limited employment opportunities, the employer could pay his workers less than he could afford to pay them without raising the price of his product. As soon as it was recognized that the existence of limited alternatives for workmen might make it impossible for them to bargain effectively and as soon as it was evident that the laws against combination preserved the bargaining power of the employer, the courts had difficulty maintaining that the conspiracy laws were being applied in the *public* interest.

Conspiracy and "the Public Interest": Doubts and Confusions. The first rejection of the conspiracy doctrine by the courts came in 1842 in the case of *Commonwealth of Massachusetts* v. *Hunt*.[7] In this case the presiding judge rejected the notion that a combination of workmen was an unlawful conspiracy against the public interest *per se*. He argued that a combination could only be an illegal conspiracy if the objective of the combination was unlawful or if the means used to enforce the combination were illegal. Since bargaining over wages was legal, and refusing to work for an employer who refused to recognize a labor union was legal, he inferred that combination to do these things could not be considered illegal. Pointing out that it would not be considered illegal for workmen to refuse to work for an employer who was intemperate, or who employed intemperate workmen, or for consumers to combine to deny patronage to a baker who sold bread at high prices, the judge noted that economic pressures might be exerted for entirely laudable purposes. The object of a conspiracy might be desirable.

The arguments used by Justice Shaw in *Commonwealth* vs. *Hunt* to justify the rejection of *per se* illegality in conspiracy cases were unfortunate in many respects because they rightly rejected an old doctrine without clarifying what uses of economic power *would* be in the public interest or at least would not be contrary to it.

Shaw argued that bargaining over wages by the individual was legal, and, therefore, collective refusal to sell labor to an employer who would not accede to a union would not be illegal. What was a legal means of exerting economic power for an individual must be a legal means for a group of individuals. This, of course, was a complete rejection of the common law notion of conspiracy. The legal right of an individual supplier to *ask* any price he wishes for his goods or services depends on the public having alternatives. The need to regulate monopoly power is a

---

[7]Supreme Judicial Court of Massachusetts, 1842. 4 Metc. III.

legitimate function of the conspiracy laws. Justice Shaw certainly would not have maintained that since one producer of a commodity could offer it for any price he pleased that a collusive group of producers could agree among themselves to sell their goods only at one price and refuse to deal with anyone who refused to pay the price.

In his example of a monopolist baker coerced into lowering his prices by a combination of consumers, Shaw makes an entirely false analogy. The members of the union, in this case, attempted to act as a monopoly and coerced a competitor to enforce their monopoly. In the example used by Shaw, conspiracy to *break* a monopoly is sanctioned as laudable. Yet, in the case at hand which is presented as analogous, conspiracy to *enforce* a monopoly is sanctioned as legitimate.

Conspiracy and the Public Interest: Uncertainty. The legitimacy of collusion by workers in the sale of their labor was not really affirmed until the Wagner Act. Justice Shaw in the *Commonwealth* v. *Hunt* case (1842) merely affirmed that the means used to enforce collusive action by a labor union or the ends sought had to be shown to be contrary to the rights of individuals economically coerced by the union or to be contrary to the interests of the public. Even the Clayton Act (1913) did not affirm the legitimacy of labor monopoly; it merely asserted that labor was exempt from the provisions of the Sherman Act.

The object of union activity, collusion to raise wages, might be increasingly recognized as permissible, but the means used to accomplish and enforce collective action were usually denied legitimacy by the courts in the period between the *Commonwealth* v. *Hunt* decision and the passage of the Wagner Act in 1935. A union is a monopoly. If it is not a monopolist in the sale of labor in a particular situation, a union cannot bargain effectively because employers will have alternatives to reaching agreement with the union. To enforce a monopoly, a union will ideally press for a *closed shop*—a situation in which it controls employment. Lacking a closed shop, a *union shop*, in which all employees must join the union, is a necessity for the maintenance of strong bargaining.[8]

The decision in *Commonwealth* vs. *Hunt* removed the *per se* conspiracy doctrine from the activities of unions. They were still limited in their bargaining power, however, by the refusal of courts to allow them to enforce union shops. Laws were passed in various states making it an offense for members of a union to bring pressure against employers of nonunion members or to intimidate workmen into joining a union.

Both the objective of forcing a union shop on an employer and the means of enforcing it by collective refusal to work were held to be illegal

---

[8]See Mancur Olsen, Jr., *The Logic of Collective Action: Public Goods and the Theory of Groups* (Cambridge: Harvard University Press, 1965), chap. iii.

in decisions by the state courts in the period after *Commonwealth* v. *Hunt*. In *The State of New Jersey v. Donaldson*[9] the presiding judge ruled that the objective of enforcing a union shop was illegal because it was "an unwarranted interference" with an employer's conduct of his business. "It is difficult to believe that a right exists in law . . . [for] workmen, by concert of action, and by taking advantage of their position, to control the business of another."

In a case brought in New York in 1867[10] collective action was held to be an illegal means of bringing pressure on a union member. While agreeing that unions had a right to bargain about wages and to collude to enforce their demands, the presiding judge, Judge Daly, also derived from the same principle which made this legal, the right of every man:

> . . . to work for whom he pleases and for any sum he thinks proper. . . . Every master workman has equally the right to determine for himself whom he will employ and what wages he will pay. Any attempt . . . to control a man in the lawful exercise of these rights is therefore an act of oppression, *and any combination for such a purpose is a conspiracy* [italics the author's].

From the principle that every man must have the right to buy or sell his labor on such terms as he could bargain individually or collectively, labor unions were deprived by the courts of their bargaining power by the denial of the right of unions to use any sort of coercion of their membership or of employers to employ only their members.

Union Power and the
Legitimacy of Economic
Coercion

In addition to the barriers placed on the growth of labor unions by the application of the conspiracy doctrine to their attempts to create and maintain bargaining power, the unions began to find themselves liable for damages in court cases brought by employers involved in labor disputes. A tortious action is one in which there is deliberate infliction of harm on one person by another *without just reason*. In granting damages against unions in tort cases the courts made the judgment that economic losses caused to employers by unions were not justified, that is, that it was wrong for unions to compete with employers over the distribution of income.

---

[9]New Jersey Supreme Court, 1867. 32 N.J.L., 151.
[10]*Master Stevedores' Association* v. *Walsh, Supreme Court of New York*, 1867, 2 Daly 1.

In cases where unions were sued for damages for their attempts to create union shops, the indictments would charge that unions were actions "in restraint of trade" since they attempted to control the supply of labor. Yet, during the same period the courts refused to stop ruthless competition by the trusts to drive small producers out of business by the use of economic power. While damages might result from this use of economic power, they were tolerated. The courts did not stop the combinations of producers to establish monopolies except in the negative sense that they would not enforce collusive agreements. It took the passage of the Sherman Anti-trust Act in 1890 to involve the courts in the positive control of economic power by the prohibition of producers' agreements to attempt to monopolize the sale of a particular commodity.

The basic disability of the labor movement until the 1930's was the refusal of the courts to recognize that bargaining between employers and employees over wages and conditions of work was the same kind of economic competition as that between producers with respect to the justification of economic damages which occurred inevitably in the pursuit of self-interest.

Strikes and Damages: Use of the Injunction. Another weapon which was used against labor unions up until 1932 was the court injunction against the strike. An injunction is a court order issued to give specific protection to a person against threatened harm to his person or property. Frequently, when a strike was threatened, an employer's attorney would petition a judge to secure an injunction against the union and its leaders to prevent their calling a strike. The pretext for this would be the protection of private property from strike damage by civil disorder. This particular weapon happened to be particularly popular with judges in threatened strikes against railroads which, in the second half of the nineteenth century, were frequently operated by court-appointed referees in bankruptcy. The injunction against the strike deprived the labor unions of their only effective sanction in bargaining, which was precisely what was sought by those who requested the injunctions.

The first legislation restricting Federal judges in their use of the injunction came in the Clayton Act in 1913 but was largely ignored until the passage of a stronger law, the Norris-LaGuardia Act in 1932. The Clayton Act also attempted to protect the labor unions against the power of the judiciary by excluding labor combinations from prosecution under the Sherman Anti-trust Act of 1890 which had most effectively been used against labor unions. The Clayton Act declared:

> The labor of a human being is not a commodity or an article of commerce. Nothing in the anti-trust laws shall be construed to forbid the existence and operation of labor . . . organizations; nor shall such organi-

zations or the members thereof, be held or construed to be illegal combinations or conspiracies in restraint of trade under the anti-trust laws.

Nevertheless, while the Clayton Act affirmed only the legitimacy of the
objectives sought by unions, it did not sanction the means used by labor
to attain these ends.

The Norris-LaGuardia Act was directed at the legal procedures used
by employers, especially during the heyday of laissez faire in the 1920's,
to prevent strikes by unions to gain recognition. Specifically, the law
forbade Federal judges to issue injunctions against strikes except where
"unlawful acts have been threatened and will be committed unless
restrained . . . and substantial and irreparable injury to the complainant's
property will follow." The judges were also required to ascertain that
greater injury would be done to the plaintiff by the denial of relief than
would be inflicted on defendants by the granting of relief. The Norris-
LaGuardia Act also prohibited the so-called "yellow dog" contract—an
undertaking which many employers had required of their employees that
they did not belong to a union and would not join one.

Political Encouragement and
Regulation of Labor Unions

The creation of effective trade unions in the 1930's depended upon a
policy for their active promotion by the government. The Wagner Act
of 1935 was a frankly "pro-labor" piece of legislation. It created a
National Labor Relations Board (NLRB) to supervise disputes and
specifically forbade the dismissal of employees for union membership
or activity. It required the employer to bargain with the duly elected
bargaining representative of the employees and the NLRB to supervise
the elections to certify unions as bargaining agents. It even allowed the
unions to negotiate closed-shop agreements.

After the Second World War, organized labor was in a strong legal
position, and a rash of strikes in 1946 and 1947 led to the passage of the
Taft-Hartley Act. This legislation sought to restore an equality of bargaining power to labor-management relations by defining unfair labor
practices as well as unfair management practices. The Act bears extensive scrutiny as it is the governing legislation at the present time and
has been for almost twenty years.

The first article of the Act states that its purpose is:

> . . . to prescribe the legitimate rights of both employees and employers
> in their relations affecting commerce, to provide orderly and peaceful
> procedures for preventing the interference by either with the legitimate

rights of the other, to protect the rights of individual employees in their relations with labor organizations whose policies affect commerce, to define and prescribe practices on the part of labor and management which affect commerce and are inimical to the general welfare, and to protect the rights of the public in connection with labor disputes affecting commerce.

Thus, the Act starts by affirming the legitimacy of government participation in labor-management relations as part of its Constitutional right to control commerce in the interests of the general welfare. The law was to define the "rights" of the parties in a positive way rather than to rely on the *ad hoc* adjudication used prior to the Wagner Act.

The Taft-Hartley Act recognized that labor unions were necessary in the modern world but also that the old common law rejection of conspiracy had relevance because the power of labor could be used inequitably against the public and individual workers and employers.

In Section 8(a), unfair practices by the employer are listed:

1. Interference with the right of employees to organize and bargain collectively.
2. Interferences with the employees' organization.
3. Rejection of union shop contracts when duly negotiated.
4. Discharge of employees who have filed charges with the NLRB or given testimony in cases heard by the board.
5. Refusal to bargain collectively.

Section 8(b) lists unfair practices by the labor union:

1. Coercion of individual members.
2. Coercion of the employer in his hiring.
3. Refusal to bargain collectively.
4. Secondary boycotts (refusing to handle the goods purchased from or sold to an employer who is involved in a labor dispute), forcing an employer or self-employed person to join a union, forcing bargaining with one union if another has been certified, forcing the assignment of work to one union when another union's members are organized and certified.
5. Requiring excessive initiation fees.
6. Extorting money from an employer.
7. Picketing an employer to force him to recognize a union when another is the duly certified bargaining representative.

The employer is obliged by the Taft-Hartley Act to accept the labor union and is forbidden to try to weaken it by coercion. The union, on the other hand, is forbidden to coerce the employer, individual workers, or other unions and employers. The purpose of unions is affirmed to be collective bargaining on equal terms with the employer, and this is defined as "the performance of the mutual obligation of the employer and the representatives of the employees to meet at reasonable times and confer in good faith with respect to wages, hours, and other terms and conditions of employment . . . but such obligation does not compel either party to agree to a proposal or require the making of a concession."

The Taft-Hartley Act affirmed the basic philosophy of market freedom. It attempts to prevent the employer from weakening the power of the union by coercing its individual members or by seeking to "divide and conquer." The employer is prevented from using his monopsonistic power in markets which are frequently far from perfect because of the absence of other job opportunities for employees.

On the other hand, the employer is given freedom from jurisdictional disputes by the unions and is protected from the economic pressure of a secondary boycott being brought against him to resolve a dispute in which he has no direct stake. Further, his traditional prerogative in hiring is preserved by the outlawing of the closed shop. The union cannot tell him who to hire.

Union Opposition to the Taft-Hartley Act. The unions, as might be expected, were bitterly opposed to the parts of the Taft-Hartley Act which restricted their powers. Their defense against social control of their actions was the same as that frequently made by management of large corporations in the defense of their powers—that is, that the abuses were few and the holders of power could be relied on to use it responsibly. In the hearings before the Senate Labor Committee in 1947 the argument was advanced that any curbing of the power of labor unions was an abridgement of traditional rights and an inexcusable interference with the operation of markets. William Green, the President of the American Federation of Labor, told the Senators that Congress should leave any questions about secondary boycotts and jurisdictional strikes up to the labor organizations involved. The head of the Congress of Industrial Organizations, Philip Murray, contended that any problems could be worked out by William Green and himself sitting down and reaching an agreement.[11] The union leaders wanted a laissez-faire policy by the government and acceptance of the "natural" or "moral" rights of unions as defined by them just like their management counterparts.

Section 14(b) of the Taft-Hartley Act: Union Opposition to State Options. One feature of the Taft-Hartley Act which has been fiercely attacked by the unions is Section 14(b). This section allows individual states to weaken greatly the bargaining power of the unions by outlawing

---

[11]*Hearings*, Senate Committee on Labor and Public Welfare, 80th Cong. 1st Sess. (1947). Quoted in Edwin F. Mason, *Economic Concentration and the Monopoly Problem* (New York: Athaneum Publishers, 1964), p. 211.

the union shop. Individual states have the option of passing so-called "right-to-work" legislation forbidding collectively bargained contracts which include union membership as a condition of employment within a specified period after an employee has been hired.

The philosophy which lies behind State legislation to prohibit a union shop is that an individual worker should have the freedom to join or not to join a union. Requiring membership in a union as a condition of employment denies an individual freedom of association. Leaving the philosophic arguments to one side, the purpose of the legislation is to weaken the power of unions by reducing their membership. If workers are not required to join a union to get the benefits of a collectively bargained contract, they may receive the benefits without contributing to the costs, and the union will be financially weaker.[12] Secondly, the employer may be able through hiring practice which illegally discriminates against union members to get rid of a specific union or get rid of a union altogether.

The States which have passed right-to-work laws have been the predominantly nonindustrial States which have hoped to attract industry from the more unionized States with promises of a more "docile" labor force. The basic premise of allowing a State option on the question of a union shop is that States should be allowed to weaken the necessity of collective bargaining on the part of the employer. It is an affirmation that a "perfectly competitive" labor market does exist in those States in which it is least likely to exist. It is an abdication of Federal control over interstate commerce which is difficult to reconcile with the philosophy and purpose of the Taft-Hartley Act.

Of course, a union shop agreement strengthens the power of the individual union against its members. If union membership is not optional, union leaders are not under such compunctions as when they have to prove their worth to the membership, actual and potential. The Landrum-Griffin Act of 1959 was an attempt to remedy this situation by giving the individual union member certain rights and remedies against the union leadership.

The most important philosophic argument to be made against Section 14(b) of the Taft-Hartley Act, which gives the individual States the option of passing laws outlawing union shops, is that it is a denial of majority rule and liberty of contract. A labor union is, in theory, chosen by the majority of workers in a particular industry as their bargaining agent. If this bargaining agent is able to get the employee to agree to a union shop contract, why should this power to contract be abridged? If an individual worker does not want to work in an industry where there is a union shop which has been bargained for by the majority of

[12]See Olsen, *op. cit.*, chap. iii.

workers in the industry, he has the option of working elsewhere. In a democratic society the individual may not vote for the levying of taxes, but he has no option in paying them, and less option exists in escaping them because the move to another country (which will also surely have taxes) is far more difficult than working for another employer.

The unions' power also poses danger for the individual worker. The worker's retention of a job depends not only on the employer but on his relations with the union hierarchy. These are the problems which confront an individual in any organization, but they are of crucial importance to the union member since his economic livelihood is in the hands of his union. The union organization is not a voluntary association in practice.

Unions and Their Members' Rights: The Landrum-Griffin Act. During the decade of the 1950's, revelations of union corruption and malpractice caused a great public outcry against the power of unions and especially against their leaders. The problem in controlling union power is that unions cannot be weakened in their dealing with employers without contradicting the philosophy of creating union monopolies for bargaining purposes. The solution adopted in the Landrum-Griffin Act of 1959 was an attempt to give guarantees to individual union members and to subject union officials to more control by the rank and file. This was an alternative to the outlawing of the union ship by "right-to-work" laws.

Section 10 of the Act gave a "Bill of Rights" to union members. Every member of a labor union was guaranteed equal rights and privileges in the nomination of officers, voting, and attendance of meetings. The freedom of speech and assembly of members was affirmed. Unions were forbidden to raise dues without a majority vote of the members. Individual members were given the right to sue the union and given safeguards against arbitrary disciplinary action by the union. The philosophy of the Act was to give union members the same guaranteed rights against deprivation of freedom and financial punishment without due process of law as exist for citizens of the United States against State and Federal governments.

Labor Monopolies and the
Public Interest

The exemption of labor unions from prosecution under the common law for conspiracy and from the anti-trust laws, coupled with the rise in importance of industrywide bargaining, has created some extremely serious problems for our society. Another set of problems has arisen in government services and publicly regulated monopolies from the existence of labor unions.

The existence of industrywide bargaining in such industries as steel, chemicals, automobiles, and truck transportation enables unions in these industries to push up wages which are then passed on to the consumer by the industries. This phenomenon has nothing to do with the competitiveness of product markets—if all producers are subject to the same wage increases, prices will go up whether the industries are oligopolistic, such as is steel, or fiercely competitive, such as trucking. This leads to a redistribution of wage incomes unfavorable to workers in unorganized industries, such as retail trade, agriculture, and the service industries.

In such services as rail and air transportation, police and fire protection, education, electricity generation, telephones, and government services, strikes in support of wage demands would lead to extremely high costs for the public and real physical suffering in some instances. Many states have legislation forbidding strikes and imposing harsh penalties for strikes by public employees. Federal intervention in strikes affecting national security can be stopped for ninety days under the Taft-Hartley Act, and local judges have dealt very severely with threatened strikes in some of the occupations mentioned above. Fortunately, little militancy has occurred in demands by employees in public industries—industries which have, consequently, experienced lagging wage scales. Shortages of workers in such critical areas as education and nursing have resulted from the lagging pay scales.

A Possible Solution to Labor Monopoly. The original logic of exempting labor unions from the conspiracy laws was to establish an equality of bargaining power for workers against their employees. The exemption of labor unions from anti-trust laws to permit industrywide bargaining does not affect union-management equality in bargaining, but it does work against the interest of the public at large by allowing workers in highly unionized industries with national unions to raise their wages at the expense of the public—not at the expense of capital in those industries.

One solution to this problem would be to prohibit collective bargaining by unions or management on an industrywide basis. It would not be necessary to dissolve the national unions to do this, and they would still be necessary to furnish legal and financial help to local unions. Each company ought to be required to bargain only with a local union under relevant legislation.

This arrangement would preserve an equality of bargaining power between labor and management. A company bargaining over wages and working conditions with a local union would know that if it failed to reach an agreement that it would suffer financial losses while its competitors supplied its customers. The union, on the other hand, would realize in pressing its demands that if they were excessive and led to contraction of operations, to movement to another area at the expiry of a contract, or to bankruptcy, that the members of the union would suffer. Both sides would have a self-interest in reaching an equitable settlement, and the union would have the bargaining power necessary to compensate for the imperfections in local labor markets.

The arrangement would undoubtedly lead to a disparity of wage scales for different firms in the same industry as firms which could afford to pay more were pressed to do so by the union. This would seem, in many ways, a preferable arrangement to the present practices of industrywide scales which allow some firms to make large profits and force others to close down operations. In a full employment economy, it would facilitate the movement of labor. It would avoid situations such as have occurred in the automobile industry where firms such as General Motors and Studebaker or American Motors pay the same wage scales with the consequence that one is able to make large profits while the other is driven out of business, with resulting unemployment which workers in the less efficient plants would probably have chosen to subsidize by taking lower wages rather than suffering unemployment.

Industrywide bargaining, of course, will be supported by both trade-union leaders and the executives of the most profitable firms in the industries concerned. It affords the national union leaders more power and authority, and it protects the executives of the most profitable firms in an industry from higher wage claims because the union leaders know that too high a wage level will drive the least efficient firms under and cause unemployment in some of their locals.

The Dilemma of Essential Services. Labor unions in government services and certain public-utility type industries pose potentially even more serious problems for the public than do national labor unions. What would happen in a large American city if the police, or the electricity-generating personnel, or the teachers or the nurses went out on strike? A strike of any length or comprehensiveness would impose enormous costs on the community—costs far in excess of the loss of wages by the individuals concerned. The costs would be born, by and large, by those people who benefitted most from the public and quasi-public services in question. Frequently, these individuals are the less fortunate members of the community and have little political power.

The community would probably be willing to pay far more for the services in question. Most of them are inadequately provided at the present time because of various difficulties in the communication of these social demands into the increased expenditures which would be necessary to provide what the public would regard as a satisfactory level of services. What is of equal importance is that many public employees who are forbidden, enjoined, or discouraged from striking receive substantially lower wage incomes than they could obtain if they were allowed to organize effectively to press their claims as workers in private industry do so effectively.

Income Distribution and
Collective Bargaining in a
Free Society

We need to emphasize that the solution of the problem of income determination by collective bargaining in a capitalist system is an extremely difficult thing to accomplish. Adherence to a policy of "laissez faire" merely abdicates decisions about income distribution to an existing set of market powers. It cannot be justified on the grounds of resource allocation or "freedom" if *freedom* is defined to mean anything more than the legal freedom to take or refuse what is offered. The other extreme alternative, government control of all prices, wages, and profits, is an alternative which is equally unacceptable to most members of our society.

We need to recognize in our control of labor markets that the protection of both individuals and the public from the power of labor union monopolies in the sale of labor services must be accomplished by legislative and judicial action to balance the bargaining power of parties in the markets for labor as well as for goods. The rejection of the old common law notions about conspiracy in the sale of labor needs reexamination, just like their affirmation in the anti-trust laws requires rethinking. Certainly, we must allow unions the necessary power to bargain effectively with employers in labor markets which are, and always will be, somewhat imperfect. On the other hand, this does not entail giving unions unlimited powers against their members or against the public.

14

The Control of Money and Capital Markets

Control of the money supply by political authority is inevitable because of the attributes of money which give it value; furthermore, its acceptability as a means of exchange and a store of value depend upon the confidence of the public that it can perform these functions. This confidence can be effectively created only by government action to insure negotiability and stability of purchasing power of the monetary unit.

While we have always recognized that only political authority could give money acceptability and negotiability, we have also realized that the power of the government to create money by making slips of paper legal tender gives it the power to make money an inconstant store of value and to alter the expectations of debtors and creditors. As a consequence, creditors, bankers, merchants, and others who depend upon a stable monetary unit for the successful conduct of their affairs have historically sought to impose limitations on the powers of governments to increase the supply of money. We emphasize "increase" rather than "change" because the fear has almost universally been a fear of inflation caused by governments financing fiscal deficits by the printing press.[1]

The Use of Gold for Monetary Purposes. The device used in the United States and other Western countries during the past few centuries to limit the power of a government to increase the supply of money too rapidly is the provision for making a national currency convertible into gold. In the absence of "paper" money, gold is the commodity best suited to use as money since it has high value relative to weight, can be easily standardized, and has a relatively constant value with respect to other commodities because the net additions to the supply of gold in the world over any short period of time are very small in relation to the total amount in existence. People have historically tended to use gold as money in preference to national currencies or debt contracts whenever they feared a rapid depreciation in the value of currencies through their overissue by governments. Until 1933 when we "went off the gold standard," United States citizens could exchange their paper money for gold. This privilege was suspended in 1933 when there was a devaluation in the value of currency relative to gold because the government did not want a large windfall gain to accrue to the hoarders of gold. This devaluation was accomplished by the Treasury changing the price at which it was willing to exchange currency for bullion. At the present time, we have a modified international gold standard as the United States Treasury and its agent, the Federal Reserve Bank of New York, stand ready to convert American dollars presented by certain cooperating foreign central banks into gold at a fixed rate.

American Attempts to Control the Supply of Money. The Constitution granted to the Congress the power "to coin money," "regulate the value thereof. . . ." and to "borrow money on the credit of the United States." It did not, however, grant to it the power to charter a bank to operate as the agent of the government, although this was debated in the Constitutional Convention. Alexander Hamilton, the first Secretary of the Treasury, did succeed in pushing through the charter of the First United States Bank which served as a rudimentary central bank over the opposition of Jefferson and his party who refused to renew its charter when it expired.

A national bank was part of Hamilton's economic strategy of active government support of the manufacturing and commercial interests of the new nation. Drawing on the analogy of the Whig creation of the Bank of England in 1694, Hamilton saw the Bank of the United States as a means of binding the financial interests of the new nation to its government. This also lay behind his insistence on the assumption of the debts incurred by the various states and the Continental Congress before the Revolution. In economic terms Hamilton argued that it would be necessary to establish the credit of the United States with domestic and foreign investors by honoring the debts incurred by the constituent states of the new union. He also noted the advantages of having the bonds and the credit instruments of the Bank of the United States supply a quantity of commercial paper to finance the trade of the new nation.

[1]For a well-written historical sketch of attempts to control inflation see Roy F. Harrod, *Policy Against Inflation* (London: The Macmillan Company, 1958), chap. i.

Political Opposition to the First and Second Banks of the United States. Jefferson's opposition to the First Bank of the United States and Andrew Jackson's opposition to the Second Bank of the United States, whose charter he refused to renew in 1836, was based on their reluctance to see the power of the state granted to a group of private individuals who could use that power to control the economic life of the nation. Jackson's veto of the renewal of the charter of the Second Bank by Congress was such a poorly reasoned and emotional document that the supporters of the Bank had it reprinted at their own expense for circulation to the public in the hope that it would increase public support for the Bank![2] Nevertheless, both Jefferson and Jackson should be credited with an early realization that the power of the central bank could be used to control the economic tempo of the nation's commercial activity. Unfortunately, their answer to the control of this power—its elimination— became an increasingly unsatisfactory solution. In the absence of a central bank, the supply of money was unstable and contracted during successive financial panics, resulting in the closing of banks, bankrupting of fundamentally sound business operations, and interrupting of commerce and agriculture.

Until the creation of the Federal Reserve System in 1913, the American distrust of financial power created a diffused and unstable banking system. Banks were chartered by the individual states. The charters were often granted as political favors, and the banks usually lacked sufficient capital to carry on the scale of operations which they attempted. In the absence of branch banking, a correspondent system grew up. Country banks would hold balances in the banks in the provincial centers which would, in turn, hold balances in New York, which became the predominant financial center after the Civil War. During financial panics which occurred with increasing frequency and seriousness, the attempts by individuals and banks to withdraw their deposits all at once would result in runs on the banks which would force them to close their doors in the absence of a lender of last resort.

Leading bankers in New York, such as J. P. Morgan, James Stillman of the National City Bank, and George F. Baker of the First National Bank, attempted to act cooperatively to function as a lender of last resort. They succeeded in finally stopping the panic of 1907 by moving deposits to banks which were experiencing "runs." This was a fundamentally intolerable situation for the bankers and the public, however. It involved private individuals in making decisions to preserve the stability of the system which were contrary to the profitability and security of their own

[2]Both Jackson's message to Congress vetoing renewal of the Bank Charter and Daniel Webster's reply to it are reprinted in Hoftadter, *Great Issues in American History*, Vol. I, *op. cit.*, pp. 291–300.

undertakings. It left control of the economy to a group of men who did not ultimately have to answer for their actions to the people through their elected representatives.

In 1912 the Pujo Committee of the House of Representatives began an investigation of the concentration of financial power in the hands of a few great banking houses.[3] The bankers, themselves, testified that they were very uneasy with the situation, and in 1913, the Federal Reserve System was established by the Congress to act as a lender of last resort—as a "banker's bank."

Creation of the Federal Reserve System. Although the Federal Reserve System was under the nominal control of Congress and the President through their appointment of the Board of Governors, the policies of the Federal Reserve System were largely determined by the banking community up to the Second World War. The supply of money was controlled by the requirement that all member commercial banks keep a fixed proportion of their deposits in deposits at the District Federal Reserve Banks. When the Board of Governors of the Federal Reserve System wished to expand or contract the supply of money, they could vary the reserve requirements, engage in "open-market" operations to change the amount of net-free reserves in the banking system, or alter the rate at which they were willing to lend additional reserves to the member banks on the security of certain credit instruments.

This volume is not the place for an exposition or evaluation of the activities of the Federal Reserve System from 1913 to the present. The Governors have been the object of detailed and incisive criticism for the actions before and during the Great Crash of 1929 and the ensuing depression. They have also been criticized for the "tight-money" policies followed during the late 1950's when their fear of inflation has been blamed for the extensive unemployment and slow growth from 1955 to 1960.

Control of the Money Supply:

The Issues

The policies of the Federal Reserve System ought to be placed in the context of our political system. Because the control of the money supply is an important determinant of the level of economic activity—the level of employment, changes in the general level of prices, the rate of growth, the allocation of income between consumption and investment, and the interpersonal distribution of income—people inevitably want to treat it

[3]*Money Trust Investigation, Report of the Sub-Committee of the Committee on Banking and Currency* (Washington, D.C.: U.S. Government Printing Office, 1913).

as a political question. The limitations on the power of a government in an "open society" to control the supply of money *as it wishes,* are the same as those limitations which pose practical limitations on other aspects of government policy, such as taxation and regulation of other markets. Segments of the community which are afraid that political control of the money supply might lead to excessive inflation have traditionally attempted to avoid having control of the money supply be treated *as a political question.* Over the years, while realizing that a government does determine the quantity of money in circulation, either they have attempted to get the government to delegate the control over the money supply to an institution which they could control or they have sought to impose constraints on the government by basing the money supply on gold, the supply of which is largely independent of political control.

Control of the United States Money Supply by the Financial Community. Our own monetary history is illustrative of the struggle to keep the money supply out of the hands of the legislature. The Constitution forbade the Legislatures of individual States to coin money, emit paper money, or make paper money legal tender. The opponents of the First and Second Banks of the United States wanted to avoid private control of the banking system by a federally chartered private monopoly, but their understanding of the role of banks in the creation of money was insufficient to lead them to put anything in its place, with the result that the monetary system was exceedingly unstable.

In the period after the Civil War, the debates about the "Greenbacks" and the purchase of silver by the Treasury were basically debates between the proponents of inflation and deflation. Contraction of the money supply relative to the rapidly expanding commerce of the country between 1873 and 1896 led to a redistribution of real income from debtors to creditors in addition to the recurrent financial crises. The Treasury was controlled by the financial community regardless of the political opinions of the Congress and the President, and the financial community kept lecturing to those pressing for increases in the money supply about the dangers of inflation, the need to insure continuing confidence by European investors in the soundness of the dollar, and the need to preserve the gold standard. In 1896, William Jennings Bryan made the monetary issue the foundation of his campaign. He invoked Jefferson and Jackson in support of his ideas for governmental control of the money supply and an end to the control by the private banking interests; he ended a speech by declaring that the financial community was not to be allowed "to crucify mankind upon a cross of gold."[4] Bryan lost the election.

[4]Reprinted in Hofstadter, *op. cit.,* Vol. II, pp. 166–72.

Recent Controversy Over Monetary Control. The only period in our history in which there was effective and complete political control over the supply of money was from 1933 until 1951. During the period of the New Deal, Franklin D. Roosevelt enforced a policy of "reflation" as a deliberate attempt to stimulate economic activity. During the Second World War and its aftermath, the role of the Federal Reserve System in national monetary policy was reduced to supporting the Treasury in its sale of bonds at high prices and low interest rates.

By 1951, it was becoming obvious that the continuance of the policy of low interest rates was going to accelerate inflation. The Board of Governors of the Federal Reserve System asserted that they would no longer support the Administration's policies in this respect. The President could have secured compliance with his policies by asking for the resignations of the Board, but he would have lacked Congressional and public support in the crisis which would have ensued; and, thus, the Federal Reserve System regained its independence. During the Eisenhower Administration from 1952 to 1960, substantial agreement existed between the "Fed" and the Administration on a restrictive monetary policy and high interest rates.

During the 1960's the Kennedy Administration sought to stimulate the economy by means of tax increases and acceded to a relatively high level of interest rates because of the necessity of attracting short-term capital and preventing its outflow, which would have aggravated the balance of payments problem for the United States. In 1966, the Federal Reserve Chairman, William McChesney Martin, Jr., came into sharp conflict with President Johnson because of Johnson's refusal to cut the deficit in the Federal budget and Martin's insistence on dealing with threatened inflation with the tightest monetary policy which had been carried out by the "Fed" since the 1920's. While Johnson might have wished to replace Martin as Chairman of the Board of Governors of the Federal Reserve System when his term expired in the spring of 1967, he did not do so. He took account of warnings that this would be interpreted by the international financial community as a decision to embark on inflationary policies and would have resulted in a massive flight from the dollar into gold, which might have forced the United States off the international gold standard.

The Economic Consequences

of Recent Monetary Policies

The control of the money supply is an extremely complex problem which depends on the maintenance of the confidence of the domestic and international banking community and on technical expertise in operations in domestic bond markets and foreign exchange markets. Monetary policy, however, is also a question on which honest men of good will may have differences of opinion. A policy choice has to be made about the rate of increase of the money supply, because this is an important determinant of the rates of growth, unemployment, and inflation. The Governors of the Federal Reserve System have followed the practice of the banking community in the past in misleading the community as to the *alternatives* in monetary policy. They have represented monetary policy as a technical matter *only* and propagated the belief that only one monetary policy can prevent financial chaos—the policy which they wish to follow. Insofar as the Federal Reserve Governors are public servants, this is a disservice to the public when it misleads the public into believing that opinions are matters of fact.

The author does not wish to suggest that there is no danger from inflation or that international financial considerations can be ignored. Inflation imposes real costs on the community, and the stability of international trade depends on confidence in a sound dollar. On the other hand, the relations between monetary stringency and inflation and the international balance of payments are very complicated. During the "tight money" period from 1957 to 1960 we had both inflation, unemployment, and an adverse payments balance. While failing to stop either inflation or the outflow of gold, monetary restraint resulted in lost production to the community, measured in the hundreds of billions of dollars and unreckoned social costs of unemployment concentrated among the members of the community least able to sustain it.

On another level, the policies of the Federal Reserve System and the Treasury during the 1950's deserve some comment, for the general public and the Congress are unaware of the implications of the policies which they allowed to be carried out. During the period the increase in the supply of money was accomplished primarily by lowering the reserve requirements for the commercial banks. This, of course, allowed them to increase their earnings by increasing the volume of loans outstanding for a given amount of deposits. At the same time, it decreased the amount of deposits which the "Fed" would have invested in government securities. This increased the cost of government borrowing, and hence, the size of the Federal budget which was devoted to financing the interest on the national debt. Interest on the national debt, of course, is merely a transfer payment from the community as a whole to the debt holders, but it is a transfer to the wealthiest segment of the community. When the "Fed" wished to decrease the supply of money during the period, it did so by selling government bonds rather than raising reserve requirements, which also had the effect of increasing the interest cost to the Federal government of financing the debt.

A second policy which the Treasury and the Federal Reserve followed during the period also had the effect of raising the interest costs of the

Federal debt. It was the policy of selling long-term debt during the up-swings to check the threat of inflation and redeeming long-term securities by the sale of short-term securities during down-swings in order to try to stimulate investment.

Neither of these policy decisions by the "Fed" during the 1950's were as important as the policy of monetary restraint, itself, for the national economy, but they were essentially carried out without an understanding of the implications of the policies by the people or the Congress. The bankers have succeeded in persuading the public and the politicians that these matters are "technical." They have not wanted to make explicit the alternatives, the costs involved or the recipients of the benefits of their policies. The public could have been saved a considerable transfer from their tax payments to the holders of the national debt if a different set of policies had been used to regulate the money supply.

Some critics, Milton Friedman for example, have argued that the increase in the supply of money ought to be controlled by rules rather than by men.[5] Friedman has marshalled some impressive arguments from the evidence of monetary history to support his view.[6] Nevertheless, his solution represents another attempt to take essentially political decisions away from the elected representatives of the community. It is a variant of the approach to monetary control represented by the pre-World War I international gold standard. It effectively withdraws the power of the community to make decisions about the supply of money on the grounds that the elected leaders will make the "wrong" decisions. It would prefer to bind the community to a set of "rules" to determine the money supply and let inflation, growth, and unemployment result from those "rules" rather than from the decisions of a popularly elected government.

Friedman's "rules" are a preferable policy to the classical gold standard in that they provide for a steady rate of increase in the money supply geared to an average rate of growth. They do not abdicate monetary control to the vagaries of world gold production and consumption. In the final analysis, however, Friedman's program is another of those counsels of despair which deny that governments can take a constructive part in the regulation of economic activity.

The control of the markets for money and credit by political authority is inevitable because the participants in those markets demand it. In this respect, the market for money and credit is the same as the market for ordinary commodities or labor. It is crucially different, however, in that in money markets, the government is in substantially complete con-

[5]Milton Friedman, *A Program for Monetary Stability* (New York: Fordham University Press, 1959).

[6]Milton Friedman and A. J. Schwartz, *A Monetary History of the United States 1867–1960* (Princeton: National Bureau of Economic Research, 1965).

trol of the supply of money, and hence of its price. While control of the money supply and money markets has ostensibly been in the hands of the government, almost without exception it has, in fact, usually been under the control of the financial community, owing to the structure of financial institutions.

This is not necessarily to be decried, but the public should know the basis of decisions and the alternatives rather than be kept in a state of ignorance on the grounds that monetary policy is purely technical.

The present struggles to secure reform of the international monetary system involve essentially the same issues as domestic control of the money supply. The use of "Special Drawing Rights" (SDRs) by the International Monetary Fund will allow the growth of the money supply to be geared to the growth of world trade and allow the sharing of benefits among all the nations of the world. Clinging to an archaic reliance on gold abandons the control of world monetary stability to gold producers and speculators and allows them to enjoy large gains at the expense of the rest of mankind.

15

Capitalism and the Distribution of Income:

theory and fact

Thus far in this volume, we have been concerned with describing the changes in economic organization, and discussing their implications. As has been argued, the primary rationale for the allocation of property rights in a capitalist system is the efficacy of property rights in promoting increases in output, from which members of society in addition to the property holder would benefit. Economic freedom, likewise, has been considered as a means to increase aggregate output, and the attempts to regulate the conditions of exchange between individuals have been explained as attempts to control socially the use of individual economic power stemming from the control of property.

Capitalism, Industrialization, and Income Inequality

While admitting the efficacy of capitalist economic organization for promoting economic growth, many critics of capitalism have been skeptical of its ability to distribute it equitably. They have particularly feared that the process of industrialization would channel an ever-increasing proportion of social output to those having property in physical assets, and that the concentration of ownership of these physical assets would also increase. Thomas Jefferson, for example, hoped that the United States could remain a nation of small farmers in order to maintain a substantial equality of income and property. He feared that the process of industrialization which he had observed in Britain and France would destroy the basis for a democratic state in the United States. Karl Marx predicted that industrialization would be accompanied by a growing "surplus," which would be appropriated by the owners of physical capital, with the resulting inequality in wealth and income leading to the abandonment of private property and free exchange.

We must look at the quantitative evidence on industrialization and income distribution. In Table 15–1 at the end of this chapter, evidence is presented on the per-capita growth of output of countries which have undergone industrialization under predominantly capitalist auspices. We use this term even though most of the European countries have had government ownership and control over substantial sectors of industry since the 1930's. Even in such socialist countries as Sweden, Denmark, and Britain, production is primarily controlled by private ownership, and, most importantly, individuals are free to bargain about the exchange of their labor and capital.

In Tables 15–2 and 15–3, historical and comparative data on income distribution is presented for countries at different stages of industrialization. The estimates presented are taken from various sources. Nevertheless, the trend of income toward greater interpersonal equality is pronounced in the historical statistics for every country undergoing industrialization.

The ratios of the incomes of the wealthiest 5 per cent of the population to the remaining 95 per cent, and of the wealthiest 20 per cent, of income units to the lowest 80 per cent of the population are an arbitrary measure of income inequality (as is any measure). The significance of the ratios, however, might be illustrated by pointing out that a ratio of .5 for the share of income received by the top 5 per cent over the bottom 95 per cent indicates that a person in the wealthiest 5 per cent is about fifty times wealthier than a member of the lowest 5 per cent population.

Of interest is to note from the historical data that the share of national income of the top 20 per cent of the population appears to increase during the process of industrialization even though the share of the top 5 per cent declines steadily. The share of the wealthiest 20 per cent of the population begins to decline substantially in the countries represented only after the Second World War. One might generalize from this about the tendency for equalization to spread gradually from the top as the rising aggressive industrial and commercial classes bargain away part of the growing surplus from the traditional holders of wealth and power.

The disparities in income distribution in developed and underdeveloped countries is manifest in Table 15–3. Income distribution is far more unequal in poor countries than in rich—despite the barrier posed by subsistence to reducing the incomes of the poor in the underdeveloped societies and the smaller amount of "surplus" over biological subsistence available for redistribution. The wealthiest 5 per cent of the population is about twice as rich relative to the rest of the population in Mexico and Colombia as it is in Britain and the United States.

Causes of Income
Inequality

The inequality in personal income, as predicted by Marx, is largely a result of inequality in the ownership of wealth. The extent of inequality in the ownership of claims to income-producing physical assets can be seen in their distribution in the two countries with the *most equal* interpersonal distribution of income. In Britain, the top 5 per cent of wealth holders held 87 per cent of total wealth in 1912 and 75 per cent in 1960.[1] In the United States, an estimated 1 per cent of the top wealth holders possessed 38 per cent of total wealth in 1929 and 25 per cent in 1953.[2]

A measure of the impact of the great inequality in the ownership of physical assets on the distribution of income can be illustrated by an example. Suppose that 25 per cent of national income went to owners of physical capital and 75 per cent went to labor. Suppose, further, that all labor income was equally distributed (everyone received the same wage). Lastly, suppose that 75 per cent of total physical assets were owned by 5 per cent of the population. On these assumptions the share of the wealthiest 5 per cent of the population would be equal to:

$$Y_5 = a_5 (L) + b_5 (1-L)$$

where Y_5 = share of total income going to the wealthiest 5 per cent of the population

L = share of national income received as labor income

a_5 = share of labor income earned by wealthiest 5 per cent of the population

b_5 = share of property income going to wealthiest 5 per cent of the population

Using our assumptions about the size of labor and capital incomes going to the wealthiest 5 per cent of the population and the share of national income represented by returns to wealth and labor, the inequality in wealth holding would give almost 25 per cent of national income to the wealthiest 5 per cent of the population *even if* everyone received the same labor income.

Causes of Inequality in Wealth. As has been perceived by companies with stock option plans for employees and the propagandists of the stock

[1]James E. Meade, *Efficiency, Equality, and the Ownership of Property*, (London: George Allen and Unwin Ltd., 1965), p. 27.
[2]Robert J. Lampman, *The Share of Top Wealth Holders in the National Wealth, 1922–1956* (New York: National Bureau of Economic Research, 1964), p. 220.

exchanges for "people's capitalism," measures to promote greater equality in wealth distribution are desirable in a society which has considerable disparities in wealth distribution. Greater equality in the ownership of physical assets, however, is not likely to occur very rapidly, if at all. The systematic accumulation of property depends upon saving and inheritance. Certain factors exist which tend to give the wealthy both a higher *rate* of capital formation by saving and a lower *rate* of capital division by inheritance. In the absence of social correctives, both these factors over time create disequalizing tendencies in wealth ownership.

The rich, of course, tend to have a higher rate of saving in proportion to income than the poor. The crucial question, however, is whether the saving of the rich relative to their capital stock is greater than the rate at which the poor save relative to their capital stock. This can be illustrated by the use of a simple formulation of the factors which affect the rate of capital formation and a comparison of these factors for the rich and the not-so-rich.

An individual's rate of capital formation is equal to the ratio of his savings to his stock of capital. Let:

$$k = S/K \qquad\qquad 1.1.1.$$

where k = rate of capital accumulation
       S = savings during a time period
       K = capital stock at a given time

We could postulate a large number of behavioral relationships for individuals between their rate of saving from current income and the size of their capital stock. The use of a simple function is not meant to rule out the use of others but only to indicate the importance of certain factors to the rate of wealth accumulation.

Assume that an individual saves a constant proportion of any income he receives above a certain minimum:

$$k = \frac{s(Y-a)}{K} \qquad\qquad 1.1.2$$

Let income be equal to the sum of labor and capital income:

$$Y = rK + wL \qquad\qquad 1.2$$

where s = rate of saving from income = S/Y
       Y = income during a time period
       a = a biologically or culturally defined minimum income
       r = rate of return on capital
       w = rate of return on labor
       L = units of labor
       K = units of capital

by substitution

$$k = S/K = \frac{s \ (rK + wL - a)}{K} \qquad \qquad 1.1.3$$

By adding subscripts to all the variables in equation 1.1.3, one can separate the various factors which will lead to differences in k_1, the rate of capital accumulation, for the wealthy and k_2 for the nonwealthy.

$$k_1 = s_1r_1 + s_1w_1L_1/K_1 - s_1a/K_1 \qquad \qquad 1.3.1$$

$$k_2 = s_2r_2 + s_2w_2L_2/K_2 - s_2a/K \qquad \qquad 1.3.2$$

If $k_1 > k_2$, the rate of capital accumulation by the wealthy will exceed that of the poor and market forces and voluntary decisions will tend to produce increasing inequality in wealth ownership over time. Both the rate of saving (s) and the rate of return on capital (r) are likely to be higher for the wealthy than the poor, so the first term (sr) in equations 1.3.1 and 1.3.2 will be larger for the rich than the poor. The last term in the equation will also tend to produce inequality.

Of crucial importance is the size of the term $[(swL)/K]$ which relates savings from labor income to wealth ownership. The larger this term is relative to the other two, and the greater the tendency toward equality in labor income for those with unequal capital ownership, the greater will be the forces leading toward equalization of capital ownership. The increasing share of labor in national income and increased equality in its distribution is the most important force leading to equalization in the distribution of wealth.

(A parenthetical comment concerning the conceptualization of the problem presented above may be of interest. Marx's argument for the increasing inequality of wealth and income in a capitalist system assumed that workers could make no net saving since $w_1L_1 = a$; that is, wage income would be at the subsistence level. He further assumed an increase in the share of national income going to capital which would emphasize the disequalizing tendency of savings from income on capital.)

For the reasons mentioned, any decrease in the inequality of wealth distribution in American society through a faster *rate* of capital accumulation by the poor has probably been slight. Further, labor incomes tend to be correlated with wealth, and, consequently, there has not been any marked tendency for the savings rates of rich and poor to converge markedly over time.

Social and Genetic Contributors to Inequality in Wealth. The amount of capital which can be amassed in one lifetime is considerable. One need only look at such individuals as Ford or Rockefeller to substantiate this statement. Nevertheless, inheritance, the passing of property from one generation to another, has profound implications for the distribution of wealth. Since individuals in our society are not "born equal" as far as the ownership of wealth is concerned, we need to ask whether the process of inheritance tends to increase or decrease the dispersion of wealth in the community.

To begin discussion of the problem, assume that we lived in a society with static population growth. Each couple produces two children and divides their property between them. In this situation the distribution of property would remain the same from one generation to the next only on the assumption that each of the two children who divided their inheritance married someone with exactly the same amount of property as themselves. If this did not occur, if there were random mating, there would quickly be a regression toward the mean as the children of the rich and poor combined large and meager estates.

Two sociological factors interfere with regression toward the mean. First, the rich tend to marry the rich. Even this, however, would tend to produce slow regression toward the mean since the nearer one rich child is toward the upper end of the distribution, the more likely he is to marry someone with less wealth than himself and their combined estate will be less than that of his parents. This will also happen on the lower end of the distribution and the effect over many generations will be to effect a movement toward the mean.

Second, let us drop the assumption that each couple reproduces itself. We have had rapid population growth in the United States and the rest of the Western world, which implies an average family size of more than two children. Our initial conclusions will hold only if the number of surviving children is the same for both rich families and poor. And, of course, it is not. There is some truth to the popular saying that the rich get richer and the poor have children. If rich families have less children, on average, than poor families, the lesser division of the property in inheritance will counteract the regression toward the mean which would otherwise take place.

A further problem exists. If fertility tends to be correlated inversely with wealth (because of more division of inheritance in large families), there may be a problem over time of relatively infertile strains of the population steadily moving toward the rich end of the population distribution, which would tend to reinforce an existing sociological tendency. Our conclusion, therefore, is that we cannot count on natural processes to cause a strong regression toward the mean in the distribution of wealth. Biological forces may instead reinforce social habits in the reproduction of the species, which in turn lead to wealth concentration. Our conclusion is that the inequality in the distribution of wealth is not likely to be equalized over time—indeed, it is likely to be exacerbated by imperfections in markets and sociological and biological tendencies which tend to concentrate wealth by inheritance.

Social Interference with Wealth Distribution. The small tendency toward increasing equality in the ownership of property must be seen largely in terms of a decline in the relative position at the very top of the distribution of wealth holders. There is nothing to indicate a substantial increase in the net wealth of the poorer three-quarters of the population of the United States except for the increase in their claims on private pension funds, which hold an increased share of claims to the national wealth. The share of top wealth holders has probably declined in response to heavy inheritance taxes and the influence these have had in the establishment of charitable foundations.

The effect of tax laws on the inheritance of wealth and of pension funds on its acquisition by large parts of the population are two prominent examples of the use of political and economic power to change the distribution of wealth. FHA and VA mortgages and free or subsidized education are important examples of other measures which have helped middle-income groups to increase and conserve their capital holdings. They might be envisaged as a continuation of the Jeffersonian philosophy of creating and protecting a nation of small property holders and avoiding an aristocracy of wealth.

The Importance of Factor
Shares to Income Equalization

The most important factor in the increasing equality of personal income distribution in the United States and other capitalist countries has not been increasing equality in the ownership of physical assets but the declining share of property income in national income. The extent of this decrease in the United States can be seen in Table 15–4. Since the turn of the century one method of estimating capital income shows that the share of property income in national income has declined from 36.8 per cent to 26.0 per cent. On the assumption that the top 5 per cent of wealth holders had maintained a constant share of 75 per cent of total wealth ownership and that there was no inequality in wage incomes (the assumptions of the example shown above in the section on "Causes of Income Inequality"), the ratio of the incomes of the top 5 per cent of the population to the rest would have declined from .48 to .32. This would represent a decline in relative shares from 32.6 per cent to 24.5 per cent of national income going to the wealthiest 5 per cent of the population. This hypothetical example shows how important the *share* of national income going to the owners of physical property is in determining the interpersonal distribution of income because of large inequalities in wealth ownership.

The factor which has contributed most to equalizing the distribution of personal incomes which took place in the United States between 1900 and 1950 (and which seems to have stabilized in the last twenty years) is the decline in the share of national income going to the owners of physical property. What underlying economic and political forces have produced this reduction?

Factor Prices and Charges in Relative Shares. Any discussion of the change in factor shares in an economic system where income distribution is determined by the sale of the factors of production must deal with the forces underlying the changes in the relative prices of capital and labor and the relative quantities of these two factors of production. Behind the changes in relative prices and quantities are supply and demand factors. Labor income in aggregate national income is equal to quantity times price. The same holds for capital. Symbolically:

$$L = Q_L \times P_L$$

and
$$K = Q_K \times P_K$$

where L = labor income
K = capital income
Q = Quantity
P = Price

and $_K$ and $_L$ = subscripts denoting capital and labor

Using the above notation K/L yields a ratio indicating the ratio of the share of capital income to the share of labor income. Q_K/Q_L gives the ratio of quantity indexes for the two factors and P_K/P_L the ratio of price indexes.

An estimate of these index numbers has been made by I. B. Kravis.[3] His estimates yield the following ratios:

Year	Q_K/Q_L	P_K/P_L	K/L
1900–1909	1.26	.309	.39
1949–1957	2.60	.092	.24

These ratios show why the share of national income accruing to capital has dropped from about two-fifths to one-fourth of that of the share of national income going to labor. While the ratio of units of capital to units of labor has roughly doubled, the relative price of capital has dropped to about one-third of what it was in the base period.

The supply of capital increased during the period much faster than the supply of labor. An index of capital roughly trebled, while an index

[3]Irving B. Kravis, "Relative Income Shares in Fact and Theory," *American Economic Review*, December 1959, pp. 917–49.

of labor hours only doubled. On the other hand, the price of labor rose markedly in relation to the price of the services of capital goods. Why did the price per unit of labor increase relative to the price per unit of capital?

Causes of Changing Relative Factor Prices. The answers to the question about relative prices can be segregated into those which emphasize, first, the changing character of technology and consumer tastes and, consequently, the demand for the two factors of production; and, secondly, those which emphasize the terms under which the factors of production were supplied.

Under the first explanation, we must emphasize that expenditure, during the period, was increasingly concentrated in sectors of the economy with lower capital/output and capital/labor ratios. During the earlier stages of industrialization, vast amounts of capital were necessary for the provision of social-overhead facilities such as railroads, urban water and sewage systems, heavy industry, and mechanization in agriculture. After 1900, expenditure was increasingly shifted to labor-intensive sectors such as education, medical care, and government services and consumer durables with a large labor content.

This author believes that the most important reasons for the change in relative shares came from changes on the supply side. First, the author thinks it is instructive to note that investments in the education of the labor force were making it more productive. While the number of hours worked by labor may have only doubled, the productivity of those hours was increased enormously by the education of the labor force and its utilization in higher productivity occupations.

Theodore Schultz has presented evidence which indicates that in the United States between 1900 and 1950, investment in education rose 3.5 times as rapidly as investment in physical capital.[4] Much of the increase in the share of labor in national income might be accounted for by the higher rate of investment in human than in physical assets. This would have been a highly rational investment from a social point of view in light of Gary S. Becker's recent estimates on the marginal return from investment in college education being in the neighborhood of 10–12 per cent,[5] with those for elementary and secondary education being somewhat higher. Some of the decline in the share of national income going to physical capital must be interpreted in terms of the diversion of capital from physical to human embodiment.

The decline of the small entrepreneur whose income is attributed to

[4]Theodore W. Schultz, "Capital Formation by Education," *Journal of Political Economy*, Vol. LXVIII, no. 6 (December 1960), p. 577.
[5]Gary S. Becker, *Human Capital* (New York: National Bureau of Economic Research, 1964).

capital and the rise of the corporate executive whose income is attributed to labor must also be given recognition in consideration of the conceptual framework used to measure factor shares.

As should be evident from the preceding chapters, the author regards institutional changes as being of prime importance in determining income distribution. Checking the power of monopoly in product markets by the encouragement of competition and limitations on conspiracy helps to lower the income which accrues to owners of physical capital as a return on capital. Checking the powers of monopsony in labor markets by the encouragement of labor unions alters the relative shares of capital and labor. Both of these types of social control help to limit the "surplus" accruing to individuals who are able to use the lack of alternatives of those with whom they strike exchange bargains to sell goods for more than they would be willing to accept and to buy labor for less than they would be willing to pay.

Another important contribution to the faster relative rise in the price of labor has been its relatively slower rate of increase. For this, social legislation has been to a large extent responsible. Minimum hours legislation, raising of the school leaving age, prohibitions on the employment of women and children under certain conditions, and restriction on immigration have all served to limit the growth of the supply of labor.

We will not speculate further on the relative importance of these explanations except to note that *if* the supply of capital from savings is inelastic (insensitive) to the rate of return and *if* it is difficult to substitute capital for labor (low elasticity of factor substitution), *then* political action to eliminate returns to capital from monopoly and monopsony and attempts to improve and limit the supply of labor will tend to alter the distribution of income between capital and labor.

The decrease in the relative share of national income accruing to capital has been accompanied by a slight decline over the last century in the rate of saving from aggregate income. Whether this has retarded the rate of aggregate growth by limiting capital formation, as suggested by Kuznets,[6] is a matter for conjecture. One could argue that the increasing share of income accruing to labor (whose lower propensity to save, could be blamed for the fall in the aggregate saving ratio) contributed to increased technological and organizational efficiency by making labor more willing to accept change. It is instructive to note that in the Soviet Union, where the rate of forced saving is much higher, that the gains from the dynamic improvements in productivity have been lower.[7] In

[6]Simon Kuznets, *Economic Growth and Structure* (New York: W. W. Norton & Company, Inc., 1965).

[7]See Bela Belassa, "The Dynamic Efficiency of the Soviet Economy," *American Economic Review*, May 1964, pp. 490–502.

the United States both Denison[8] and Solow[9] have called attention to the importance of improved organizational and technological efficiency in contrast to the traditional emphasis of economists on capital formation.

In connection with the supply of labor one could argue that the limitations on the participation of the labor force have retarded the rate of growth in per-capita income, but it is equally likely that shorter hours and delayed entry into the labor force have improved labor productivity per hour by more than the loss of hours.

Inequality in the Distribution
of Labor Income

While the decrease in the share of national income going to capital has helped to equalize income distribution, considerable inequality still exists because of the unequal distribution of labor income. The decreasing scope for increasing the equality of interpersonal income distribution through limiting the share of income accruing to capital makes inequality in labor incomes an increasingly important source of income inequality. Differential investment in human capital is one reason for the considerable differentials in labor income among employed workers.

Between 1945 and 1965 the poorest 20 per cent of the United States population received about 5 per cent of national income.[10] On the assumption that they had *no* property income, this would have meant that they received only about 7 per cent of labor income. This disparity, while not as great as that in per-capita income, is still enormous.

Differential public expenditures on education may be a contributing cause of income differentials resulting from the quality and quantity of education. Albert Fishlow has recently called attention to the fact that during the nineteenth and early twentieth centuries in the United States, public provision of free primary and secondary education benefitted the well-to-do more than the poor because the poor could not forego the income earned by their children in sending them even to free schools.[11]

A Syracuse University study of educational finance showed that significantly higher expenditures were made per pupil in high-income suburbs than in contiguous cities with concentrations of low-income families. The same study also showed that the suburbs were receiving more state aid than the city educational systems and that the gap was increasing.

[8]Edward F. Denison, *The Sources of Economic Growth in the United States and the Alternatives Before Us* (New York: Committee for Economic Development, 1960).

[9]Robert Solow, "Technological Change and the Aggregate Production Function," *Review of Economics and Statistics*, Vol. 39 (August 1957), pp. 312–20.

[10]See Table 15–5.

[11]Albert Fishlow, "Levels of Nineteenth-Century American Investment in Education," *Journal of Economic History*, Dec. 1966, pp. 418–36.

The effect of this on achievement was indicated by the correlation found between locality expenditure on education and National Merit Scholarship finalists.[12]

An equally important source of differential expenditure on investment in education is private disparities. Children from upper-income groups are far more likely to go to college within similar intellectual aptitude groups than children from lower-income families.[13]

The ability of upper-income groups to pass on wealth in the form of superior education and to divert public expenditures to superior education for their children helps to make possible the continuation of substantial inequality in labor income. From the standpoint of both economic growth and political stability in a democratic society, we must in the future divert more resources to the education of those segments of the population which are having inadequate educational investments made in them at the present time.

Underinvestment in the education of the poor (and investment with a lower rate of return in physical assets) results from the inability of private investors to secure property rights in the income streams produced by other people in contrast to the property rights in income from investment in physical assets. This disability of a capitalist system has been recognized by thoughtful observers for a long time.[14]

Not beyond the realm of possibility is the conception of a public corporation establishing itself to finance the higher education of individuals in return for a claim to part of their future income. This would constitute a form of limited property by the public corporation in the income of another—a form of slavery entered into voluntarily and contractually. Slaves held in involuntary servitude in ancient Rome occasionally became extremely wealthy from carrying on trade on their master's account in return for a share in the gains. In our own day, life insurance companies finance medical education for prospective doctors by guaranteeing repayment of loans through insurance contracts in case of death. The resulting insurance business, at least, has proved profitable, and the doctors are very willing to enter into the agreements in view of their high expected future incomes. Many industrial corporations make similar investments in the education of their employees with little more than "gentlemen's agreements" about the continuing employment of those in whom extensive educational investments are made.

These programs only go a small way toward dealing with underin-

[12]Results summarized in S. M. Miller et al., "Poverty, Inequality, and Conflict," *Annals of the American Academy of Political and Social Science*, September 1967, p. 38.

[13]*Ibid.*, p. 40.

[14]See, for example, the comments of the eminent nineteenth century economist, Alfred Marshall, on the social underinvestment in education of children from working class families. Alfred Marshall, *Principles of Economics, op. cit.*, Book VI, chap. IV.

vestment in education in poorer segments of the community. The real needs are in primary and secondary education where the costs, risks, and administrative problems necessitate actions by the federal government. The problem for local communities is the lack of congruence between the incidence of cost and receipt of returns. What self-interest can the citizens of a small Southern textile town or the residents of a Northern ghetto see in taxing themselves highly to provide high-quality education for recipients whose very success will consist in leaving? The parents, of course, will have an interest, but their limited incomes pose a barrier which can only be mounted by the intervention of the state. The state must provide increased investment in education, either through progressive taxation in the present or by a loan program financed by progressive taxes on the recipients of higher future incomes made possible by present investments in their education.

Recent Changes in

Income Distribution[15]

Between 1947 and 1965, the median family income in the United States, measured in constant, 1965 dollars increased from $4300 to $6900. The percentage of families with incomes less than the "poverty line" of $3000 in 1965 dollars declined from 30 per cent of the total population to 17 per cent. The income of the poor is growing as fast as the rich. The relative gap is remaining constant. But the absolute gap is increasing. In 1947, about 30% of American families had more than twice the income of the "poverty line." By 1965 almost 60% of U.S. families had more than double "poverty line" income. To rephrase the old adage, the rich get rich, and the poor get richer . . . but not so fast.

There has not been any perceptible equalization of income in the United States since the end of the Second World War. (See Table 15–5). In 1947, the poorest quintile of U. S. families received 5% of aggregate personal income. In 1965 they received the same share. In 1947 the upper 40% of the population received two-thirds of aggregate income. In 1965 they received almost an identical proportion of an aggregate which had increased enormously. The estimates of the income of the poor included such sources of income as welfare assistance and unemployment compensation. The income reported for the rich did not include such income as capital gains, expense accounts, or medical and educational programs

---

[15]All the statistics used in this section are taken from *U.S. Department of Commerce, Current Population Reports,* Series P-60, no. 51 (Washington: U.S. Government Printing Office, 1966).

provided by employers. These are the hard facts about income distribution in the United States. They do not identify the poor.

Who are the poor behind these figures? First it should be pointed out that the figures cited above do *not* include individuals living alone, i.e., apart from family groups. In 1965, 40% of the "unrelated individuals," 5 million Americans, had incomes less than $1500 per year—most of them were old, eking out a lonely and precarious existence. Of all "unrelated individuals," about 60% were over 55 years of age. It bears emphasis that these unrelated persons were living outside institutions. The institutional population of the United States is not included in any income group.

In other cultures, the elderly are retained within the extended family group where they continue to occupy a recognized status and socially useful functions in the care of infants, the performance of household and agricultural tasks, or the transmission of a cultural heritage to a young generation. In our own society they are institutionalized or isolated and left to fend for themselves.

There are 8 million American families who live beneath the "$3000 poverty line." (In New York City, the City Welfare Department estimates that a family with an income of less than $8900 per year suffers "deprivation.") Who are they? Almost 2 million of those families are Negro—about a quarter of non-white families have incomes below the poverty line. About 2 million of the families below the poverty line have a female head. Almost 3 million families below the poverty line are over 65. Only 9% of the families of four prsons have incomes below the poverty line. Almost 15% of the families of 7 persons or more have incomes below $3000.

Poverty, in our society, is heavily concentrated among the old, broken families with female heads, non-whites, and the poorly educated. Their lot is growing worse. In 1947, the median income of a family with a head over 65 was 58% of that of a family with an under 65 head. By 1965, the ratio had declined to 47%. In 1947, the median income of the family with a female head was 70% of the family with a male head. In 1965 it was 49%. To be poor in our society means to be outside the labor force. Exclusion from the labor force is the fate of the Negro, the elderly, the poorly educated, and the woman with a family and no husband.

The Social Explanation of
American Poverty

Poverty in the United States is not primarily a matter of physical hardship—it is a matter of social deprivation. It is not a matter of hunger but of malnutrition and poor diet. It is not a matter of no roof over one's head, but of a leaking roof over a room too small to house one's family. It is not a matter of no education and medical care but of grossly inadequate social services. In a poor society, deprivation can be accepted as inevitable. In a rich society this explanation of poverty is unacceptable.

The American rationalization of poverty, however, has never rested on the assumption of the inevitability of poverty. Quite the contrary. It has always attributed responsibility for personal poverty to the poor, themselves. This explanation finds its classical statement in John Locke's *Second Treatise on Civil Government* (1688) where the plight of the poor is explained by their failure and that of their forefathers to work and save. The "Puritan ethic" not only commends industry and thrift, it explains poverty as the failure of men to observe the ethic. Poverty in the United States has not only been viewed as a personal misfortune, it has been accepted as *per se* evidence of individual sloth and profligacy.

There was more correspondence between the "Puritan ethic" and economic reality in the past than there is in the present. The possibility of agricultural activity or unskilled labor in the nineteenth century may not have promised very high incomes to the mass of the population but the social definition of an acceptable standard of living was considerably more modest. In comparative terms the richest 1/5, or 20 per cent of the population was wealthier than today but the poorest segment of the population did not lag so far behind the rest. And the poor did not eke out a precarious existence on welfare, public assistance, and unemployment compensation with the resulting social stigma and personal alienation. They might not earn much but they did *earn* and they hoped that their children would do better even when they abandoned hope for themselves.

There are striking differences between the past and the present in the demographic characteristics of the population. A significant portion of the population now ends employment by retirement rather than illness and death. And when they do reach retirement, they no longer live with their children. Most individuals have not yet adjusted their intertemporal expenditure of earnings to take account of this change and our present Social Security benefits to the elderly have not kept pace with the rise in incomes and prices.

A serious economic problem has been created by the more prevalent current practices of divorce, separation, and abandonment. Welfare legislation in some areas exacerbates this problem by making families with able-bodied males ineligible for welfare payments. The economic effects of the broken home are as bad for the children as the psychological effects. Does the Puritan ethic really explain the poverty of the elderly or of the fatherless home?

Income Distribution, Race, and

History: A Challenge to Capitalism

For certain groups, the poverty of the present decade has a distressing permanence and personal quality to it. It is no longer primarily explained by transient conditions of crop failure, business cycle, or making a new start in the new world. Poverty is seen as a permanent condition for those who are black, uneducated, and the progeny of parents with similar social characteristics. The sins of the father are visited on the sons unto the n'th generation. Children are now being born whose parents and grandparents have accepted "the dole" as a way of life.

But why is it a sin to be black and/or uneducated? It is a social deficiency, a modern sin, because those who are uneducated have been adjudged incapable of socially productive labor. Those who are black are prejudged as incapable of acquiring education or performing skilled work. And those incapable of performing skilled work have been replaced by machines.

In the United States, the "Puritan ethic" has often been invoked to explain the high incidence of poverty among Negroes. The inferior income and inferior social status of the black man in a predominantly white society has been explained by the laziness and lack of motivation to work and save by the Negro. This explanation has been used to justify the very considerable differentials which persist in our society between the relative incomes of whites and blacks.

In 1965, the median income of the employed white male in the United States was $5,135. His Negro counterpart had a median income of $2,672. The ratio of the median income of the employed Negro male to the employed white male was 53% in 1965. It had not changed substantially in the 20 years since the Second World War. The percentage of Negro families below the poverty line of $3000 was twice as great in 1965 as for white families.[16]

Much of the economic disparity could be explained by the differences in white/Negro educational attainment. Yet the average Negro high school graduate over 25 years of age had a median income only 69% of that of his white counterpart. Almost exactly the same relative income positions attached when both had only 8 years of school. Thus, it is not only the greater educational attainments of whites which have assured them higher incomes than their black counterparts. Men with equal educational attainments receive unequal incomes. A Negro college graduate has lifetime earnings equal to a white with 8 years of school.

[16]*Ibid.*

But even an explanation of contemporary income differentials on the basis of educational differences fails to provide a *social* explanation of poverty. Why do such large educational differences exist? Why are they passed on from generation to generation? Why do they continue to have such differential impact on the basis of race a century after emancipation and a decade after the Supreme Court decision outlawing school desegregation?

The contemporary answer is a complex of sociological factors which deprive the Negro of educational opportunity, motivation and employment opportunity even when he possesses the requisite qualifications. But the real explanations must be sought in history. The sociological matrix which determines educability is hereditary. It is an inheritance as important in our society as was status or title to physical assets in those which preceded it. The contemporary relative poverty of the Negro and other groups who are seemingly in permanent poverty must be explained in terms of a long-run disparity of educational advantage.

The origin of this disparity, the "original sin," must be found in slavery. For over two centuries, white society systematically dispossessed Negro slaves of their contributions to the growing economic wealth of the United States. When the slaves were emancipated they were thrust onto the labor market without land, physical assets, or skills. The replacement of the "Black Codes" by "Jim Crow" kept the Negro in permanent subjection and allowed his continued exploitation as tenant farmer or unskilled labor. His educational opportunities, both North and South, past and present, were separate and unequal.

The consequence of three centuries of deprivation is the continuance of two societies—one largely white and rich, the other largely black and poor. The Negro child has difficulty acquiring an education because he comes from a home where there is no tradition of education and no value placed upon it because of past experiences with labor market discrimination. His school is overcrowded and obsolete because he comes from a poor community. Educational subsidies from the larger community are usually made on a matching basis which channels the largest portion of state and federal funds to the richest school districts. Disparities in educational expenditure enforce a continuing cycle of inequality.

In our society, the estate of one generation is passed to the next after the subtraction of liabilities incurred. On the same logic, the debts incurred by our white forefathers in the deprivation of Negroes by slavery and discrimination calls for the repayment of debts from our massive inheritance. It is a repayment of accrued liabilities because part of our inheritance was accumulated by the systematic underpayment of a minority race which was suppressed by law and violence.

It is honoring our own system of social accounting which necessitates the repayment of old debts with interest. The same logic which led America to impose payments by the Germans to the State of Israel for crimes against the Jewish people should lead America to make reparations for the dispossession of a minority race by concerted political action in our own land. Otherwise, we are open to the criticism of Karl Marx who argued that immorality in a capitalist economic system was originated and compounded by the capitalists who drove the serfs from the land and then exploited their economic necessity to deprive them of part of the value of what they produced. Exploitation consisted of paying them wages of less value than their output so that what was passed from one generation of the wealthy to the next was the labor value stolen from the poor who had been transformed into a property-less proletariat.

The Negroes, Spanish-Americans, and American Indians do not merit charity. They demand justice. They do not disregard the logic of a "free-enterprise" system. They ask for the repayment of old debts so that they will be able to compete in an industrial state which the unrequited toil of their ancestors helped to create. If they are denied justice by the system, they will turn from peaceful demonstration to violence and in the repression which would certainly follow, the system, itself, would become unworkable. A system which is unfair will not merit the voluntary loyalty of those it oppresses. It is questionable whether it merits the respect of those it blesses.

TABLE 15-1

Long-term Growth Rates in Output Per Capita for Selected Industrialized Countries

	1870–1913	1913–1950	1950–1960
Belgium	1.7	0.7	2.3
Denmark	2.1	1.1	2.6
France	1.4	0.7	3.5
Germany	1.8	0.4	6.5
Italy	0.7	0.6	5.3
Netherlands	0.8	0.7	3.6
Norway	1.4	1.9	2.6
Sweden	2.3	1.6	2.6
Switzerland	1.3	1.5	3.7
United Kingdom	1.3	1.3	2.2
Canada	2.0	1.3	1.2
United States	2.2	1.7	1.6

Source: Angus Madison, *Economic Growth in the West* (New York: The Twentieth Century Fund, 1964), p. 30. All figures are annual compound percentage growth rates.

224 Private Enterprise and Public Interest

TABLE 15-2

Long-term Trends in the Concentration of Income (Ratios of shares of income received by the top 5 per cent and top 20 per cent on income units to the share of incomes received by the rest of the population of selected countries for selected dates)

Country	Ratio						
		1880	1913	1929	1938	1947	1957
Great Britain	5/95	.92	.76	.50	.45	.32	.22
Great Britain	20/80	1.38	1.44	1.04	1.08	.85	.71
		1854	1875	1896	1913	1928	
Prussia	5/95	.27	.35	.37	.43	.35	
Prussia	20/80	n.a.	.92	.82	1.00	.96	
		1913	1928	1936	1950	1959	
Germany-W. Germany	5/95	.45	.24	.39	.31	.22	
Germany-W. Germany	20/80	1.00	.82	1.13	.98	.75	
		1870	1908	1925	1939	1955	
Denmark	5/95	.59	.43	.35	.33	.22	
Denmark	20/80		1.22	1.13	1.04	.79	
		1913–19	1919–28	1929–38	1939–43	1944–48	
United States	5/95*	.32	.33	.33	.24	.21	
United States	5/95**	.28	.32	.32	.22	.16	
		1929	1935–36	1941	1944–47	1955–59	
United States	20/80†	1.17	1.08	.96	.85	.82	
United States	20/80‡	1.17		.88	.75	.78	

Source of Data: Simon Kuznets, "Quantitative Aspects of the Economic Growth of Nations," *Economic Development and Cultural Change*, January 1963, pp. 60–63.

*Before Federal tax, Kuznets, National Bureau of Economic Research, estimates.
**After Federal tax, Kuznets, National Bureau of Economic Research, estimates.
†Before Federal tax, Department of Commerce, estimates.
‡After Federal tax, Department of Commerce, estimates.

TABLE 15-3

International Differences in the Size Distribution of Income

Country		Share of Ordinal Group in National Income			Ratio of Top 20%
		Top 5%	0–80%	81–100%	Bottom 80%
India	(1950)	33%	45%	55%	1.22
Ceylon	(1952)	31	46	54	1.17
Mexico	(1950)	40	40	60	1.50
Columbia	(1953)	42	44	56	1.27
Puerto Rico	(1953)	23	50	50	1.00
Italy	(1948)	24	52	48	.92
Great Britain	(1952)	21	55	45	.82
West Germany	(1950)	24	52	48	.92
Netherlands	(1950)	25	51	49	.96
Sweden	(1948)	20	54	46	.85
United States	(1950)	20	54	46	.85

Source of Data: Simon Kuznets, "Quantitative Aspects of the Economic Growth of Nations," *Economic Development and Cultural Change*, January 1963, p. 13.

TABLE 15-4

U. S. Distribution of Income by Functional Shares

Years	Employee Compensation	Entrepreneurial Income	Rent, Interest and Corp. Profits	Property Share*	Labor Share
1900–1909	55.0%	23.6%	21.4%	36.8%	63.2%
1920–1929	60.5%	17.6%	22.0%	32.3%	67.7%
1930–1939	66.8%	15.0%	18.1%	23.9%	76.3%
1949–1957	67.1%	13.9%	18.9%	26.0%	74.0%

Source of Data: I. B. Kravis, "Relative Income Shares in Fact and Theory," *American Economic Review*, December 1959, p. 919.

Property share is estimated as the sum of incomes received as rent, interest, corporate profits, and an imputed share of the income from unincorporated enterprises (entrepreneurial income). The basis of the imputation was the assumption that the share of entrepreneurial income attributable to capital was equal to the rate of return on capital for the economy as a whole.

TABLE 15-5

Distribution of Personal Income by Quintiles, in the United States: 1947-1960

Distribution of Income Shares Before Federal Income Tax				
Quintile	1947	1950	1955	1960
Lowest	5.0	4.8	4.8	4.6
Second	11.0	10.9	11.3	10.9
Third	16.0	16.1	16.4	16.4
Fourth	22.0	22.1	22.3	22.7
Highest	46.0	46.1	45.2	45.4
Top 5 Per Cent		21.4	20.3	19.6
Distribution of Income Shares After Federal Income Tax				
Lowest		5.1	5.2	4.9
Second		11.4	11.9	11.5
Third		16.8	17.0	16.8
Fourth		22.7	22.7	23.1
Highest		44.0	43.2	43.7
Top 5 Per Cent		19.2	18.2	17.7

Source of Data: U. S. Department of Commerce, *Survey of Current Business*, April 1958 and April 1963.

16

The Character of American Capitalism:

conclusions

Value judgments and prescriptive language have intruded themselves into the description of the development of capitalism at many points in the preceding chapters. However, the exploration and explanation of institutional arrangements has not primarily been undertaken to support a particular set of policy recommendations. Rather it has been undertaken to clear an accretion of myths about the uniqueness, morality, and indispensability of an existing set of economic arrangements. Having (hopefully) disposed of some of the aura of sanctity and mystery which attaches to idealized conceptions of property and freedom, the market and the state, the corporation and the union, the author would like to conclude by commenting on the implications of the view of capitalism developed in this book.

Parallels with Marx. To claim that this volume is "an answer to Marx" would be pretentious. It has not been the author's purpose to present an *apologia* for capitalism on the same scale as his criticism. Yet, in conclusion, the writer would like to draw attention to some similarities in method between Marx's treatment of the logic and development of capitalist institutions and his own.

Marx's purpose in writing *Das Kapital* was the demonstration of the historical relativity of economic arrangements. He sought to explain the institutions of private property and free markets, especially the market for labor, as devices designed by the bourgeoisie for the exploitation of the proletariat. This exploitation occurred when the bourgeoisie paid the proletariat less than the labor value of the goods which they produced.

226

Like Marx, the author has emphasized the historical relativity of economic organization. However, the author has laid stress on property and economic freedom as devices used by society to increase output. The text has emphasized the logic of social guarantees of property to individuals for increasing output in which society would share. Similarly, free markets have been explained as instrumentalities which could be used by societies to organize production more efficiently and which could allow individuals to realize the value of their contribution to output.

Marx explained the origin of economic freedom and private property in the overthrow of feudal economic relationships by force. The author has explained them as the economic consequences of changes in technology. His analysis has attempted to show that while industrialization increases the scope of possible "exploitation" by increasing the productivity of the worker, social controls and the enhancement of the bargaining power of labor by unions have prevented an increasing share of output from going to "capital." Marx did not foresee the possibility of gradual change in a capitalist society. In the past century, the great mass of the United States population (and the populations of most Western "capitalist" countries) has shared in the gains from economic growth as they have used their political power to secure favorable legislation and their economic power to bargain for a more secure and egalitarian society.

The approach to economic institutions in the preceding chapters, like Marx's, has been both analytic and synthetic. Marx analyzed the process of capitalist exchange in order to demonstrate the way in which the capitalist was able to appropriate "surplus value." The author has demonstrated the social utility of property and voluntary exchange and has analyzed the limiting conditions under which society will be "better off" through the creation of property and the exchange of goods and services.

Differences with Marx. A considerable difference exists in the historical view of Marx and that expounded in the present book. The author would agree that economic institutions in any society are structured to allocate a "surplus." However, the view of history as a series of conflicts between cohesive classes is difficult to accept on the basis of the historical evidence. The writer further finds it at odds with his view of man as a calculating social being. While Marx was influenced by the Hegelian philosophy of history being dominated by the ongoing life of social groups, the author's own historical view is conditioned by the existentialist view of the individual man struggling to adapt himself to the changing conditions of the physical environment. The author believes that the economic arrangements of capitalist society have originated in the contractual arrangements of self-interested individuals. They have been sanctioned by the rest of society on a pragmatic basis as long as their recognition and maintenance did not involve other members of society in coercion. The end of state-enforced monopolies and the recognition of labor unions, for example, have both been considered in terms of the political costs of continued maintenance.

This writer finds little explanatory value in the "dialectic" for the illumination of social development. On the other hand, inspecting the way in which particular practices came into use as the result of the particular needs of societies is extremely informative. An historical perspective on the development of capitalism is not conducive either to a view of contemporary American capitalism as the ultimate form of socio-economic organization or as merely a transitional stage in the inevitable passage to some form of communist utopia. Both Marx and many of the current defenders of "private enterprise" have been led astray in failing to take account of the historical relativity and changing functions of private property, market freedom, the corporation, the union, and the political arrangements we refer to as "the state."

Where the author is most at odds with Marx is in the implications of the analysis. This is not surprising because different conclusions are reached from the synthetic and analytic treatment of economic institutions in this volume. Marx concluded that capitalism was only maintained by force and that the proletariat who were coerced by the capitalist-controlled state would inevitably overthrow it by force when it had reached a certain state of economic development.

The writer's analysis of private property and market freedom indicates that their acceptance, *even by the members of society having little property or effective freedom,* is a matter of self-interest. Further, the quantitative evidence on economic growth and income distribution in capitalist societies corroborates the analytical expectation that property and market freedom will be defined to allow society collectively to enjoy a substantial part of the gains from economic growth.

The major difference between Marx's analysis and predictions about the effect of economic growth on income distribution in a society based on private property and the author's own arises from a different assessment of the bargaining power of the individual who possesses no physical assets. Marx predicted that he could never bargain effectively for a larger part of increasing social output, and he posited that the oppressed individual would, consequently, receive only a "subsistence" income. With the benefit of hindsight, we can see that the individual in many capitalist societies has obtained and wielded power *within* the system. Capitalism, and the increasingly universal franchise which accompanied capitalism, gave the individual both property in his own labor and a voice in choosing the government. The power to withhold either has forced the employers and the political leaders of capitalist societies to strike acceptable bargains with the mass of the population.

Marx's work accomplished a conceptual revolution in the social sciences. The author has no illusions about this slight work accomplishing a similar result. Marx's great contribution to intellectual history was a framework of class conflict which manifested itself in the institutions of society and a dynamic of change which depended on the changing character and control of the means of production. The author's theory of institutional change emphasizes the increasing power of the individual and the inability of societies, classes, or despotic governments to impose unacceptable arrangements upon him because of his power to withhold his cooperation and disrupt production.

The Justification of
Capitalist Institutions

In the opening chapter of this book it was stated that a fundamental source of misunderstanding in American society was the conflict between those who believed in the efficacy of the power of the state and those who insisted on the rights of the individual. The argument which has run through succeeding chapters has emphasized that the specification of the rights of individuals and groups of individuals associated in corporations or labor unions is made by society, subject to the assent of its individual members.

The distinguishing feature of capitalism, and American capitalism in particular, is a cost-benefit calculation of social interest in maintaining a wide dispersion of power among individuals in society and recognizing private claims to property and freedom. While rights are what a society defines them to be, the powers of the state are limited by the social cost-benefit calculation; society, acting through the state, cannot take away some rights from the individual without the costs of coercion outweighing the benefits which are sought. A society is forced by the self-seeking of its members to offer and guarantee certain rights as incentives to obtain socially desirable behavior.

This rather stark view of society does not originate with twentieth century technocrats or nineteenth century utilitarians. It finds its earliest statement in the political philosophy of Thomas Hobbes. It was rejected by John Locke, the philosopher of the capitalist revolution of the seventeenth century in England, as being too harsh, too difficult of acceptance by the common man, and dangerous to established wealth. As a consequence, we have labored on with the cumbersome justifications of "natural rights" and procedural checks on the power of the legislature.

Economists who have been willing to adopt the crudest models of material self-interest in the analysis of the behavior of men within given social framework have largely failed to use the same models on the analysis of the social framework. This is particularly true for the economists of the last two generations who have devoted their very considerable intellectual abilities to such marginal projects as the mathematical demonstration of second-order stability conditions in abstruse economic models, while neglecting the primary requisites for social stability in their own society. The most penetrating benefit-cost analysis of capitalism ever made was accomplished by Marx a century ago. He concluded that the proletariat had nothing to lose from the overthrow of capitalism but their chains. The subsequent development of capitalism and very considerable institutional changes in the delimitation of freedom and property in capitalist countries invalidated his calculations. Still, the calculations need to be made—not to justify capitalism as an economic system but to make it work better. The social cost of not making the system work better will be the riots we have observed in the streets of our cities in the last decade and the alienation of some of our most talented young people into withdrawal from society.

One hears a great deal about "rights" in our society; businessmen talk about their rights to "reasonable" profits after taxes; labor leaders talk about the rights of unions to strike, negotiate union-shop contracts, and determine their qualifications for membership; old-age pensioners assert their right to be protected against inflation; young people assert their right of freedom to smoke "pot" and demonstrate against the war in Viet Nam; Negroes assert their rights to equal opportunity in jobs, housing, and education; whites assert their rights to discriminate.

This book has attempted to make a case for a conceptual revolution in the way we look at "rights" in a capitalist society. This is more than a matter of linguistic exactness. If the guarantees of property and freedom which individuals, corporations, and unions claim from the state are no more than incentives, no more than instrumentalities offered by the society to secure certain objectives, then their maintenance requires continual justification by their holders. The corporation has to make society aware of the rate of interest necessary to pay savers after taxes to induce them to save, and it needs to justify the use which is made of profits in excess of that amount; the union needs to demonstrate the social utility of its powers to economically coerce employers, its own members, and the public.

If inflation imposes burdens on some groups and benefits on others, then a social decision about the costs and benefits to various groups must be balanced in the framing of national policy. Safeguards on the purchasing powers of pensions must either be negotiated by their owners, or their holders must safeguard them at the ballot box. No sacred and inviolable contract exists between a government and its people to maintain the purchasing power of money, although the failure to do so may have certain bad effects.

A Digression on Personal Freedom. We have not been concerned with the personal freedoms of the individual in this book; in fact, in Chapter 9 we argued that economic freedom was fundamentally different from some other types of freedom in that there was always a problem with the division of the gains from exchange in economic transactions. Nevertheless, the author believes that his view of economic freedom as a means to achieve certain ends and secure the cooperative participation of the individual has implications for personal freedom.

The author does not believe that individuals have any inalienable rights to personal freedom any more than they have absolute rights to make any bilaterally voluntary exchange transaction. The freedom of the individual to do or speak as he wishes must always be balanced with the effect of his actions on the rest of society. Civilized societies, for example, restrict the freedom of their members to consume opiates because of the possible harm inflicted on other members of society by the behavior of those under their influence and because of the possibility of those who take them becoming burdens on the rest of society. As John Donne wrote in the age which witnessed the renunciation of a sense of community:

> No man is an island, entire of itself; every man is a piece of the continent, a part of the main; if a clod be washed away by the sea, Europe is the less, as well as if a promontory were, as well as if a manor of thy friends or of thine own were; any man's death diminishes me, because I am involved in mankind; and therefore, never send to know for whom the bell tolls; it tolls for thee.

Personal freedoms cannot be absolute any more than freedom of exchange can be absolute because society is inevitably affected by the actions of its members.

Freedom of Speech. There are some close parallels between the arguments for market freedom and freedom of speech. The freedom of speech and dissent is one of the most closely guarded possessions of a free society. The freedom is well recognized as having certain limits, and those limits are connected with the possible effects of one person's freedom on another person's welfare. The important positive reason for freedom of

---

[1]John Donne, Meditation XVIII, reprinted in *The Complete Poetry and Selected Prose of John Donne,* Charles Coffin, ed., (New York; Modern Library, Inc., 1952), p. 441.

speech and freedom of dissent, however, is the emergence of truth and good counsel from the dialectic of opposing views. Competition in argument is supposed to have the same beneficial effects for society as competition between buyers and sellers in the marketplace. This pragmatic argument for freedom was eloquently made by John Milton in 1643:

> As therefore the state of man now is; what wisdom can there be to choose, what continence to forbear without the knowledge of evil? . . . Since, therefore, the knowledge and survey of vice is in this world so necessary to the constituting of human virtue, and the scanning of error to the confirmation of truth, how can we more safely, and with less danger, scout into the regions of sin and falsity than by reading all manner of tractates and hearing all manner of reason?[2]

What is profoundly disturbing about much of the contemporary dialogue about the freedom of speech and the freedom to dissent, like the claims for economic freedom, is the absence on both sides of an understanding of the place of individual freedom in a free society. Freedom of speech is denied and suppressed in totalitarian societies on the grounds that there is no possible benefit and considerable danger to the "Revealed Truth" possessed by the "Leader of the Party" from allowing error to be propagated. In our own society, the authorities often are willing to allow that people have a right to their own opinion, but their attitude is that they have a right to it only as long as they keep it to themselves and do not try to interfere with the policies presently being carried out. They deny the freedom of the minority to put forward their view for serious debate and refuse to come to terms with the arguments advanced. As a result, they frequently provoke demonstrations which accomplish little more than the venting of frustration.

Many of those who claim the freedom of speech and dissent have little appreciation of the basis of social guarantees of freedom. They are not interested in a real debate with the established views. They are interested in sabotage and chaos and in the disintegration of an existing society which they hope to replace with one of their own making which they plan to impose without debate or criticism.

The defense of freedom against those who would use it to destroy society can only be accomplished by denying them freedom or by ensuring that freedom is recognized as a means to the attainment of social objectives. The denial of freedom exposes a society to great dangers and difficulties. The alternative entails the acceptance of the obligation by all members of society to conduct their argument about social arrange-

---

[2]John Milton, *Areopagetica* (London: 1643) quoted in *John Milton: Complete Poems and Selected Prose*, Merritt Y. Hughes, ed. (New York: The Odyssey Press, Inc., 1957), pp. 728–29.

ments and policies on the basis of explicit value judgments and frank exchange of views on how to reconcile and achieve them.

If genuine discussion is lacking in our society, freedom of speech will not work as it is intended to work, and it will have lost the value for which it is guaranteed by society. It will be restricted in what is construed to be "the public interest." If effective debate breaks down in a society and the freedom to speak permits demagogues to inflame the populace with lies and claims which go unanswered, the public will respond with suppression of free speech as it no longer serves the ends of society.

Most men have an instinct to suppress the ideas they do not agree with and the men who publish them. When intelligent debate about alternatives ceases in a society, the right of free speech will allow the circulation of increasingly repugnant opinions which go unrefuted. After a short period of time, the public will suppress free speech with all the dangers for a good society which this entails. The blame for the end of freedom will rest not only with the demagogues; it will rest equally with those who allowed the errors and distortions to go unanswered. The same considerations pertain to economic freedom, private ownership, and the survival of competition.

Capitalism and Racial Problems. Some will think that the problem of racial discrimination and the relative deprivation of the American Negro has been given too much attention in a book primarily concerned with the nature and evolution of a capitalist society. Those who make this criticism will have failed to understand the logic and development of our institutions. The Negro problem is a racial problem only to the extent that it was largely this racial group which was excluded from the prerogatives of the members of a capitalist society. Having been excluded for a long period of time, they are losing patience with their continued relegation to an inferior position, and they find little reason to obey and honor a system which they find denies them the rights of property they are asked to respect. The future of American capitalism and liberal democracy will not be threatened by Negro violence and disaffection because the Negroes are too small a proportion of the total population. It is entirely possible, however, that the creation of the police state which would be necessary to suppress wide-scale disaffection of Negroes and other underprivileged groups would lead to the demise of our liberal, individualist society. The danger in denying equality of opportunity in a society is that the denial of rights to one part of the population may lead to the denial of rights to other parts of the population and thereby lead to a totalitarian society.

Negroes do not have any natural rights to property, freedom, equality of education, or employment opportunity any more than any other members of society. However, the cost of denying them equal rights which are socially created and enforced is too high to make it a rational policy by the members of society. Social reform will come much more easily when reformers sit down and sharpen up their pencils to figure the production lost by the high rates of unemployment and the low levels of skill resulting from the Negro exclusion from adequate educational opportunity. Social reform may also be hastened when communities add up the cost of threats of civil violence to their expenditure on police and insurance, and the income lost when employers no longer want to situate their activities in an area of racial conflict. The tea leaves of history which have been analyzed in this volume all point to the growth of personal freedom as the result of economic calculation. The American Civil War and the Emancipation Proclamation present an historical aberration because the South seceded in protest against the unwillingness of the North to continue to sanction the institution of slavery.

Capitalism and Planning. We have not considered in this volume the problems raised by economic planning for the relationship between the state and private groups. This stops being a fundamental question when the conceptual framework which has been used in this volume is used to analyze the relationship between the individual and society. The divorce between politics and economics becomes untenable when the social origin of property and economic freedom is admitted. The constraints on state action remain the practical ones of securing performance. The absolute sanctity of private property, individual freedom, and the impersonal self-regulating market were classical myths designed to prevent political interference with the status quo. When they are dispelled, the propriety of overtly political decisions can no longer be entertained as a meaningful question.[3]

A Capitalist Ethic

The socio-economic systems which preceded capitalism—the imperial systems of Greece and Rome and the feudalism of medieval Europe—had a well-defined philosophy of the individual's relationship to the society of which he was a part. The rights of freedom and property which were held by the members of the privileged classes were recognized as the arbitrary creations of the state and certain well-defined obligations were accepted by them as necessary for their continuance.

The emergence of capitalism was accompanied by the egalitarian doc-

[3]For an interesting discussion of the effect of ideology and tradition on economic planning in France, Britain, and the United States, see Andrew Schonfeld, *Modern Capitalism* (London: Oxford University Press, 1965).

trine that freedom and property were universal and inalienable rights—protected but not created by the state. The possession of these rights imposed no obligations on their possessors other than the prudential obligation to support the society which guaranteed them. The protection and security of the individual members of the society was to be guaranteed, not by a system of positive law and social responsibility, but by "the self-regulating market" and the guarantees of absolute property rights on which it was based.

What did not emerge with modern capitalism was a public philosophy which reconciled the interests of the individual with the interests of society. The doctrine of natural rights lacks intellectual acceptance. The way in which the self-regulating market operates is not accepted as inevitable. The increasing disaffection of the poor in the midst of unprecedented affluence indicates that they feel little prudential obligation to support a system which they feel offers them less than they are entitled to.

The evolution of capitalism has been accompanied by the modification of the doctrine of "natural rights" and the "self-regulating market." Interference by the state has been increasingly accepted as the privileged classes in a capitalist society have realized the prudence of increasing the stake which the less privileged members of the society have in its maintenance. The operation of the market has been altered to increase the share of "surplus" which accrues to the less privileged.

The major difficulty with the unspecified theory of prudential obligation, which has replaced the natural rights theory as the intellectual basis of capitalist organization, is that it lacks definitive guidelines for ordering the relationship between individuals. This writer is not arguing that it has not served capitalist societies well in the past. It has allowed individual freedom to flourish (at least for a part of the population), it has allowed economic growth to proceed at a rapid rate, and it has permitted substantial equalization of interpersonal income distribution. However, its shortcoming, once the absence of limits on the arbitrary power of the state is realized to be the consequence of the rejection of the natural rights theory, is that it provides no standard of reference to guide the definition of the freedom and property allocated to the individual by society.

As was noted in the opening chapter of this book, the term *capitalism* has never enjoyed great popularity with the American people as a description of our economic system and the application of the term has long been in dispute among scholars. The author has no desire to popularize or resurrect the term, he does hope, however, that the distinctions which have been made about property and freedom and their historical evolution will contribute to an understanding of the relationship between individual rights and social interest.

In conclusion, the author would like to state simply a view of the philosophy of the relationship between the individual and society which he thinks *ought* to underlie the structuring of capitalist organization. It is the philosophy of "the commonwealth" which formed the basis for the capitalist revolution of the seventeenth century in England and which was adopted in Massachusetts by its founding fathers. In his economic transactions with other members of society, each individual was to be free to enrich himself as long as his actions also enriched the rest of society. Transactions which merely redistributed existing wealth or income were not to be socially condoned. The analysis of property and of freedom of exchange elaborated in preceding chapters have been informed with this ethic. This writer believes such an ethic does provide a reconciliation between private enterprise and public interest, between individualism and community.

Appendix:

the Edgeworth-Bowley Box diagram

The Edgeworth-Bowley Box diagram is an expositional device which allows the demonstration of the limits of gains from exchange. The assumptions underlying the device are that two individuals with independent and fixed preferences for two types of goods which are in fixed supply bargain about their final distribution. The device can also be used to talk about hypothetical exchange bargains struck between an "individual" and "society."

The total quantities of the two goods are "given" by the productive capacity of available resources and technology. The quantities are measured along the horizontal and vertical axes. The assumption is made that the quantities of each good possessed by each of the two parties are measured from origins at the lower left and upper right hand corners of the "Box." Thus, any point within the "Box" represents a distribution of the goods between the parties. In Fig. 5-1 (p. 67), "Society" initially produces and consumes total output at point C. The expansion of output enlarges the size of the "Box" to $AB'C'D$.

The "preference" functions represented by the convex lines indicate the hypothetical choices of the parties between an infinite number of choices of goods. Each preference function represents the border between all combinations of goods considered inferior and superior to any combination of goods represented by a point on the preference function. The convexity of the preference functions to the origins at the lower left and upper right hand corners of the "Box" indicates that each good has a decreasing rate of substitutability for the other good in the judgment of each of the consuming parties. Because it is defined to be rational behavior to prefer "more" of both goods to "less," one moves away from the origin to preferred combinations of more goods.

The limits of voluntary exchange are defined by the ellipse formed by the preference functions of the two parties which pass through the point representing the initial distribution of goods. Any point within the ellipse would be preferred by both parties to the point representing the initial distribution because at any point within the ellipse, both parties would be on a higher preference function and, therefore, in a preferred position by definition.

Bibliographic Note: F. Y. Edgeworth is generally credited with the development of the box-diagram technique. (*Mathematical Psychics*, London: C. Kegan Paul and Co., 1881.) The diagram was first used extensively by A. L. Bowley. (*Mathematical Groundwork of Economics*, Oxford: Clarendon Press, 1924.) The best introduction I know of the logic and difficulties of the analytic techniques is I. M. D. Little, *Critique of Welfare Economics*, Oxford: Oxford University Press, 1950. An article which places the box diagram in relation to equilibrium analysis in both production and consumption is F. M. Bator, "The Simple Analytics of Welfare Maximization," *American Economic Review*, March, 1957, pp. 22–59.

Index

A

B

C

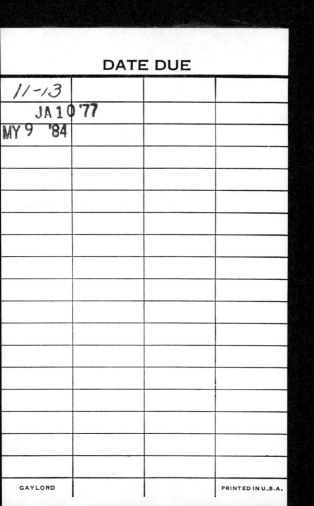

DATE DUE

11-13			
JA 10 '77			
MY 9 '84			

GAYLORD

PRINTED IN U.S.A.